WEISER ✚ CLASSICS

THE WEISER CLASSICS SERIES represents the full range of
subjects and genres that have been part of Weiser's publishing
program for over sixty years, from tarot, divination, and
magick to alchemy and esoteric philosophy. Drawing
on Weiser's extensive backlist, the series offers works by
renowned authors and spiritual teachers, foundational texts,
as well as introductory guides on an array of topics.

PSYCHIC
SELF
DEFENSE

Violet Firth, aka Dion Fortune, ca. 1906, a publicity photo from the *Bystander UK* newspaper, announcing release of her second self-published volume of poetry, *More Violets*. Photo courtesy of Diane Champigny.

PSYCHIC
SELF
DEFENSE

The Definitive Manual for Protecting
Yourself Against Paranormal Attack

DION FORTUNE

Foreword by Mary K. Greer

WEISER BOOKS

This edition first published in 2020 by Weiser Books, an imprint of
Red Wheel/Weiser, LLC
With offices at:
65 Parker Street, Suite 7
Newburyport, MA 01950
www.redwheelweiser.com

The publisher wishes to thank Diane Champigny for kindly providing the
image of Violet Firth on p. iv.

ISBN: 978-1-57863-731-7
Library of Congress Cataloging-in-Publication Data available upon request.

Cover design by Kathryn Sky-Peck

Printed in the United States of America
IBI

10 9   8 7 6 5 4 3 2 1

CONTENTS

PART III

THE DIAGNOSIS OF PSYCHIC ATTACK

PART IV

METHODS OF DEFENCE AGAINST PSYCHIC ATTACK

FOREWORD

I FIRST BECAME ACQUAINTED with the works of Dion Fortune (hereafter, D. F.) in 1971 while living in London, where I expanded on my budding astrological and Tarot studies. I devoured her occult novels, *Moon Magic* and *The Sea Priestess* and looked for anything else by this writer who so exquisitely evoked the magic for which I was yearning. Even after reading her other novels, I willingly struggled through *The Cosmic Doctrine* and *The Mystical Qabalah* even though the concepts and much of the vocabulary were new to me. It was with great relief that I came upon *Psychic Self-Defense*, probably D. F.'s most popular nonfiction book, as something understandable and applicable to my life. However, it is only on rereading it that I've come to realize how many of my own early magical concepts and practices stemmed from this work.

In 1974 I was living in an apartment in Florida that felt strangely haunted. Several friends, when visiting, asked how I could stay there by myself. With no option to move, I set about changing the vibe. I remember explaining to others that the apartment wasn't haunted but rather it was like there was a tape loop of emotional violence and fights that kept playing over and over, probably stemming from earlier tenants. I set about changing this by filling the space with images I visualized of love and light. It was a slow and rather naive process but, by the time I moved out—within a year—the apartment felt totally different. Friends even commented on how pleasant the place was. I forgot how I came to the idea of a tape loop replaying emotional states, but as I reread *Psychic Self-Defense* I kept coming across this concept and many other practices that now seem intuitive or second nature to me. As a liberated hippie of the 1960s, I didn't seem to imbibe the more problematic prejudices expressed by D. F., instead I've spent a lifetime excavating my own.

If you are reading this book you probably have had some kind of experience with the efficacy of spells, affirmations, and/or visualization to create a change in your circumstances or interactions with others. Or it could be that you or someone you know is experiencing troubles that seem to stem from a deliberately destructive intent meant to harm. This book can help you to more deeply understand the multidimensional interactions of conscious and unconscious intents, emotions, and their material plane effects.

This book goes far beyond mere techniques. In the nearly one hundred years since *Psychic Self-Defense* was published it has provided a significant framework for evaluating and diagnosing a wide range of psychic phenomena by integrating the findings of science, psychology, ancient and modern occult and mystery traditions, and the ever practical "art of living." Regarding self-defense, D. F. insists that one differentiate first among actual psychic attack, mental illness, and situations that are merely unethical, illegal, or unhealthy. Rather than jumping to conclusions about what you are facing, she provides a methodology and steps to first determine the forces with which you are dealing and, only then, the best response. Mostly, D. F. warns against a simplistic understanding of psychic attack, with explanations that lead to a broader comprehension of the mundane effects of psychic stimuli. According to D. F., the real basis of psychic attack is telepathic suggestion, however it requires that the recipient's aura be pierced due to their own fear or desire. Strengthening one's own defenses through self-knowledge and a connection to Spirit becomes paramount.

While this book will hone the skills of professionals, it is also a great place for a neophyte to start, even if it seems to lead down trails and byways that are frustrating to a reader seeking quick tips and instant results. Despite its flaws, this book will widen your understanding of muggle/magical coexistence and provide practical guidelines for identifying and respecting the effects and needs of the multiple planes of an expanded reality.

One thing about *Psychic Self-Defense* that struck me negatively when I first read it in the early 1970s and even more so half a century later, is a bias, even extreme prejudice, against certain groups of people. This attitude seems beneath such a psychologically and magically developed individual as D. F. I'm sure many people will be put off by her derogatory comments regarding hypnotism and mind-power techniques, as well as witches, "apaches," and East Indians, among many others. We have to realize that D. F. was a product of pre-Gardnerian witchcraft and stuck in her era. As a ceremonial magician with a Christian focus, she sought to separate high, theurgic magic from what she believed was low magic, and especially from magic she feared had a manipulative twist or was sourced in a different race. I'll ask you to treat such references with compassion. The strengths of this book far outweigh its weaknesses. I urge you to use your own reactions to her overt prejudices as opportunities to examine what might be your personal 21st century unacknowledged assumptions.

Dion Fortune is the assumed name of Violet Mary Firth, born in Bryn-y-Bia, Llandudno, Wales on January 6, 1890 to a wealthy middle-class family. Her father was a lawyer. Her mother's family ran a hydrotherapeutic establishment (a healing spa). By the time Violet was in her teens, both parents had become Christian Scientists. From an early age she experienced visions of what she later came to believe were previous lives and showed an interest in writing, demonstrated by two privately published books of poetry and scripts for school dramas. When she was sixteen, her family moved to London, eventually buying property in an early suburban communal housing project where the family became friends with several people having close ties to the mystical aspects of Glastonbury.

At age twenty-one, Violet enrolled at a horticultural college that specialized in creating career opportunities for girls with nervous or psychological problems. Within two years, as a result of her success with poultry and some canny detective work that uncovered a thief, Violet became an instructor. Issues arose regarding the seemingly unethical methods of the warden, Dr. Lillias Hamilton, an experienced administrator who had lived an adventurous life in India, Afghanistan, and South Africa. Violet opposed her, resulting in one of the detailed examples of psychic attack given in this book. Violet's resulting nervous breakdown led her to enroll for training at the Medico-Psychological Clinic where she both received and conducted counseling for others, primarily women with sexually related problems. She acknowledged, though, that it was not until she came to the study of the Zurich School (Jungian psychology) that she "found psychology which could be correlated with esoteric psychology." (Knight, Gareth. 2000. *Dion Fortune & the Inner Light*, Thoth Publications. p. 133.)

From 1914 to 1921, Violet threw herself into a search for meaning through the esoteric realm. She joined the Theosophical Society where she eventually ran their Christian Mystic Lodge. At one of their lectures, she met Dr. Theodore Moriarty and joined his school of occult studies. Her experiences with Dr. Moriarty became the basis for her first fiction book, *The Secrets of Dr. Taverner*, and for several of the examples in this book. Other examples of psychic self-defense can be found in fictionalized form in her novels and short stories.

Around 1919, Violet joined a theosophy-based group run by B. P. Wadia, a labor activist advocating home rule for India, who came to be highly respected for his activism and for setting up theosophy centers in several different countries. Gareth Knight, in his biography, *Dion Fortune & the Inner Light*, points out that the psychic attack involving "an Indian gentleman" may have been an issue of ideological conflicts between D. F. and Wadia that created an energy short-circuit on the astral plane, rather than nefarious intent on the part of Wadia.

Soon thereafter Violet was initiated into the Alpha et Omega Temple of the Stella Matutina (formerly the Hermetic Order of the Golden Dawn) under J. W. Brodie-Innes, having been introduced by a family friend and member, Maiya Curtis-Webb (later, Tranchell-Hayes). Violet assumed the name Dion Fortune, taken from a family motto, *Dio Non Fortuna*, meaning "God, not fate."

In 1922, D. F. met Charles Loveday in Glastonbury where she subsequently established a second home. Together they formed the Fraternity of the Inner Light (later, the Society of the Inner Light) guided by a series of masters, especially the "Master Jesus," via trance mediumship. This resulted in her first book, *The Esoteric Philosophy of Love and Marriage*, which is based on transcriptions of her own trance communications. Moina Mathers, widow of Golden Dawn founder MacGregor Mathers, subsequently chastised D. F. for revealing Golden Dawn secrets; D. F. protested that she had learned none of this through her initiations but rather from spirit contacts.

D. F.'s tale of a battle with another magical group may have stemmed from this schism and reveals her tendency to exaggerate and sensationalize her examples. We find something similar in the story of the mysterious death of Netta Fornario, found naked upon the "fairy hill" on the mystical Scottish island of Iona. Coming, as this story does, immediately following another account of a magical struggle suggests that Fornario's demise may have resulted from an occult encounter with what D. F. calls "Green Ray elementals" (the faery folk), rather than her ill health and an overnight exposure to the elements.

Almost a decade after writing this book, from 1939 through the end of World War II, D. F.'s application of psychic defense strategies took on a whole new import. Through the society's newsletters, she opened her training to those willing to take part in daily meditations to link with and support the work of the Universe: "Our work is to formulate and re-formulate day-by-day the mental link between the spiritual influences and the group mind of the race . . . . We cannot do better than to continue on our work of realizing the all-powerful nature of spiritual law." Although many urged her to use knowledge and power to make personal attacks on the leaders of the German nation, D. F. concluded such action would be wrong. According to her follower and biographer, Gareth Knight, experience taught her that nothing and nobody is altogether evil, therefore it is never justifiable to try to destroy any person or thing by direct action, but only to open a channel whereby spiritual forces are brought to bear upon the problem. "Our work is a work of healing, and no hate must come of it." (Knight, Gareth. 2012. *The Magical Battle of Britain:* Dion Fortune. Skylight Press. p. 10-11.)

Dion Fortune died rather suddenly of leukemia on January 6, 1946. She is buried at St. John's Church, Glastonbury.

In contrast to the pre-1930s prejudices in this book, during the last ten years of her life, D. F. gave much more credence to ancient Pagan mysteries. She became an inspiration to the development of 20th-century goddess spirituality and modern Wicca with her portrayal of women who were independent, wise, and powerful. She provided role models to those who consciously initiated others into the secrets of the esoteric realm. Her works on occult theory and doctrine form the bedrock of much 20th-century magic and witchcraft, influencing both individuals and groups like Starhawk's Reclaiming Collective and Dolores Ashcroft-Nowicki's Servants of Light, among many others. With her emphasis on self-mastery and examples of magic performed by non-initiates she promulgated the idea that magic is more a learned technique based on discipline, knowledge, and practical tools than one belonging to a magical order. I've personally taken part in a great many rituals drawn from words and practices that came directly from her writings, and I've benefited from them greatly.

Each generation has its thought forms and blind spots. The integration of Buddhism, meditation, and visualization into the human potential movement of the late 20th century has given us a whole new raft of methods and techniques beyond what is found here. Yet it is rare, indeed, to find such a detailed analysis of conditions and methodologies that clarify the forces with which we operate in the psychic realms. Work with spirit animals and soul retrieval derived from medicine traditions of indigenous peoples has also expanded our skills and options. New Age practices and modern-day Wicca have contributed to an understanding of how to navigate the realms deemed light and dark. They have opened the way for the recognition that sexual energy, while a significant force in magic, is not limited to old concepts of masculine and feminine duality. The internet has brought occult wars out into the open. We have seen Pagan gatherings close down as differences of opinion fracture the delicate balance among Pagan groups. Even psychic vampirism is no longer always seen as inherently bad, resulting from the explorations of pioneers into the psychic realm who have recognized a need to sometimes draw energy from others, for they've begun to both define what's involved and to describe mutually acceptable ethical practices that harm none. Furthermore, we now acknowledge cultural appropriation, political incorrectness, bullying, and even binding rituals as some of today's forms of psychic attack that need to be addressed with esoteric as well as mundane methods. D. F.'s methodology, as outlined here, can serve as a model for approaching the many sides of such issues.

There is still much work to be done. Dion Fortune's *Psychic Self-Defense* provides an essential bedrock to our journey.

—Mary K. Greer

EXPLANATORY NOTE

THIS IS A WARNING to the curious: Times, points of view, and fashions change, but never principles. Those who have formed the impression they are suffering from some form of psychic attack should take note of this. In the end, isn't your own projection simply exaggerated into a dramatic scenario? For the ultimate answer to most of life's problems almost inevitably lies within oneself.

Sometimes the little 'self' craves for attention at all costs, even attention that most people would think was unwelcome attention. Whatever you do, don't dwell on the problem; stand back from it and give yourself space! Believe and put your trust in something much more positive, bigger, and better. There are some practical steps that you can take to restore the balance in your life. Please consider the following:

1. Sever all connections with the suspected originator(s) of the attack, in so far as this is practical, e.g., if you are living with your attacker, in which case you should detach and distance yourself as much as you can, and vigorously assert your own will and don't give in to someone else.

2. Keep away from drugs.

3. Don't meditate while the episode continues. If you have a religious belief, concentrate on that; e.g., go to Holy Communion, or whatever, regularly, for example.

4. Keep to a healthy diet, get plenty of sleep and fresh air, and take physical exercise.

5. Find something positive to do, such as sports or gardening.

6. Some counselors or psychotherapists are sufficiently open-minded, knowledgeable, and experienced to help you with your problem. In any case, before taking that step, it is generally advisable to have a thorough physical check up, which should be done anyway. The supposed "attack" may be a simple physical malfunction.

Then and Now: Different Perspectives

This book was written shortly after the beginning of a major change in the West that brought with it the recognition of the positive contribution psychology was likely to make in the future. Written over sixty years ago, Dion Fortune inevitably reflects many commonly held beliefs and attitudes of that time.

Times have changed, but the underlying principles have not. "Psychic attack" is really a form of bullying of one sort or another. It is the drive to dominate, if not crush, a person by invalidating that person—breaking his or her will. It can take many forms, such as sexual harassment, or political or religious persecution. It is generally an assault on free will by the assertion of "superior" power which, so far as the persecutor is concerned, is best carried out in a controlled environment from which the "victim" cannot easily escape. Obvious environments would include the workplace, any close group, institutions of one kind or another including schools, service units, prisons, cults and sects, the family even. As well as the victim's own mind.

One solution, after weighing the pros and cons, is leaving that environment and the "psychic bully" to his or her own devices. What such a person craves is the means to exercise power over others. Once that is removed, he or she has failed and is no different from anyone else. The second Achilles heel of the "persecutor" is activated when he or she is not taken seriously. He or she *must* be taken seriously at all costs, otherwise the power is lost. To be laughed at, or not to be taken seriously, is to turn the tables on the bully. That it is *all very serious* is the name of the silly negative game.

However, it is needless to point out that walking away from an environment is not always easy, and, in doing so, one may simply be exchanging one problem for another. One should be able to appeal to higher authority, though a sympathetic response from human "superiors" or law enforcers cannot always be relied on. A third solution is direct confrontation with the oppressor, as Dion Fortune relates; a similar run-in of the sort described between East and Flashman in *Tom Brown's Schooldays*. And while that was physical confrontation, it is equally true to say that in the end all bullies are, at heart, cowards in whatever context.

Negative thought-streams are not always easy to handle since they tend to be attuned and attracted to the weak spots in a person's psyche. Hence the particular vulnerability of the inexperienced of either sex when confronted by an older and therefore seemingly more experienced "adept."

Without a modicum of self-confidence, or a firm trust in one's ability to handle the situation using good judgement, one becomes a relatively easy target.

However, we repeat, the ultimate solution is in the mind of the "victim"; until the weak spot attracting negative attention and thought-flows is eliminated or balanced, the problem cannot be properly dealt with. Strength to bear with, rise above, and overcome the negative influence can be obtained by sincerely and silently invoking the Christ Force as the temporarily veiled aspect of one's own Higher nature.

Objective Phenomena

The world mood has swung, to some extent, from demons of the night and various elementals, some of which are sadly missed, to corn circles, alien sightings, and abductions, UFOs, etc. However, poltergeists are still in evidence, though largely linked to young girls approaching puberty. Similarly, haunt-ings—the likely consequence of unresolved fragmented per-sonalities "stuck" in the beyond and unable to proceed in the normal after-death sequence, still obsessed by a particular habit pattern or event from which they seem powerless to rid themselves.

Recent Developments

It must be pointed out that recent developments in quantum physics, namely Bell's Theorem, confirmed experimentally by John Clause (1978) and Alain Aspect's team (1982) confirms the proposition that our world is supported by an unmediated invisible reality, which allows instantaneous communication faster than light. This interaction does not diminish with dis-tance and links up locations without crossing space.

This reinforces the reality of thought transfer (ESP) from one person to another. The ability to concentrate is a key factor in this though, and with the present level of mind and will development, that is probably a somewhat rare talent.

The use of such a technique negatively is unlikely to be successful where distance is involved. Again the key to disengaging oneself from this kind of involvement consists in severing all mental, emotional, and physical links, so far as is possible. In extreme emergency, one should sincerely invoke the Higher Powers in the form of the Christ Force.

Here is a formula you can use to calm yourself when unduly stressed. Use it in private! Face the East, visualising yourself standing in the Sign of Stability and raise your right hand in the Sign of Evocation, saying:

By the Power of the Christ within me Whom I serve . . .

Make the Sign of the Cross on the breast and forehead.

with all my heart and with all my soul and with all my strength . . .

Draw a Circle of Protection right round you, using the pointed index finger of your right hand, now saying:

I encompass myself about with Divine Circle of His protection, across which no error may set foot.

PREFACE

It is with a sense of the seriousness of the issues involved that I set myself to the task of writing a book on psychic attack and the best methods of defence against it. The undertaking is beset with pitfalls. It is hardly possible to give practical information on the methods of psychic defence without at the same time giving practical information on the methods of psychic attack. It is not without reason that initiates have always guarded their secret science behind closed doors. To disclose sufficient to be adequate without disclosing sufficient to be dangerous is my problem. But as so much has already been made known concerning the esoteric teachings, and as the circle of students of the occult is becoming rapidly wider every day, it may well be that the time has now come for plain speaking. The task is not of my seeking, but as it has come into my hands, I will do my best to discharge it honourably, making available the knowledge which has come to me in the course of many years' experience of the strange by-ways of the mind which the mystic shares with the lunatic. This knowledge has not been attained without cost, nor, I suspect, will the divulging of it be altogether free from cost, either.

I have endeavoured to avoid, as far as possible, the use of second-hand material. We all know the person who has a friend whose friend saw the ghost with her own eyes. That is not of very much use to anybody. What we need is to have the eye-witness under cross-examination. For this reason I have not drawn upon the vast literature of the subject for illustrations of my thesis, but have preferred to rely upon cases that have come within the range of my own experience and which I have been able to examine.

I think I may fairly claim to have practical, and not merely theoretical, qualifications for the task. My attention was first turned to psychology, and subsequently to occultism as the real key to psychology, by the personal experience of a psychic attack which left me with shattered health for a considerable period. I know for myself the peculiar horror of such an experience, its insidiousness, its potency, and its disastrous effects on mind and body.

It is not easy to get people to come forward and bear witness to psychic attacks. First, because they know there is very little likelihood of their being believed, and that they will be more likely to earn themselves a reputation for mental unbalance than for anything else. Secondly, because any tampering with the foundations of the personality is an experience of such peculiar and unique horror that the mind shrinks from the contemplation of it and one cannot talk about it.

I am of the opinion that psychic attacks are far commoner than is generally realised, even by occultists themselves. Certainly the general public has no conception at all of the sort of things that are done by people who have a knowledge of the powers of the human mind and set to work to exploit them. I am convinced that this factor played a large part in the witch-cult, and was the real cause of the universal horror and detestation of the witch. These powers have always been known to students of occultism, but nowadays they are known and used by people who would be exceedingly surprised to find who are their fellow practitioners. Mrs. Eddy, the founder of Christian Science, stumbled on to these methods empirically without ever acquiring any rational knowledge as to their *modus operandi*. She endeavoured to teach them in such a way that they could only be used for good and their power for evil should be concealed; but that she herself was well aware of their possibilities if abused is witnessed by the dread of what she called "Malicious Animal Magnetism" which shadowed her whole life.

The methods of Christian Science, without its strict discipline and careful organisation, were developed and exploited by the innumerable schools and sects of the New Thought Movement. In many of the developments the religious aspect was lost sight of, and they simply became a method of mental manipulation for purely personal ends, though not necessarily deliberately evil. Their exponents advertised that they would teach the art of salesmanship, of making oneself popular and dominant in society, of attracting the opposite sex, of drawing to oneself money and success. The amazing number of these courses advertised shows their popularity; in a recent issue of an American magazine. I counted advertisements for sixty-three different courses in various forms of mind-power. They would not be so popular if they achieved no results at all.

Let us consider some of these advertisements and see what they indicate, reading between the lines and drawing our own conclusions.

"Transfer your thoughts to others. Send for free folder. *Telepathy*, or *Mental Radio*."

"Troubled-health, love, money? Let me help you. No failures, instructions being followed. Strictly personal and professional. Careful as family physician. Five dollars must accompany enquiry. Money back if not satisfied."

"What do you want? Whatever it is, we can help you to get it! Just give us the chance by writing for 'Clouds Dispelled.' Absolutely free. You will be delighted."

"HYPNOTISM. Would you possess that strange mysterious power which charms and fascinates men and women, influences their thoughts, controls their desires and makes you supreme master of every situation? Life is full of alluring possibilities for those who master the secrets of hypnotic influence, for those who develop their magnetic powers. You can learn at home, cure diseases and bad habits without drugs, win the friendship and love of others, increase your income, gratify your ambitions, drive worry and trouble from your mind, improve your memory, overcome domestic difficulties, give the most thrilling entertainment ever witnessed and develop a wonderfully magnetic will-power that will enable you to overcome all obstacles to your success."

"*You can hypnotise people instantly*—quick as a flash—put yourself or anyone else to sleep at any hour of the day or night, or banish pain and suffering. Our free book tells you the secrets of this wonderful science. It explains exactly how you can use this power to better your condition in life. It is enthusiastically endorsed by ministers of the gospel, lawyers, doctors, business men and society women. It benefits everybody. It costs nothing. We give it away to advertise our institution."

These are a few specimens chosen from among the sixty-three similar advertisements counted in this single issue of a popular weekly magazine. They are given *in extenso,* in no way edited save by the omission of addresses.

Let us now consider what such advertisements as these signify from the point of view of the persons to whom they are not addressed, the persons over whom the reader is presumed to want to acquire power. What will be their position should he break the tenth commandment and covet his neighbour's Wife, or his ox, or his ass, or any of his other valuables? Supposing the diligent student of these methods wants something he ought not to have? Supposing he is on the shady side of the law? Or is nursing a sense of injury and desires to be revenged? Or merely loves power for its own sake? What is the fate of the cannon fodder that supplies the student of mind-power with the material for his experiments? What does it feel like to be dominated by these methods, and what results may ultimately be obtained by a competent experimenter?

Let me give my own experience, painful though it is, for someone has got to be the first to come forward and uncover these abuses which are only able to flourish because of the general failure to realise their significance.

As a young girl of twenty I entered the employment of a woman who I now know must have had a considerable knowledge of occultism obtained during a long residence in India, and concerning which she used to drop hints that I could make nothing of at the time, but which, in the light of later knowledge, I have come to understand. It was her custom to control her staff by means of her knowledge of mind-power, and she had a steady succession of most peculiar breakdowns among the people working under her.

I had not been with her very long when she wanted me to give evidence in a lawsuit. She was a woman of violent temper, and had dismissed an employee without notice and without wages, and he was suing her for the money due to him. She wanted me to say that his behaviour had been such that she was justified in thus dismissing him. Her method of collecting my evidence was to look into my eyes with a concentrated gaze and say, "Such and such things happened." Fortunately for all concerned I had kept a diary and had a day-to-day record of the whole transaction. If it had not been for this I should not have known where I was. At the end of the interview I was dazed and exhausted, and lay down on my bed in my clothes and slept the sleep of utter exhaustion till the next morning. I suppose I slept for about fifteen hours.

Soon after this she wanted my testimony again. She wished to get rid of my immediate superior, and wanted to find sufficient grounds to justify her in doing so. She repeated her previous manoeuvres, but this time I had not got a diary record to fall back upon, and to my intense surprise I found myself agreeing with her in a series of entirely baseless charges against the character of a man I had no reason to believe to be otherwise than perfectly straight. The same exhaustion and the same dead sleep descended upon me immediately after this interview as after the preceding one, but an additional symptom now manifested itself. As I walked out of the room at the end of the interview I had a curious sensation as if my feet were not in the place I expected them to be. Anyone who has walked across a carpet that is bellying up with the under-floor draught will know what I mean. Occultists will recognise it as having to do with the extrusion of the etheric double.

The next incident to occur in this curious menage did not concern myself, but another girl, an orphan with considerable means. My employer kept this girl constantly with her, and finally persuaded her to put the whole of her capital into her schemes. However, trustees descended in wrath, forced my employer to disgorge, and took the girl away with them then and there, leaving all her belongings behind, to be packed up and sent on to her afterwards.

Another incident followed quick on the heels of this one. There was an elderly woman in the establishment who was slightly "minus" mentally. A dear old thing, but childlike and eccentric. My employer now turned her attention to her and we watched the same process of domination beginning. In this case there were no trustees to interfere, and the poor old lady was being persuaded to take her affairs out of the hands of her brother, who had hitherto managed them, and commit them to the tender mercies of my employer. My suspicions had by now been thoroughly aroused. It was more than I could bear to see old "Auntie" rooked, so I took a hand in the game, woke "Auntie" up to the situation, pushed her belongings into a box, and got her off to her relatives while my employer was away for a brief absence.

I hoped my complicity in the affair would not become known, but I was soon disillusioned. My employer's secretary came to my room one night, after "lights out," and warned me that the Warden, as we called our employer, had found out who it was that had engineered "Auntie's" escape, and I had better look out for trouble. Knowing her to be of an exceedingly revengeful nature, I knew that my best refuge was flight, but flight was not altogether easy to achieve. The institution in which I was employed was an educational one, and a term's notice had to be given before leaving. I did not look forward to working out that term under the unchecked control of a spiteful woman. So I watched for an opportunity that should justify me in walking out. With my employer's uncontrolled temper it was not long to seek. I was up late the following night packing, in preparation for my intended flight, when there came to my room another member of the staff, a girl who seldom spoke, had no friends, and went about her work like an automaton. I had never had any dealings with her, and was more than surprised at her visit.

It was soon explained, however.

"You are going to leave?" She said.

I admitted that it was so.

"Then go without seeing the Warden. You will not get away if you don't. I have tried several times, and I cannot get away."

However, I was young and confident in my untried strength, with no means of gauging the forces arrayed against me, and next morning, dressed for the journey and suitcase in hand, I went down and bearded my formidable employer in her den, determined to tell her what I thought of her and her methods, quite unsuspicious that anything save ordinary knavery and bullying was afoot.

I was not allowed to get started with my carefully prepared speech, however. As soon as she learnt that I was leaving, she said:

"Very well, if you want to go, go you shall. But before you go you have got to admit that you are incompetent and have no self-confidence."

To which I replied, being still full of fight, that if I were incompetent, why did she not dismiss me herself, and anyway, I was the product of her own training-school. Which remark naturally did not improve matters.

Then commenced a most extraordinary litany. She resumed her old trick of fixing me with an intent gaze, and said:

"You are incompetent, and you know it. You have no self-confidence, and you have got to admit it."

To which I replied, "That is not true. I know my work, and you know I know it."

Now there was no doubt that much could be said concerning my competency in my first post at the age of twenty, with a great deal of responsibility on my shoulders, and newly inducted into a disorganised department; but nothing whatever could be said against my self-confidence, except that I had too much of it. I was quite prepared to rush in where archangels would have hung back in the collar.

My employer did not argue or abuse me. She kept on with these two statements, repeated like the responses of a litany. I entered her room at ten o'clock, and I left it at two. She must have said these two phrases several hundreds of times. I entered it a strong and healthy girl. I left it a mental and physical wreck and was ill for three years.

Some instinct warned me that if I admitted I were incompetent and had no self-confidence my nerve would be broken, and I would never be good for anything afterwards, and I recognised that this peculiar manoeuvre on the part of my employer was an act of revenge. Why I did not pursue the obvious remedy of taking refuge in flight, I do not know, but by the time one realises that something abnormal is toward on these occasions, one is more or less glamoured, and just as the bird before the snake cannot use its wings, so one cannot move or turn away.

Gradually everything began to feel unreal. All I knew was that I had to hold on at all costs to the integrity of my soul. Once I agreed to her suggestions, I was done for. We went on with our litany.

But I was getting near the end of my resources. I had a curious sensation as if my field of vision were narrowing. This, I believe, is a characteristic phenomenon of hysteria. Out of the corners of my eyes I could see two walls of darkness creeping up behind me on either side, as if one stood with one's back to the angle of a screen, and it were being slowly closed upon one. I knew that when those two walls of darkness met, I should be broken.

Then a curious thing happened. I distinctly heard an inner voice say:

"Pretend you are beaten before you really are. Then she will let up the attack and you will be able to get away." What this voice was, I have never known.

I immediately followed its advice. With my tongue in my cheek I asked my employer's pardon for everything I had ever done or ever should do. I promised to remain on in my post and to go softly all the days of my life. I remember I went down on my knees to her, and she purred complacently over me, well satisfied with the morning's work, as she had every reason to be.

Then she let me go, and I went up to my room and lay down on the bed. But I could not rest until I had written her a letter. What that letter contained, I do not know. As soon as I had written it and put it where she would get it, I fell into a sort of stupor, and lay in this state with my mind completely in abeyance till the following evening. That is to say, from two o'clock one afternoon till about eight o'clock of the following day—thirty hours. It was a cold spring day with snow on the ground. A window close to the head of the bed was wide open and the room unheated. I had no covering over me, but I felt neither cold nor hunger, and all the processes of the body were in abeyance. I never stirred. Heartbeat and respiration were very slow, and continued so for several days.

I was found eventually by the housekeeper, who revived me by the simple application of a good shaking and a cold sponge. I was dazed, and disinclined to move or even to eat. I was left to lie in bed, my work taking care of itself, the housekeeper coming to look at me from time to time, but making no comment on my condition. My employer never showed herself.

After about three days my especial friend, who thought I had left the house, learnt of my continued presence, and came along to see me; an act requiring some courage, for our mutual employer was a formidable antagonist. She asked me what had happened at my interview with the Warden, but I could not tell her. My mind was a blank and all memory of that interview had gone as if a sponge had been passed over a slate. All I know was that out of the depths of my mind a most terrible state of fear was rising up and obsessing me. Not fear of any thing or person; just plain fear without an object, but none the less terrible for that. I lay in bed with all the physical symptoms of intense fear. Dry mouth, sweating palms, thumping heart and shallow, hasty breathing. My heart was beating so hard that at each beat a loose brass knob on the bedstead rattled. Fortunately for me, my friend saw that something was seriously wrong and she sent for my family, who fetched me away. They were exceedingly suspicious. The Warden was exceedingly uncomfortable, but no one could prove anything, so nothing was said. My mind was a blank. I was thoroughly cowed and very exhausted, and my one desire was to get away.

I did not recover, however, as had been expected. The intensity of the symptoms wore off, but I continued to be exceedingly easily tired, as if I had been drained of all my vitality. I knew that, somewhere at the back of my mind, was hidden the memory of a terrible experience, and I dared not think of it, because if I did, the shock and strain would be so severe that my mind would give way altogether. My chief consolation was an old school arithmetic book, and I used to spend hour upon hour doing simple sums to keep my mind from racing itself to pieces in wondering what had been done to me and sidling up towards the memory, and then shying away from it like a frightened horse. Finally I gained some measure of peace by coming to the conclusion that I had simply had a breakdown from overwork, and that the whole queer transaction was the fruit of my imagination. And yet there was a lingering feeling that it was real, and this feeling would not let me rest.

About a year after the incident, my health still being very poor, I went away to the country to recuperate, and there came across a friend who had been on the spot at the time of my breakdown. It had apparently caused a good deal of talk, and I found here one who was not inclined to explain away my experience, but asked pertinent questions. Another new friend became interested in my case and hauled me off to the family doctor, who bluntly gave it as his opinion that I had been hypnotised. It was before the days of psycho-therapy, and his ministrations to a mind diseased were limited to patting me on the back and giving me a tonic and bromide. The tonic was useful, but the bromide was not, as it lowered my powers of resistance, and I speedily discarded it, preferring to put up with my discomfort rather than to render myself defenceless. For all the time I was obsessed by the fear that this strange force, which had been applied to me so effectually, would be applied again. But although I feared this mysterious power, which I now realised was abroad in the world, I cannot tell what a relief it was to me to find that the whole transaction was not an hallucination, but an actual fact that one could rise up and cope with.

I obtained my release from the bondage of this fear by facing the whole situation and determining to find out exactly what had been done to me and how I could protect myself against a repetition of the experience. It was an exceedingly unpleasant process, in fact, the reaction caused by recovering the lost memories was only a little less violent than the original one; but I finally succeeded in freeing myself from my hag-ridden condition of fear, although it was a very long time before my physical health became normal. My body was like an electric battery that had been completely discharged. It took a long time to charge up again, and every time it was used before the charging was completed, it ran down again rapidly. For a long time I had no reserves of energy, and after the least exertion would fall into a dead sleep at any hour of the day. In the language of occultism, the etheric double had been damaged, and leaked prana. It did not become normal until I took initiation into the occult order in which I subsequently trained. Within an hour of the ceremony I felt a change, and it is only upon the rarest occasions since then, after some psychic injury, that I have had a temporary return of those depleting attacks of exhaustion.

I have told this story in detail because it is a useful illustration of the manner in which the little-known powers of the mind can be abused by an unscrupulous person. Firsthand experience is of far more value than any amount of illustration from the pages of history, however well authenticated.

If such a transaction had taken place during the Middle Ages, the parish priest would have organised a witch-hunt. In the light of my own experiences, I am not at all surprised that people who had acquired a reputation for the practice of witchcraft were lynched, the methods are so terrible and so intangible. We may think the records of the witch-trials are ridiculous, with their tales of wax images melting in front of slow fires, or the crucifying of christened toads, or the reciting of little jingles, such as "Horse, hattock, To ride, to ride." But if we understand the use of mindpower we soon realise that these things were simply aids to concentration. There is no essential difference between sticking pins into a wax image of an enemy and burning candles in front of a wax image of the Virgin. You may think that both these practices are gross superstition, but you can hardly think that one is real and potent and deny reality and potency to the other. "The weapons of our warfare are not carnal" may as truly be said of the practitioners of Black Magic as of the Church.

My own case belongs more to the realm of psychology than to occultism, the method employed being an application of hypnotic power to improper ends; I have given it, however, because I am convinced that hypnotic methods are very largely used in Black Magic, and that telepathic suggestion is the key to a large proportion of its phenomena. I cite my own case, painful as it is to me to do so, because an ounce of experience is worth a pound of theory. It was this experience which led me to take up the study of analytical psychology, and subsequently of occultism.

As soon as I touched the deeper aspects of practical psychology and watched the dissection of the mind under psychoanalysis, I realised that there was very much more in the mind than was accounted for by the accepted psychological theories. I saw that we stood in the centre of a small circle of light thrown by accurate scientific knowledge, but around us was a vast, circumambient sphere of darkness, and in that darkness dim shapes were moving. It was in order to understand the hidden aspects of the mind that I originally took up the study of occultism.

I have had my full share of the adventures of the Path; have known men and women who could indubitably be ranked as adepts; seen phenomena such as no seance room has ever known, and borne my share in it; taken part in psychic feuds, and stood my watch on the roster of the occult police force which, under the Masters of the Great White Lodge, keeps guard over the nations, each according to its race; kept the occult vigil when one dare not sleep while the sun is below the horizon; and hung on desperately, matching my staying-power against the attack until the moon-tides changed and the force of the onslaught blew itself out.

And through all these experiences I was learning to interpret occultism in the light of psychology, and psychology in the light of occultism, the one counterchecking and explaining the other.

Because of my specialised knowledge, people came to me when an occult attack was suspected, and their experience reinforces and supplements my own. Moreover, there is a considerable literature on the subject to be found in quarters where one would least expect it—in accounts of folklore and ethnology, in the State Records of witch trials, and even under the guise of fiction. These independent records, by people in no way interested in psychic phenomena, confirm the statements made by those who have experienced occult attacks.

On the other hand, we have to distinguish very carefully between psychic experience and subjective hallucination; we have to be sure that the person who complains of a psychic assault is not hearing the reverberation of his own dissociated complexes. The differential diagnosis between hysteria, insanity and psychic attack is an exceedingly delicate and difficult operation, for so frequently a case is not clear-cut, more than one element being present; a severe psychic attack causing a mental breakdown, and a mental breakdown laying its victim open to invasion from the Unseen. All these factors have to be borne in mind when investigating an alleged occult attack, and it shall be my task in these pages not only to indicate the methods of occult defence, but also to show the methods of differential diagnosis.

It is very necessary, with so much occult knowledge about, that people should know an occult attack when they see it. These things are much more common than is generally realised. The recent tragedy in Iona gives point to this assertion. No occultist is under any illusion as to that death being from natural causes. In my own experience I have known of similar deaths.

In my novel, *The Secrets of Dr. Taverner,* there were presented, under the guise of fiction, a number of cases illustrative of the hypotheses of occult science. Some of these stories were built up to show the operation of the invisible forces; others were drawn from actual cases; and some of these were written down rather than written up in order to render them readable by the general public.

So much first-hand experience, confirmed by independent evidence, should not go unregarded, especially since rational explanations are difficult to find save in terms of the occult hypotheses. It may be possible to explain away each individual case mentioned in these pages by alleging hallucination, fraud, hysteria, or plain lying, but it is not possible to explain the sum-total of them in this way. There cannot be so much smoke without some fire. It is not possible that the prestige of the magician in antiquity and the dread of the witch in the Middle Ages could have arisen without some basis in experience. The vapourings of the wise woman would be no more heeded than those of the village idiot if no painful consequences had ever been found to follow upon them. Fear was the motive of these persecutions, and fear founded upon bitter experience; for it was not officialdom which incited the witch-burnings, but whole countrysides that rose up for a lynching. The universal horror of the witch must have some cause behind it.

The labyrinthine windings of the Left-hand Path are as extensive as they are devious; but while exposing them in something, at any rate, of their horror, I still maintain that the Right-hand Path of initiation and occult knowledge is a way to the loftiest mystical experiences and a means of lifting the burden of human suffering. Not every student of this knowledge necessarily abuses it; there are many, nay, the great majority, who hold it selflessly in trust for mankind, using it to heal and bless and redeem that which is lost. It may well be asked: If this knowledge can be so disastrously abused, why should its veil ever be lifted? What answer is made to this question is a matter of temperament. Some will maintain that knowledge of whatever kind cannot be without its value. Others may say we had better let sleeping dogs lie. The trouble is, however, that sleeping dogs have an unfortunate knack of waking up spontaneously. So much occult knowledge is abroad in the world, so much of the kind of things described in these pages is going on unknown and unsuspected in our midst, that it is very desirable that men of goodwill should investigate the forces which men of evil will have perverted to their own ends. These things are the pathologies of the mystic life, and if they were better understood, many tragedies might be averted.

On the other hand, it is not well that everybody should indulge in the study of textbooks of pathology. A vivid imagination and a weak head are a disastrous combination. The readers of that onetime "best seller," *Three Men in Boat,* may remember the fate of the individual who spent a wet Sunday afternoon reading a medical textbook. At the finish he was firmly convinced he had got every single disease described therein with the single exception of housemaid's knee.

This book is not intended merely to make the flesh creep, but is designed as a serious contribution to a little-understood aspect of abnormal psychology, perverted, in some instances, to the purposes of crime. It is a book intended for serious students and for those who find themselves confronted by the problems it describes, and who are trying to understand them and find a way out. My chief aim in speaking so frankly is to open the eyes of men and women to the nature of the forces that are at work below the surface of everyday life. It may happen to anyone of us to break through the thin crust of normality and find ourselves face to face with these forces. Reading of the cases cited in this book, we may well say that there, but for the grace of God, goes anyone of us. If I can give in these pages the knowledge which protects, I shall have fulfilled my purpose.

PART I

Types of Psychic Attack

1 SIGNS OF PSYCHIC ATTACK

The mind-side of nature ◆ The Unseen not necessarily evil ◆
Causes of the rending of the veil ◆ Signs of psychic attack ◆ Fear and
oppression ◆ Nightmares ◆ Hypnagogic visions between sleeping and waking ◆
Nervous exhaustion ◆ Wasting and loss of strength ◆ Changes of temperament ◆
Projection of thought-forms ◆ Materialisations ◆ Hauntings ◆ Vampirism ◆
Repercussion ◆ Evil odours ◆ Precipitation of slime ◆ Phantom footprints ◆
The astral bell ◆ Poltergeist phenomena ◆ Outbreaks of fire ◆ Necessary to
consider: (a) Possibility of a natural explanation, (b) Deliberate fraud ◆
An open mind essential.

IF WE LOOK AT the universe around us we cannot fail to realise that there must be some overruling plan coordinating its infinite complexity. If we take into our hands and examine minutely any living thing, however simple, equally must we realise that the order of its parts is built up on a determining framework. Science has sought in vain for this organising principle; it will never find it on the physical plane, for it is not physical. It is not the inherent nature of atoms which causes them to arrange themselves in the complex patterns of living tissues. The driving forces of the universe, the framework upon which it is built up in all its parts, belong to another phase of manifestation than our physical plane, having other dimensions than the three to which we are habituated, and perceived by other modes of consciousness than those to which we are accustomed.

We live in the midst of invisible forces whose effects alone we perceive. We move among invisible forms whose actions we very often do not perceive at all, though we may be profoundly affected by them.

In this mind-side of nature, invisible to our senses, intangible to our instruments of precision, many things can happen that are not without their echo on the physical plane. There are beings that live in this invisible world as fish live in the sea. There are men and women with trained minds, or special aptitudes, who can enter into this invisible world as a diver descends to the ocean-bed. There are also times when, as happens to a land when the sea-dykes break, the invisible forces flow in upon us and swamp our lives.

Normally this does not occur. We are protected by our very incapacity to perceive these invisible forces. There are four conditions, however, in which the veil may be rent and we may meet the Unseen. We may find ourselves in a place where these forces are concentrated. We may meet people who are handling these forces. We may ourselves go out to meet the Unseen, led by our interest in it, and get out of our depth before we know where we are; or we may fall victim to certain pathological conditions which rend the veil.

The Threshold of the Unseen is a treacherous coast on which to bathe. There are potholes and currents and quicksands. The strong swimmer, who knows the coast, may venture in comparative safety. The non-swimmer, who takes counsel of nothing but his own impulses, may pay for his temerity with his life. But we must not make the mistake of thinking that these invisible forces are necessarily evil and inimical to humanity. They are no more inimical in themselves than are water or fire, but they are potent. If we run counter to them, the result is disastrous for us, for we have broken a natural law; but they are not out to attack us, any more than we are out to attack them. We must face the fact, however, that men and women with knowledge of these things, have, both in the past and in the present, used that knowledge unscrupulously, and that we may find ourselves involved in the results of their actions. It may safely be said that the Unseen is only evil and inimical to humanity when it has been corrupted and perverted by the activities of these unscrupulous men and women, whom initiates call adepts of the Left-hand Path.

We must consider the outward and visible signs of psychic attack before we are in a position to analyse the nature of such attacks and indicate their source of origin. It is a fundamental rule that diagnosis must precede treatment. There are many different kinds of psychic attacks, and the methods that will dispose of one will be ineffectual against another.

The commonest form of psychic attack is that which proceeds from the ignorant or malignant mind of our fellow human beings. We say ignorant as well as malignant, for all attacks are not deliberately motived; the injury may be as accidental as that inflicted by a skidding car. This must always be borne in mind, and we should not impute malice or wickedness as a matter of course when we feel we are being victimised. Our persecutor may himself be a victim. We should not accuse a man of malice if we had linked hands with him and he had stepped on a live rail. Nevertheless, we should receive at his hands a severe shock. So it may be with many an occult attack. The person from whom it emanates may not have originated it. Therefore, we should never respond to attack by attack, thus bringing ourselves down to the moral level of our attackers, but rely upon more humane methods,which are, in reality, equally effectual and far less dangerous to handle.

People also come into touch with the Unseen through the influence of places. Someone who is not actually psychic, but who is sufficiently sensitive to perceive the invisible forces subconsciously, may go to a place where they are concentrated at a high tension. Normally, although we move in the midst of these forces (for they sustain our universe), we are oblivious of them. Where they are concentrated, however, unless we are very dense-minded, we begin to be dimly conscious of something that is affecting us and stirring our subliminal self.

It may happen that the barrier between consciousness and subconsciousness is dense in some people, and they are never able clearly to realise what is going on. They merely have the sense of oppression and general malaise, which lifts when they go away to another place. Consequently, the condition may never be detected, and lead to years of ill-health and misery.

More commonly, however, if there is a definite psychic attack of sufficient force to make itself noticeable at all, there will soon begin to appear characteristic dreams. These may include a sense of weight upon the chest, as if someone were kneeling on the sleeper. If the sense of weight is present, it is certain that the attack emanates locally, for the weight is due to the concentration of etheric substance or ectoplasm, and is sufficiently tangible to press down the scale of a balance when it is possible to capture it for measurement. A great deal of research has been done with materialising mediums upon the nature of this tangible subtle substance, and the reader is referred to the books on the experiments conducted by Crawford with the Goligher Circle at Belfast, and in Paris with Eva C. by other experimenters, for further information and evidence on this subject. It may be noted that Crawford eventually committed suicide for no known reason.

A sense of fear and oppression is very characteristic of occult attack, and one of the surest signs that herald it. It is extremely rare for an attack to make itself manifest out of the blue, as it were. We are not in our normal state of mind, body and circumstance, and then find ourselves suddenly in the midst of an invisible battle. An approaching occult influence casts its shadow on consciousness before it makes itself apparent to the non-psychic. The reason for this is that we perceive subconsciously before we realise consciously, and a line of creeping shade indicates the penetrating of the subconscious censor from below upwards.

As the attack progresses, nervous exhaustion becomes increasingly marked, and there may, under certain conditions, which we will consider later, be such wasting of the tissues that the victim is reduced to a mere bloodless shell of skin and bones, lying on the bed, too weak to move. And yet no definite disease can be demonstrated.

Such a case is an extreme example, proceeding unchecked to its logical conclusion. Other issues are possible, however. The resistance may be good, in which case the attack is unable to gain a foothold on the physical plane, and is limited to that borderland between matter and mind which we perceive upon the threshold of sleep. This is a very terrible experience, for the victim is afraid to sleep and cannot keep awake indefinitely. Worn out by fear and lack of sleep, mental breakdown soon supervenes.

Nervous exhaustion and mental breakdown are the commoner results of astral attack among white people, for in Europe, at any rate, it is not often that an attacker is able to bring the attack to a conclusion in the death of the victim. There are, however, records of cases where the victim has died of pure fright. Kipling's terrible story, *The End of the Passage*, gives an account of such an occurrence.

But in addition to the purely subjective phenomena, there will also be objective ones if the attack has any degree of concentration. The phenomenon of repercussion is well known, the phenomenon wherein that which befalls the subtle body is reflected in the dense body, so that after an astral skirmish during sleep, bruises are found on the physical body, sometimes bruises of a definite pattern. I have seen the print of a goat's hoof and the ace of clubs marked upon the skin as well-defined bruises, passing from blue to yellow and dying away in the course of a few days, as bruises will.

Evil odours are another manifestation of an astral attack. The characteristic smell is of decomposing flesh, and it comes and goes capriciously; but while it is manifesting, there is no doubt whatever about it, and anyone who is present can smell it, whether they are psychic or not. I have also known a frightful stench of drains arise when a ritual belonging to the Element of Earth was being incorrectly performed.

Another curious phenomenon is the precipitation of slime. I have not actually seen this myself, but I have first-hand information upon good authority of one such case. The marks are sometimes as if an army of slugs had been marching in ordered formation; sometimes there is a broad smear of slime, and at others, distinct footprints, often of gigantic size. In the case to which I refer, of which I heard from an eyewitness, the marks were like the footprints of an elephant, enormous tracks on the floor of the drawing-room of a bungalow situated near the sea.

Odd footprints appearing from nowhere and leading nowhere, are sometimes observed when there is snow about. I have seen them on two occasions on the roof of an outbuilding. They alighted upon the edge of it, as if the walker had stepped off an aeroplane, went straight across, and ended abruptly at the wall of the main building upon which the lean-to abuts. They did not return. A single line of footprints came from nowhere and ended in a lofty wall.

A similar happening took place on a very extensive scale in Devon some fifty years ago, and an account of it is to be found in that very curious book, *Oddities*, by Commander Gould. In this case, however, the prints were not human, but were those of what was apparently the hoof of a donkey, proceeding in a single line and going straight through walls and over roofs and covering the best part of a couple of hundred miles in a single night on both sides of an unbridged estuary. Those who want confirmatory evidence would do well to consult Commander Gould's book, where the incident is given in detail.

There is a curious phenomenon known to occultists as the astral bell; Sir Arthur Conan Doyle makes use of it in one of his Sherlock Holmes stories. This sound varies from a clear, bell-like note to a faint click. I have often heard it resemble the sound made by striking a cracked wine-glass with a knife-blade. It commonly announces the advent of an entity that is barely able to manifest, and need not necessarily be a herald of evil at all. It may simply be a knock on the door of the physical world to attract the attention of the inhabitants to the presence of one who stands without and would speak with them. If, however, it occurs in the presence of other symptoms of an astral attack, it would give strong evidence in confirmation of the diagnosis.

Inexplicable outbreaks of fire are also sometimes seen in this connection. These indicate that elemental forces, not human, are at work. Poltergeist phenomena also occur, in which objects are flung about, bells rung and other noisy manifestations take place. Of course, there may be multiplicity of phenomena, more than one type appearing in the same case.

Needless to say, the possibility of some natural, material explanation must never be ignored, even in cases where the supernatural element appears most obvious. It should always be diligently sought in every possible direction before any supernormal hypothesis is considered worthy of attention. But, on the other hand, we should not be so wedded to materialistic theories that we refuse to take a psychic theory as a working hypothesis if it shows any possibility of being fruitful. After all, the proof of the pudding is in the eating, and if, working on an occult hypothesis, we are able to clear up a case which has resisted all other methods of handling, we have pretty good evidence in support of our contention.

We must also bear in mind that the element of deliberate fraud may enter into the most unexpected places. I have seen a drug addict successfully pass himself off for a considerable length of time as the victim of an occult attack. A recent writer in the British Medical journal declared that whenever he came across a case of bell-ringing, knocks, the dripping of water and oil from ceilings, and other untoward happenings, he always looked for the hysterical maidservant. Occultists would be very well advised to do likewise before they begin to worry about the Devil. But, on the other hand, the wise man, whether occultist or scientist, will not insist upon the hysterical maidservant unless he can catch her red-handed, as he surely will do sooner or later if she is the guilty party.

Forged bank-notes would never gain currency unless there were such a thing as genuine bank-notes. It would never occur to anyone to produce fraudulent psychic phenomena unless there had been some genuine psychic phenomena to act as a pattern for the forgery.

The acceptance of an explanation should rest upon the weight of evidence in its favour, not upon one's dislike of its alternatives. I plead that the possibility of a non-material explanation should be investigated in cases where the materialistic hypothesis does not yield results. Not in diseases of the brain and nervous system, nor of the ductless glands, nor in repression of the natural instincts, shall we find the explanation in all cases wherein the mind is afflicted. There is more to man than mind and body. We shall never find the clue to the riddle of life until we realise that man is a spiritual being and that mind and body are the garments of his manifestation.

2 ANALYSIS OF THE NATURE OF PSYCHIC ATTACK

THE ESSENCE OF A psychic attack is to be found in the principles and operations of telepathic suggestion. If we put together what we know of telepathy and what we know of suggestion, we shall understand its *modus operandi*.

Suggestion is of three kinds: Auto-suggestion, Conscious Suggestion and Hypnotic Suggestion. The distinction, however, is not as fundamental as at first sight appears; for the goal of all suggestions in the subconscious mind is the same, and they do not become operative until it is reached. Suggestion is distinguished from threats and appeals to reason by the fact that these aim at a mark in the conscious mind. If they succeed, they owe their success to the acquiescence of the conscious personality, whether coerced or voluntary. But suggestion does not make its appeal to consciousness, but aims at laying its hands upon the springs of action in the subconsciousness and manipulating them from there.

We might compare these two processes to the operation of pulling at the bell-knob outside the front door and taking up a floor-board and twitching the *bell-wires* themselves. The result will be the same in both cases, the bell will ring. Threats and argument pull the bell-knob with varying degrees of emphasis, from the persistent tinkling of moral suasion to the resounding peal of the blackmailer. Suggestion twitches the wires at various points in their course.

Auto-suggestion is given by one's own conscious mind one's own subconscious mind. Now, you may ask, why can I not give orders to my subconscious mind direct, without having to resort to the paraphernalia of suggestion? The answer to this question is very simple. The subconscious mind belongs to a much earlier phase of evolution than the conscious mind; belongs, in fact, to a phase prior to the development of speech. To address it in words, therefore, is like speaking to a man in a language he does not understand. In order to deal with him we must have resort to sign-language. So it is with the subconscious mind. It is no use to say to it, Do this: or, Don't do that. We must make a mental picture of the thing we want done and hold it in consciousness till it begins to sink into the subconsciousness. The subconscious mind will understand this picture, and act upon it.

The actor who wishes to cure himself of stage-fright, will fail to do so if he say to his subconscious mind, "Don't be frightened," for a nod is as good as a wink to a blind horse. Equally, if he makes a mental picture of stage fright and says to his subliminal self, "Now don't do that," the result will be disastrous, for the subliminal self will see the picture and omit the negative, because the word "not" means nothing to it. In order to handle the subconscious mind effectually, we make a mental picture of the thing we want done and hold it in mind by repeated applications until the subconscious begins to be influenced and takes up the task of its own accord.

This is the end result of all suggestion, and the different kinds of suggestion are distinguished, not by the difference in end result, but by the gate through which they enter the subconscious mind. Auto-suggestion originates in our own consciousness; waking suggestion originates in the mind of another and is conveyed to our mind by the ordinary channels of the spoken or written word; hypnotic suggestion enters the subconscious mind direct, without impinging upon consciousness at all.

Hypnotic suggestion (which means, literally, suggestion made during sleep, and is to some extent a misnomer) is of three kinds: firstly, true hypnotic suggestion, made when the subject has been rendered insensible by magnetic passes or fixation of the eyes on a bright object; secondly, suggestion given during normal sleep, as Coué advises should be done with children, in my opinion a most undesirable proceeding; and, thirdly, telepathic suggestion. All these modes of suggestion enter the mind behind the censor; that is to say, they are independent of consciousness, which is neither asked to cooperate, nor has the power to inhibit them.

In most cases, suggestions made in this way are never recognised as coming from outside, but are only discovered after they have matured in the subconsciousness and are beginning to take effect. We do not see the invisible seed, that has been sown in our mind by the mind of another, but in due course germination takes place and the strong-growing shoot appears above the threshold of consciousness as if it were a native growth. The skilful suggestionist always aims at making his suggestions harmonise with the bias of the personality; for if they do not, the established sub-conscious complexes will expel them before they have time to strike root. All he can really do is to reinforce and stimulate the ideas and impulses that are already there, though perhaps latent. He cannot plant an entirely alien seed. He cannot graft a rose shoot on a lilac bush, for it will merely wither and die.

For growth of the thought-seeds of suggestion to take they must find a congenial soil. It is herein lies the strength of the defence. We may not be able to prevent the minds of others from sending us suggestions, but we may so purify the soil of our own natures that no harmful ones can find a congenial seed-bed. It is a simple matter to pull up a seedling nettle, but it is quite a different business to eradicate a thickset bank of tangled roots and stinging shoots, many years old.

It has been said, and not untruly, that a person cannot be hypnotised into doing anything which is contrary to his real nature. But what is the real nature of each one of us ? Have we all overcome the ape and tiger, or are they merely caged? Suggestion can unbar the cage of all our secret temptations and let them loose upon us. None but the saint is naturally immune. It is possible to reduce anybody to anything provided suggestion has unchecked scope for a sufficient length of time. The purest woman can be made a harlot, the noblest man a murderer under certain conditions. Knowledge is necessary to protect, and it is that knowledge which I intend to give in these pages.

Let us now consider exactly how a psychic attack operates. In the realms of mind there is neither time nor space as we understand them. I do not propose to argue this statement philosophically but state it as a fact of experience which anyone who is accustomed to operating on the Inner Planes will have shared. If we think of a person, we are in touch with that person. If we picture them clearly, it is as if we were face to face with them. If we picture them vaguely, it is as if we saw them in the distance. Being in the mental vicinity of a person, we can create a thought-atmosphere by dwelling upon certain ideas in connection with him. This is how spiritual healing is done. The affirmations of Christian Science are used in order to get the mind of the healer into a certain emotional state, and his condition effectually influences the mind of the patient with whom he has put himself en *rapport*.

This power, however, can be used for evil as well as good; the Founder of Christian Science was wise enough to put her teaching in such a way that her students would not readily discern the second edge of the sword. As long as the world in general was ignorant of the powers of the mind, it was better that nothing should be said by those who knew, because the knowledge, if spread abroad indiscriminately, might do more harm than good, giving information to those who ought not to have it. But now that so much is generally known and even practised concerning the powers of the human mind, it is as well that the real facts should also be known and the whole matter brought out into the open, and as far as lies in my power I am prepared to do this.

Any message to the subconscious mind must be couched in very simple terms, because subconscious thought is a primitive form of mentation, developed before spoken language was known to mankind. The primary aim of the suggestion is to create a mental atmosphere about the soul of the person, whether that person is to be attacked or healed, until a sympathetic response or reaction is elicited within the soul itself. (I use the term soul to include both the mental and emotional processes, but to exclude the spiritual ones.) Once this reaction is achieved, the battle is half over, for the gate of the city has been opened from within, and there is free ingress. The telepathic suggestion of definite ideas can now proceed rapidly.

It is this point which is the critical one in any occult attack. Up to this point, the defender has the advantage. If he has sufficient knowledge, the knowledge I hope to make available through this book, he can without any undue exertion retain that advantage indefinitely, and wear his attackers down, even if unable to meet them on their own ground of occult knowledge. There is nothing in this world or the next that a hypnotist can do with the person who keeps his nerve and won't pay attention.

There are two gates, and two only, by which the attacker can gain entrance to the city of Mansoul, and these are the Self-preservation Instinct and the Sex Instinct. The hypnotic appeal must be couched in terms of one or both of these if it is to be successful. How does the attacker proceed? He has to create an atmosphere about the soul of his victim on the

Inner Planes. He can only do this by creating that atmosphere within his own consciousness while he thinks of his victim. If he wants to perform a psychic murder, he must fill his own soul with the rage of destruction until it overflows. If he wants to perform a psychic rape, he must fill his soul with lust and cruelty. The cold rage of cruelty is essential to effectual operations of this nature. Now what happens when he does this? He has sounded a ringing keynote in the Abyss. It will be answered. All beings who have this keynote for the basis of their nature will respond - " Dark Uriel and Azrael and Ammon on the wing" - and will join in the operation. But they do not operate direct upon the victim, *they work through the operator*. It is like the old game of Nuts and May, in which the one who is sent "to fetch her away" is gripped round the waist by the leader of a chain of supporters. The real pressure comes on his own abdominal muscles, as anyone who has played the game will remember.

And when the magical operation is over, what then ?
Will the operator be left to enjoy his victim in peace ?
IS IT LIKELY ?

This is the mystical basis of the story of Faust. The Devil might be not only willing but anxious to enable Dr. Faustus to win Margarita, but he came for his soul at the appointed time. We may also remember that if Margarita had not responded to the lure of the Jewel Song she would not have fallen a victim. The weak spot in the defence was after all in her own nature.

We have considered the *modus operandi* of telepathic suggestion in detail because it forms the real basis of every kind of occult attack. Whether it be a discarnate entity, a being of another order of evolution, a demon from the Pit, or merely the panic-stricken soul of a selfish friend, clinging to the life of form regardless of consequences, in all cases the opening gambit is the same. Until the aura is pierced, there can be no entrance to the soul, and the aura is always pierced from within by the response of fear or desire going out towards the attacking entity. It we can inhibit that instinctive emotional reaction, the edge of the aura will remain impenetrable, and will be as sure a defence against psychic invasion as the healthy and unbroken skin is a defence against bacterial infection.

It happens sometimes, however, that a rapport has been formed with the attacking entity in a previous incarnation, and therefore it holds, as it were, the key to the postern. Such a problem is a very difficult one, and external assistance is needed for its solution. The difficulty is increased by the fact that the victim is often disinclined to allow the break to be made, being bound to the attacking entity, whether discarnate or incarnate, by bonds of fascination, or even genuine affection.

A case with which I was acquainted throws so much light on various aspects of psychic interference by incarnate souls operating out of their bodies that it is of value to quote it at length.

In the summer of 1926 I saw in the papers a short paragraph describing the death of a certain man and his wife, which took place within a few hours of each other. A couple of years previously I had been consulted by a friend of the wife, who was deeply perturbed about the state of affairs, and suspected psychic interference. The wife, Mrs. C. we will call her, had begun to be troubled by nightmares, waking up in a state of intense fear, hearing the echoes of menacing words ringing in her ears. At about the same time the husband, Mr. C., developed what at first sight looked like epileptic fits. A careful diagnosis by specialists, however determined that although epileptiform, they were not true epilepsy. Epilepsy is due either to a congenital tendency whose nature is not fully understood by medical science, or to some injury or disease of the brain. In congenital epilepsy the disease shows itself early in life; in fits due to disease, other symptoms are present which can be detected by a physical examination, such as changes in the eye that are revealed by the ophthalmoscope. The diagnosis can therefore be definitely established. Moreover, there is one sure sign by means of which an epileptic fit can be distinguished with certainty from a hysterical or psychic seizure. In true epilepsy the urine is involuntarily voided in the course of the fit. This is a sure sign, and when it is absent we are safe in saying that the fit is not epileptic, whatever else it may be. This is a useful point for those who have to deal with the pathologies that afflict the psychic temperament, for they will see plenty of seizures, and a sure method of distinguishing those that are of organic origin is very useful. We must not, however, conclude that all cases of such incontinence are epileptics, for there are many other causes, both organic and functional.

In the case of Mr.C. this cardinal symptom was lacking. The attacks, moreover, always took place in sleep, and it seemed as if they were more of the form of severe nightmare, verging on somnambulism. It was a curious factor in the case that Mrs. C.'s nightmares usually heralded Mr. C.'s attacks.

These occurrences showed a certain cyclic regularity, occurring about once a month. In the case of a woman this would naturally be referred to the twenty-eight day cycle of her nature, but in the case of a man, no such explanation was forthcoming, and we therefore had to look for another twenty-eight day cycle to explain his periodicity. The only other cycle of this period is that of the phases of the moon.

We were then confronted by a correlation of epileptiform attacks, which had no organic basis, the nightmares of a second person, and the phases of the moon. Some theory had to be found which would resume these three and explain their inter-relationship.

A dream is commonly the first way in which psychic manifestations make themselves known, the subconscious perceptions being reflected into consciousness in this form.

It is held by many occultists that congenital epilepsy, as distinguished from that due to tumours of the brain, has its roots in the operations of black magic or witchcraft in which the sufferer participated in a past life, whether as practitioner or victim, the fit being an astral struggle with a discarnate entity, reflected on the physical body by means of the well-known phenomenon of repercussion.

The moon plays a very important part in all occult operations, different tides being available at different phases of her cycle. Persephone, Diana and Hecate, all aspects of Luna, are three very different persons.

It therefore appeared probable that as the physical investigation had drawn blank, a psychic investigation might yield fruits. One was performed. And with the following results. Nothing at all was discerned with regard to Mrs. C. She was merely what lawyers call an accessory after the fact. But the psychic trail of Mr. C. was soon picked up and followed, and it appeared that in his last incarnation he had been associated with two women, mother and daughter, who had practised witchcraft for his benefit. The younger of the two women had been for a short time his mistress. Mother and daughter had paid the penalty for their crimes, but their male partner had escaped.

The diagnosis was as follows: It is the younger witch that is at the bottom of the trouble. It is her astral visits which cause the seizures of Mr. C. and the nightmares of Mrs. C., and they correlate with the phases of the moon because certain phases are favourable for the operation she performs and she therefore takes advantage of them. The question now remains, is this woman in incarnation or not ? That is to say, is the midnight visit paid in an astral body projected from a living human being, or by an earth-bound spirit which has succeeded in evading the Second Death ?

Mrs. C. had by now been taken into the confidence of their mutual friend who was concerned for her welfare, and lent a ready ear to the suggestion that some psychic influence might be at the bottom of the trouble, for this explanation coincided with her own intuitions in the matter, intuitions she had not dared to divulge for fear of ridicule.

When asked if she could identify anyone in the circle of her husband's acquaintances who might prove to be the younger witch, she replied immediately that she could without any difficulty, identify both the women, and told the following curious story.

The older witch she identified as her husband's mother, an aged lady who occupied a suite of rooms in their house. For this inoffensive old creature Mrs. C. had always had a peculiar horror and repulsion, although admitting there were no rational grounds for it, and honestly endeavouring to do her duty by her. So great was her horror of the old lady that she would never remain in the house after her husband had left for his office in the morning, but went out herself to her club if she had no other engagement.

Among the frequenters of the house was an intimate friend of the elder Mrs. C., a woman of peculiar psychic temperament, who always called the old lady mother and was singularly attached to her. She was also very attached to Mr. C., but her feelings never exceeded, outwardly at any rate, the bounds of propriety, and Mr. C., who was sincerely attached to his own wife, never paid the slightest attention to her, looking upon her as his mother's friend, and as such to be tolerated.

Mrs. C. unhesitatingly identified Miss X., as we will call her, as the younger witch. Enquiries were then made regarding her history, and a very curious story unfolded.

As a young girl she had become engaged to a man who, soon after the engagement was announced, had developed galloping consumption and died after a short illness with a violent haemorrhage.

Soon after this, Miss X's sister also became engaged, and by a strange fatality her lover shared the same fate, dying as died the other man, in a flood of his own blood.

Years went by, and Miss X. became engaged again. Soon the second lover fell ill, not, this time, with galloping consumption, but with a more lingering form of the complaint, in which haemorrhage was the principle symptom. He seemed to linger on from haemorrhage to haemorrhage, and this went on for years. Miss X., a woman of considerable private means, took a house, installed an aunt as a chaperone, and took her fiancé to live there and be nursed by her. Soon the aunt developed symptoms of illness; she appeared to be drained of all vitality and for days at a time would lie unconscious, but no specific cause was ever discovered for her illness. This peculiar menage continued for years, Miss X. living in her big house with these two moribund creatures lingering on from attack to attack.

She was a constant visitor at the home of the C.'s, both during the lifetime of Mr. C.'s first wife and that of his second, the friend of my friend. On the death of Mr. C.'s first wife she had great hopes, it was observed, that his attentions would turn towards herself, but they did not; nevertheless she swallowed her chagrin, and succeeded in maintaining her foothold as an intimate friend of the family when the new Mrs. C. came to preside over the household.

Certain methods of protection were suggested to Mrs. C. which helped her considerably, but it was not possible to exclude Miss X. from the house owing to her intimacy with the old lady. In due course, however, old Mrs. C. was gathered to her fathers, and then young Mrs. C. put her foot down and said she would have no more to do with Miss X. Mr. C. concurred in this, as he had always had a repulsion for Miss X., and had only tolerated her for his mother's sake.

Soon after this Mrs. C. began to feel unwell, the indisposition slowly progressed, until finally, although she had no definite symptoms, she was obliged to consult a doctor on account of her steadily increasing weakness and sense of malaise. A diagnosis of rapidly growing cancer of the womb was made. An operation was performed, which gave temporary relief, it was not expected to do any more, and she went downhill steadily.

Towards the end she lapsed into unconsciousness, and at the same time, Mr. C. also became unconscious, apparently having one of his seizures in sleep, from which he never awakened. They died within a few hours of each other.

Mr. C.'s first wife had also died of cancer of the womb.

About this time Miss X.'s aunt and fiancé died within short time of each other, and the last that was heard of Miss X. was that she had been removed to a nursing-home in the country with a severe mental breakdown.

Taken separately, any of the incidents in this strange, eventful history can be explained away, but taken together they make a curious story, especially when it is remembered that without any previous information a psychic investigation had "spotted" the existence of a person with abnormal faculties who was interested in Mr. C.

Cancer is a disease upon which certain occult hypotheses throw a good deal of light. It is believed to be a disease of the etheric double, not of the physical body, and that a "Cancer Elemental" is the infective factor.

To prove or disprove anything concerning the foregoing story is impossible, but the following occult hypothesis may explain much. If this hypothesis be not accepted, readers may find an interesting exercise for their ingenuity in constructing another that shall explain more satisfactorily the circumstances of the case.

Miss X. retained subconsciously the knowledge and powers that had been hers during the previous life when she was implicated in the witch-cult. She also retained her passion for Mr. C., a passion which was obviously unrequited. She employed her power of projection of the astral body to visit Mr. C. at night, during sleep. In the absence of details it is impossible to decide definitely whether the "fit" of Mr. C. was a struggle or an embrace. It might be either, or it might be both, an initial struggle ending in an embrace. The dreams of

Mrs. C. obviously related to the same astral visitant who caused the seizures of Mr. C. There is, unfortunately, no record to show at what phase of the moon these attacks took place, but presumably at the Hecate phase, which is the period of evil witchcraft.

The condition of Miss X.'s fiancé and aunt and the death of her first lover point markedly towards vampirism. It is difficult to believe that a consumptive would continue for so many years without his disease either being checked or making definite progress. It is difficult to say what the connection, if any, might be between Miss X. and the death of her sister's lover, but it is a curious thing that three men, associated with this ill-omened household as prospective husbands, should lose their lives in the same way. This, together with the mysterious illness of the aunt, are very suspicious. As noted before, any one of these incidents could be explained away, but taken together they call for thought. It is also curious that Miss X. should keep her fiancé in her house and yet not marry him, from every normal point of view an arrangement with many drawbacks and no advantages. On the other hand, if her feelings were fixed upon Mr. C. and were obtaining satisfaction by astral visits, she would naturally not want to break her rapport with the man she loved by giving herself to the man she did not love. If she were a vampire, her motive for keeping the aunt and lover in her house, and their condition, would be readily explained. Also her breakdown, which followed immediately upon their deaths.

The fact that Mr. C.'s first wife died of cancer of the womb does not in itself call for remark, but it is a curious thing that he should lose his second wife from the same disease. Cancer is not as common as all that, and in any case, there are many available sites beside the womb. On the other hand, Diana, one of the aspects of Luna, of whom Hecate, the goddess of witches, was another, presides over the female reproductive organs.

The illness of Mrs. C. began to show itself soon after Miss X. was excluded from the house.

Finally, what shall we say concerning the deaths of the three people most intimately associated with Miss X. within a short time of each other, and her immediate breakdown? In the absence of details any conclusion must be guesswork, but we have good grounds for supposing that Miss X.'s magical operations were attended by some mishap.

It may be said that such a theory is the wildest improbability and does violence to all the laws of evidence. Let it, however, be borne in mind that two years before these matters eventuated, the work of a witch in connection with Mr. C.'s epileptiform attacks was suspected and the nature of her relationship to him was indicated; and subsequent enquiries revealed the curious facts in connection with Miss X.'s history and menage; let it also be noted that the happenings which subsequently occurred are such as have been recorded in many accounts of witch-trials. It is a scientific maxim that the power to foretell the course of phenomena is a good indication of the truth of a theory.

3 A CASE OF MODERN WITCHCRAFT

Effect of witchcraft in previous incarnations ♦ Case of an occult attack by an
ex-witch ♦ Antipathy of animals to her ♦ Nightmares of the other occupants of
the house ♦ Psychic discernment of danger ♦ Maniacal attack ♦ Method of
handling the case ♦ Use of pentagram ♦ Its effect ♦ Incident of
magnetised cross ♦ Dread of sacred symbols ♦ Her confession.

THE PART PLAYED by the ex-witch in occult attack is very
marked. Again and again do the investigations of
independent psychics point to witchcraft in a previous
incarnation when trouble of this sort is afoot. The motive is
nearly always vengeance, but there is also good reason to
believe that the projection of the astral body takes place
involuntarily during sleep, and is not deliberately willed by
the offender. Very many people who are at present psychics
and sensitives got their training in the covens of mediaeval
witchcraft, and for this reason experienced occultists are very
wary of the natural psychic, as distinguished from the initiate
with his technique of psychism. Where psychism and mental
unbalance are found conjoined with a malevolent disposition,
there is strong presumption that the cult of Diabolus is not
far to seek.

A curious set of happenings, in which I myself was one of the
actors, throws a good deal of light on this by no means
uncommon occurrence. It was in the early days of my interest
in occultism, when I was still buying my experience by the
expensive but effectual method of running my head into
obstacles. I made the acquaintance of a woman who was
interested in psychic matters. She was a person of the most
extreme sensitiveness to anything unclean or ugly, fastidious
to a degree in her personal habits, living almost exclusively

on uncooked vegetarian foods, even refusing eggs as too stimulating. Although not an animal lover, she was morbidly humanitarian, reading with gusto those papers which give lurid and detailed descriptions of vivisection experiments. Had I been older and wiser I should have recognised the significance of her ultra-cleanliness and ultra-sensitiveness as marking the abreaction of a sadistic temperament - sadism being a pathology of the emotional nature in which the sex instinct takes the form of an impulse to inflict pain. Not having learnt then many things I now know, I looked upon her characteristic, as indicative of an exalted spirituality.

At the time I knew her she was verging on a breakdown which was alleged to be due to overwork, and she was very anxious to get away from cities and back to nature. I was just leaving London to take up my residence at an occult college which was hidden away in the sandy fastnesses of the Hampshire barrens. In the innocence of my heart I suggested that she might come down there and help with the domestic duties. The suggestion was acted upon, and a few days after my own arrival Miss L. joined us. She seemed quite normal, made herself agreeable, and was well liked. One incident, however, in the light of subsequent events, was significant. On getting out of the ancient fly in which she had driven from the station, she immediately went and patted the still more ancient horse that drew it. That beast, usually sunk in all apathy from which he was with difficulty roused when action was required of him, galvanised into life at her touch as if she had stung him. He threw up his head, backed, snorted, and nearly turned the equipage over in the ditch, to the amazement of his jehu, who declared he had never been known to do such a thing before, and viewed our visitor with disfavour.

Miss L., however, appeared quite normal, made herself agreeable, and was given a friendly reception by the humans at any rate.

That night I was awakened by nightmare, a thing to which I am not usually subject. I struggled with a weight on my chest, and even after consciousness had fully returned, the room seemed full of evil. I performed such simple banishing formulae as I knew, and peace was restored.

At breakfast next morning an assembly of blear-eyed people met together, complaining of having passed disturbed nights. We compared notes, and found we had all, some six or seven of us, had similar nightmares, and proceeded to exchange experiences. The effect of this upon Miss L. was curious. She squirmed upon her chair as if it had suddenly become red-hot and said with much emphasis:

"These things should not be discussed, it is most unwholesome."

Out of deference to her feelings we desisted. But presently up to the open window came another member of our community, a woman who slept in an open-air shelter at some little distance from the house. We enquired after her health, as usual, and she replied that she was not feeling very well, as she had slept badly, and proceeded to recount the same nightmare as the rest of us.

Later on in the morning, another lady, who had a house a little way down the road, arrived, and she in her turn told of a similar nightmare.

These nightmares continued, on and off for the next few days, to afflict different members of the community. They were vague and nebulous, and there was nothing we could pitch upon for diagnostic purposes, and we put it down to indigestion caused by the village baker's version of war bread.

Then one day I had a quarrel with Miss L. She had conceived a "crush" for me; I have a constitutional repulsion for crushes and give them scant politeness, and she complained bitterly of my lack of responsiveness. Whatever may be the rights and wrongs of the case, I had roused her resentment in good earnest. That night I was afflicted with the most violent nightmare I have ever had in my life, waking from sleep with the terrible sense of oppression on my chest, as if someone were holding me down, or lying upon me. I saw distinctly the head of Miss L., reduced to the size of an orange, floating in the air at the foot of my bed, and snapping its teeth at me. It was the most malignant thing I have ever seen.

Still not attaching any psychic significance to my experiences, and being firmly convinced that the local baker was responsible, I told no one of my dream, thinking it one of those things that are better kept to oneself, but when the members of the community came to talk matters over in the light of subsequent events, we found that two other people had had similar experiences.

A night or two later, however, as it came to bed-time, I was overcome with a sense of impending evil, as if something dangerous were lurking in the bushes around the house threatening attack. So strong was this sensation that I came down from my room and went all round the house, testing the catches of the windows to make sure that all was secure.

Miss L. heard me, and called out to know what I was doing.

I told her of my feelings.

"You silly child," she said, "it is no use latching the windows, the danger is not outside the house but in it. Go to bed, and be sure and lock your door."

She would give no answer to my questions except to reiterate that I should lock my door. This was the first night I had slept in that house, previously having been in a cottage on the opposite side of the road.

I did not lock my door because the night was intolerably hot and the room and the window small. I compromised, however, by putting an enamel slop-pail at a strategic spot in the fairway, trusting that any intruder would fall over it and give the alarm.

Nothing happened, and I slept quietly.

Next morning, however, the storm broke. Miss L. and I were peacefully at work in the kitchen when she suddenly caught up a carving-knife and started after me, as mad as a March hare. Fortunately for me I had in my hands a large saucepan full of freshly boiled greens, and I used this as a weapon of defence, and we danced round the kitchen table, slopping hot cabbage-water in all directions.

We neither of us made a sound; I fended her off with the hot and sooty saucepan, and she slashed at me with an unpleasantly large carving-knife. At a psychological moment in walked the head of the community. He took in the situation at a glance, and handled it by the tactful method of scolding us both impartially for making so much noise and telling us to get on with our work. Miss L. finished whatever she was doing with the carver, I dished up the cabbage, and the incident passed off quietly.

After lunch Miss L. experienced the reaction from her excitement and went to her room completely prostrated with exhaustion. I was somewhat perturbed. Although used to mental cases, and therefore not as disturbed by the recent fracas as anyone else might have been, I did not relish the prospect of being the housemate of a dangerous lunatic who was under no sort of control.

The head of the community, however, said there was no cause for alarm, he would soon have the case in hand. He went up to the bathroom, filled a soap dish with water from the tap, made certain passes over it, and dipping his finger in the water, proceeded to draw a five-pointed star upon the threshold of Miss L.'s room.

Miss L. made no attempt to leave her room until forty-eight hours later when he fetched her out himself.

As he had promised, he soon had her in hand. He had several long talks with her, at which I was not present, and at the end of a few days a very chastened Miss L. began to go about her household duties again. There were relapses, and there were struggles, but in the course of a few weeks she became comparatively normal, and when I met her again some eighteen months later there had been no relapse.

Two curious incidents occurred during the period of her treatment at the hands of this man, an adept if ever there was one. The house in which she had a room was a very old one, and the front door exceedingly massive. It was secured at night by two enormous bolts that extended right across it, a chain that could have moored a barge, and a huge lock with a key the size of a trowel. When the door was opened in the morning it acted as an alarm clock for the entire village. It creaked, it groaned, and it clanged. Yet night after night we came down in the morning to find this door standing ajar. We all slept with our doors open on to the small landing. To go down the ancient, creaking stairs was like walking on organ stops. The back door was a modern affair, which could have been opened easily. The windows were modern casements of the most gimcrack description. Who opened the heavy front door, and why?

We exchanged recriminations several mornings at breakfast as to who had left the door open the night before, but no one could ever be convicted of the blame. Finally the matter came to the knowledge of the head of the group.

"I will soon put a stop to that," he said, and each night he resealed Miss L.'s room with the pentagram. We had no more trouble with the front door coming open after that.

While he was dealing with Miss L. he made a practice of sealing the threshold of his own room in the same way, only in this case he drew the pentagram point outwards, to prevent

Miss L. from coming in; whereas when he sealed her room, he put its point inwards, to prevent her coming out. She did not know this, nor was it likely to reach her ears indirectly, for he was very uncommunicative, I only knew that he was sealing his room because I chanced to see him doing it.

Nevertheless, one day I heard a knock at my door, and there was Miss L. with her arms full of clean linen. She asked me if I would be good enough to take it into the room of the head of the community, and put it away. I asked her why she did not do so herself, for I knew he was out, and it was her work to put away the linen. She replied that she had been to his room for that purpose, but there was a psychic barrier across the threshold that prevented her entering.

She also asked me, on several occasions, to put inside my frock out of sight a little silver cross that I habitually wore, as she said she could not bear the sight of it. This cross I had purchased just before coming to this occult college, and had taken it to a priest of my acquaintance to be blessed, for I had not been altogether easy in my mind concerning the nature of the group I was joining, and during the early days of my association with it was poised on tiptoe, as it were, ready for instant flight. Naturally I had kept my own counsel concerning the psychic precautions I had taken against my new friends, and no one was aware that the cross had been specially magnetised against psychic attack. Nevertheless, the woman who would have attacked if she could, felt its influence and feared it.

Auto-suggestion and imagination play so large a part in so-called psychic impressions that one is chary of accepting confirmatory testimony from a psychic who knows what is expected of him, but a spontaneous reaction is in my opinion evidential. When the treatment of Miss L. had progressed some way towards her final recovery, much interesting information was elicited. She told us that she had distinct memories of dealings with black magic in her previous lives. This, she said, had been confirmed by several independent psychics, and I would certainly have been willing to add my testimony to theirs had I been asked. As a child, she used to daydream that she was a witch, willing the death or misfortune of those who annoyed her, and she also averred, though whether this was true or not I cannot say, that her wishes were so effectual that she was frightened and tried to abandon the practice. She also volunteered that she was in the habit of visualising herself standing before people she was angry with, scolding them, and projecting malignant force at them. This, of course, would explain our nightmares. She also said that she had been in the habit of attacking her mother and sister in this way, and had made her sister very ill, so that they now refused to have her in the house. This statement was later confirmed by the mother.

She told us that she felt as if she were two distinct persons, her normal self being spiritually-minded, intensely compassionate and idealistic. Her other, and lower self, which came to the surface when she was crossed, upset, or over-tired, being intensely malicious and subject to paroxysms of hate and cruelty.

These characteristics had been particularly marked when she was little. But as she grew older she recognised the wrongfulness of them, and her lofty idealism represented her endeavour to rise above them. This endeavour was, I am convinced, an honest one; unfortunately it was not always successful.

She referred to the incident in which she told me to lock my door, and said she had done so in the hope of affording me some measure of protection against the astral projection in which she knew she was tempted to indulge.

At first sight her case had looked like one of obsession, and had been so diagnosed by one or two members of the community, but wise handling revealed otherwise.

This case reveals another interesting point in that, true to the witch-tradition, she had a horror of sacred symbols. She would not occupy a room where there was a picture of a religious subject. Nothing would induce her to wear any piece of jewellery in the form of a cross, and it was impossible for her to enter a church.

This case has many points of interest, especially in the fact that what was apparently a case of well-marked insanity was cleared up by occult methods.

4 PROJECTION OF THE ETHERIC BODY

BEFORE WE CAN leave the subject of attack by incarnate human beings, we must consider the subject of etheric projection. In this case not only is the mind at work, but also something which is pretty nearly physical; sufficiently physical, at any rate, to leave bruises on the flesh of the victim, throw the furniture about, or at least make a considerable amount of noise.

Where such manifestations take place, it is obvious that we are dealing with something more substantial than the mind, for although mind can influence mind, and through it the body to an extent to which in the present state of our knowledge it is difficult to set limits, mind cannot manipulate matter directly: that is to say, you cannot smash a window by means of a thought. There must be some physical vehicle that can be manipulated by the mind if effects are to be wrought on the physical plane. The living body is such an instrument; it is manipulated by the mind every time a voluntary movement takes place, and the operations of spiritual healing are simply an extension of this principle to the involuntary muscles and physiological processes not ordinarily directed by the conscious mind. Occultists maintain that mind affects body by means of the etheric double, as it is called, the "mortal mind" of the Christian Scientists. We may not unreasonably conclude that when physical action is produced at a distance by occult means, it is done by employing this etheric double.

The etheric double is primarily a body of magnetic stresses in the framework of whose meshes every cell and fibre of the physical body is held as in a rack. But intermediate between this and the dense physical body as we know it, there is what may be called the raw material out of which dense matter is condensed. This was called by the ancients, Hyle, or First Matter, and by the moderns, Ectoplasm. It is this projected ectoplasm which produces the phenomena whenever physical manifestations are in question. It may be projected as long rods, which will operate up to a distance of a dozen feet or so; or it may be projected as a nebulous cloud, connected with the medium by a tenuous thread. This cloud can be organised into distinct forms, having the semblance of life and acting as vehicles for conscious wills. There is a great deal of information available on this subject in the literature of spiritualism, to which reference may be found in the bibliography at the end of this book.

The adept who was head of the occult college to which I have previously referred, and from whom I received my first training in occultism, was able to perform this operation, and I have many times seen him do it. He would go into a deep trance, after a few convulsive movements, somewhat like a slow tetany, and would then lose about two-thirds of his weight. I have many times helped to lift him, or even lifted him single-handed, when he was in this state, and he weighed no more than a child. A man can fake many things, but he cannot fake his weight. I have lifted him single-handed from the floor on to a sofa when in this state. It is quite true that, being rigid as a board, he was much easier to handle than the ordinary limp, unconscious human form; but there is a certain ratio between the weight of a grown man and the strength of a woman of average physique.

What became of the missing weight on these occasions I found out one night. He had been ill, with some delirium, and the lion's share of the nursing, especially the night work, had fallen to my lot. There came a time, however, when we decided that he was so far recovered that it was unnecessary for anyone to sit up with him, so to bed we all went, for the first time for several days. I shared a room with another member of the community. It was a comparatively small cottage we were in, and our two beds were close together, side by side, right under the uncurtained open window. It was the time of the full moon, and I remember that I had no need to light a candle in order to see to undress.

I fell asleep at once, for I was very tired. I could not have been asleep very long, however, when I was awakened by the sensation of a weight upon my feet. It was as if a good-sized dog, say, a collie, had jumped up and lain down on the bed. The room was flooded with moonlight, and as bright as day, and I clearly saw, lying apparently asleep across the foot of my bed, the man whom we had left safely tucked up for the night in the room below. It was a somewhat embarrassing situation, and I lay still, taking thought before I did anything. I was wide enough awake by now, as may well be imagined. I concluded that Z., as I will call this man, had either had a return of the delirium, or was sleep-walking. In any case I was very anxious to get him safely back to bed again without a fuss or a scene. My companion had a bad heart, and I did not want her to get a shock; neither did I want him to get a shock in his weak state. I was afraid that if I asked my room-mate first, she might scream, and wake Z. up with a start, with disastrous consequences. I decided therefore to wake him gently, as being the worse case of the two, and let her take her chance. Having cogitated these matters for several moments at least, I finally took action. I sat up in bed and leant quietly forward with the intention of touching him gently on the shoulder and so arousing him. In order to lean forward, I had to withdraw my feet from under him, for they were pinned by his weight, which until now had rested upon them, for I had been careful not to stir while thinking out my plan of campaign.

Z. was plainly visible in the moonlight, clad apparently in his dressing-gown, or so I took the muffling folds of material to be that swathed him about. Both his face and wrapping appeared grey and colourless in the moonlight, but there was no question in my mind as to his solidarity, for not only could

I see him, but I could feel his weight resting upon my feet. But the moment I moved, he vanished, and I was left staring in amazement at the smooth fold of the blankets over the end of the little camp-bed on which I lay. It was then, and only then, that I realised he had appeared all grey and colourless, more like a shaded pencil sketch than a human being of flesh and blood.

I asked him about this incident in the morning, but he said he had no recollection of it; he had been dreaming the uneasy, broken dreams of a sick man, but could not recall them.

This, of course, was in no way an occult attack, but rather the visit of a friend, who had come to lean upon me in the course of his illness, and instinctively came to me for consolation when out of his body in trance at a time when his weakened condition prevented him from retaining his normal control over his psychic activities. Nevertheless, it serves to illustrate what could be done if the etheric form that visited me had been energised by a malignant will. It may explain the nature of the sense of weight that oppresses the victims of a certain type of nightmare.

I have heard of more than one case wherein bruises resembling finger-marks were found on the throats of people who had been victims of an astral attack. I have never actually seen such bruises myself, but I have been told of them by people who have either had them themselves, or seen them. It is a well-known fact that if an occultist, functioning out of the body, meets with unpleasantness on the astral plane, or if his subtle body is seen, and struck or shot at, the physical body will show the marks. I myself have many times found curiously patterned bruises on my body after an astral skirmish. The mechanism of the production of such marks must, I think, be of the same nature as that which produces the stigmata of saints and the curious physical marks and swellings sometimes seen in hysterics - the mind, powerfully stirred, affects the etheric double, and the etheric double acts upon the physical molecules held in its meshes. I dare to prophesy the next advances in medicine will be bound up with the knowledge of the nature and function of the etheric double.

The next type of psychic attack which we must consider is that conducted by means of artificial elementals. These are, distinguished from thought-forms by the fact that, once formulated by the creative mind of the magician, they possess a distinct and independent life of their own, though strictly conditioned as to nature by the concept of their creator. The life of these creatures is akin to that of an electric battery, it slowly leaks out by means of radiation, and unless recharged periodically, will finally weaken and die out. The whole question of the making, charging, recharging, or destruction of these artificial elementals is an important one in practical occultism.

The artificial elemental is constructed by forming a clear-cut image in the imagination of the creature it is intended to create, ensouling it with something of the corresponding aspect of one's own being, and then invoking into it the appropriate natural force. This method can be used for good as well as evil, and "guardian angels" are formed in this way. It is said that dying women, anxious concerning the welfare of their children, frequently form them unconsciously.

I myself once had an exceedingly nasty experience in which I formulated a were-wolf accidentally. Unpleasant as the incident was, I think it may be just as well to give it publicity, for it shows what may happen when an insufficiently disciplined and purified nature is handling occult forces.

I had received serious injury from someone who, at considerable cost to myself, I had disinterestedly helped, and I was sorely tempted to retaliate. Lying on my bed resting one afternoon, I was brooding over my resentment, and while so brooding, drifted towards the borders of sleep. There came to my mind the thought of casting off all restraint and going berserk. The ancient Nordic myths rose before me, and I thought of Fenris, the Wolf-horror of the North. Immediately I felt a curious drawing-out sensation from my solar plexus, and there materialised beside me on the bed a large wolf. It was a well-materialised ectoplasmic form. Like Z., it was grey and colourless, and like him, it had weight. I could distinctly feel its back pressing against me as it lay beside me on the bed as a large dog might.

I knew nothing about the art of making elementals at that time, but had accidentally stumbled upon the right method - the brooding highly charged with emotion, the invocation of the appropriate natural force, and the condition between sleeping and waking in which the etheric double readily extrudes.

I was horrified at what I had done, and knew I was in a tight corner and that everything depended upon my keeping my head. I had had enough experience of practical occultism to know that the thing I had called into visible manifestation could be controlled by my will provided I did not panic; but that if I lost my nerve and it got the upper hand, I had a Frankenstein monster to cope with.

I stirred slightly, and the creature evidently objected to being disturbed, for it turned its long snout towards me over its shoulder, and snarled, showing its teeth. I had now "got the wind" up properly; but I knew that everything depended on my getting the upper hand and keeping it, and that the best thing I could do was to fight it out now, because the longer the Thing remained in existence, the stronger it would get, and the more difficult to disintegrate. So I drove my elbow into its hairy ectoplasmic ribs and said to it out loud:

"If you can't behave yourself, you will have to go on the floor," and pushed it off the bed.

Down it went, meek as a lamb, and changed from wolf to dog, to my great relief. Then the northern corner of the room appeared to fade away, and the creature went out through the gap.

I was far from happy, however, for I had a feeling that this was not the end of it, and my feeling was confirmed when next morning another member of my household reported that her sleep had been disturbed by dreams of wolves, and she had awakened in the night to see the eye of a wild animal shining in the darkness in the corner of her room.

Now, thoroughly alarmed, I went off to seek advice from one whom I have always looked upon as my teacher, and I was told that I had made this Thing out of my own substance by revengeful thoughts, and that it was really a part of myself extruded, and that I must at all costs recall it and reabsorb it into myself, at the same time forgoing my desire to "settle accounts" with the person who had injured me. Curiously enough, just at this time there came an opportunity most effectually to "settle" with my antagonist.

Fortunately for all concerned, I had enough sense left to see that I was at the dividing of the ways, and if I were not careful would take the first step on to the Left-hand Path. If I availed myself of the opportunity to give practical expression to my resentment, the wolf-form would be born into an independent existence, and there would be the devil to pay, literally as well as metaphorically. I received the distinct impression, and impressions are important things in psychic matters, for they often represent subconscious knowledge and experience, that once the wolf-impulse had found expression in action, the wolf-form would sever the psychic navel-cord that connected it with my solar plexus, and it would be no longer possible for me to absorb it.

The prospect was not a pleasant one. I had to forgo my dearly-loved revenge and allow harm to be done to me without defending myself, and I also had to summon and absorb a wolf-form which, to my psychic consciousness at any rate, looked unpleasantly tangible. Nor was it a situation in which I could either ask for assistance or expect much sympathy. However, it had to be faced, and I knew that with every hour of the Thing's existence it would be harder to deal with, so I made the resolution to let the opportunity for revenge slip through my fingers, and at first dusk summoned the Creature. It came in through the northern corner of the room again (subsequently I learnt that the north was considered among the ancients as the evil quarter), and presented itself upon the hearthrug in quite a mild and domesticated mood. I obtained an excellent materialisation in the half-light, and could have sworn that a big Alsatian was standing there looking at me. It was tangible, even to the dog-like odour.

From it to me stretched a shadowy line of ectoplasm, one end was attached to my solar plexus, and the other disappeared in the shaggy fur of its belly, but I could not see the actual point of attachment. I began by an effort of the will and imagination to draw the life out of it along this silver cord, as if sucking lemonade up a straw. The wolf-form began to fade, the cord thickened and grew more substantial. A violent emotional upheaval started in myself; I felt the most furious impulses to go berserk and rend and tear anything and anybody that came to hand, like the Malay running amok. I conquered this impulse with an effort, and the upheaval subsided. The wolf-form had now faded into a shapeless grey mist. This too absorbed along the silver cord. The tension relaxed and I found myself bathed in perspiration. That, as far as I know, was the end of the incident.

I had had a sharp lesson, and a highly instructive one. It may not be convincing to other people, owing to the lack of corroborative evidence, but it was exceedingly evidential to me, and I put it on record for what it is worth to those who, having personal knowledge of these things, can see its significance.

It is a curious point that, during the brief twenty-four hours of the Thing's life, the opportunity for an effectual vengeance presented itself.

5 VAMPIRISM

Vampirism supposed to have died out ♦ Curious effect of certain persons upon
their associates ♦ Effect of the same persons upon electric batteries ♦ Morbid
rapports ♦ Oedipus complex ♦ Psychic parasitism ♦ The Berberlangs ♦
Description of case of vampirism ♦ Necrophilia on the Western Front ♦
Vampirism in South-Eastern Europe ♦ Contagiousness of vampirism ♦
Abnormal "mosquito-bites." ♦ Where to look for vampire marks ♦
The characteristic teeth of vampires.

THE ALLEGED VAMPIRE has always been a popular character
in tales of mystery and imagination. There is a
considerable literature concerning his doings, from the
famous novel *Dracula* to serious studies of the mediaeval
witch-trials, for which the reader is referred to the
bibliography at the end of the book. In these pages, however,
I do not want to avail myself of second-hand evidence, nor of
incidents which took place in other centuries and under
primitive conditions, for it might be argued that with the
passing of such conditions from our midst, the problem of
vampirism, like the problem of typhus, has gone too, and
need not trouble us. From my own experience I am of the
opinion, however, that this is not so, and that the peculiar
condition which the ancients called vampirism may account
for certain forms of mental disturbance and the physical ill-
health associated therewith.

When psychoanalysis was first introduced into England I
took up the subject, and became a student, and eventually a
lecturer at a clinic that was founded in London. We students
were soon struck by the fact that some cases were exceedingly
exhausting to deal with. It was not that they were
troublesome, but simply that they "took it out" of us, and left
us feeling like limp rags at the end of a treatment. Someone

happened to mention this fact to one of the nurses engaged in the electrical department, and she told us that the same patients equally "took it out of" the electrical machines and that they could absorb the most surprising voltages without turning a hair.

At the same place, in the course of my psychoanalytical work, I came across a number of cases where a morbid attachment existed between two people, most commonly mother and daughter, or two women friends; sometimes also between mother and son, and in one case I met socially, between a man and a woman. It was always the negative one of the pair who came for treatment, and we were able to benefit them considerably by psycho-therapeutic means.

They always showed the same symptom-complex, a sensitive temperament, pallid complexion, wasted form and general debility, sense of weakness, and were easily fatigued. They were also invariably highly suggestible, and were therefore easy to handle. Consequently we were usually able to get good results pretty quickly in such cases.

The curious point, however, was that the breaking of the morbid rapport caused a marked disturbance and even semi-collapse of the dominant partner in the alliance. We found it necessary to insist upon a separation if a cure were to be effected, and the separation invariably disagreed very actively with the dominant partner.

At that time I explained everything in terms of the psychology, but even so, I could not help being struck by the curious effect a separation had upon the person who was not supposed to be ill, and that as the one went uphill, the other went down.

I am of the opinion that what Freud calls an Oedipus complex is not altogether a one-sided affair, and that the "soul" of the parent is drawing upon the psychic vitality of the child. It is curious how aged Oedipus cases always look, and what little old men and women they are as children. They never have a normal childhood, but always are mentally mature for their years. I persuaded various patients to show me photographs of themselves as children, and was much struck by the elderly, worried expression of the childish faces, as if they had known all of life's problem and burdens.

Knowing what we do of telepathy and the magnetic aura, it appears to me not unreasonable to suppose that in some way which we do not as yet fully understand, the negative partner of such a rapport is "shorting" on to the positive partner. There is a leakage of vitality going on, and the dominant partner is more or less consciously lapping it up, if not actually sucking it out.

Such cases are by no means uncommon, and clear up rapidly when the victim is separated from the vampire. Whenever there is a record of a close and dominating bond between two people with the devitalisation of one of them, it is a good plan to recommend a temporary separation and observe the results.

Such cases as these, however, may more justly be described as parasitism than vampirism. Such psychic parasitism is exceedingly common, and explains many psychological problems. We will not pursue the subject in these pages, however, as it is outside the scope of our present enquiry, and is merely mentioned for illustrative purposes. Vampirism, as generally understood, is a very different matter, and we shall do well to reserve the term for those cases wherein the attack is deliberate, applying the term parasitism to the cases wherein it is unconscious and involuntary.

In my opinion, true vampirism cannot take place unless there is power to project the etheric double. All the records of vampirism that we have give an account of something much more tangible than a haunting. In Western Europe the occurrence seems to be comparatively rare in modern times, but in Eastern Europe and in primitive countries it appears to be by no means uncommon, and innumerable well-authenticated cases occur in books of travel.

Commander Gould, in his exceedingly interesting book, *Oddities*, gives an account of vampirism among the Berberlangs of the Philippine Islands. His account is based on a paper printed in the *Journal of the Asiatic Society, Vol. LXV, 1896.* These unpleasant people, according to Mr. Skertchley, the author of the article which Commander Gould quotes, "are ghouls, and must eat human flesh occasionally or they would die.... When they feel a craving for a meal of human flesh they go away into the grass, and having carefully hidden their bodies, hold their breaths and fall into a trance. Their astral bodies are then liberated. . . . They fly away, and entering a house, make their way into the body of one of the occupants and feed on his entrails.

"The Berberlangs may be heard coming, as they make a moaning noise, which is loud at a distance and dies away to a feeble moan as they approach. When they are near you, the sound of their wings may be heard, and the flashing lights of their eyes can be seen dancing like fire-flies in the dark."

Mr. Skertchley declares that he himself saw and heard a flight of Berberlangs pass by, and, visiting next day the house he saw them enter, found the occupant dead without any sign of external violence.

Compare Mr. Skertchley's account of the Berberlangs lying in the long grass and throwing themselves into trance with Mr. Muldoon's account of *The Projection of the Astral Body*, with which every student of occultism ought to be familiar, for it is undoubtedly a classic of occult literature, being a practical account of occult experiences and detailed instructions how to go and do likewise.

But to return nearer home. In the course of my experience of the byways of the human mind, which, from the nature of my work, has been, like Sam Weller's knowledge of London, extensive and peculiar, I have only known one case of genuine vampirism, according to the sense in which I use the term, and this was not one of my own cases, though I knew the persons concerned, but was handled by my original teacher, whom I have already referred to in connection with the case of the good lady who chased me with a carving-knife. I have made use of the facts of this case as a groundwork for one of the stories in *The Secrets of Dr. Taverner*, but the actual facts are such that they were unsuitable for a work supposedly designed to amuse.

At that time I was doing the tutorials in abnormal psychology at the clinic I have spoken of, and, supervising the work of the other students, one of them took counsel with me concerning a case that had come to her in private practice, the case of a youth in the late 'teens, one of those degenerate but intellectual and socially presentable types that not infrequently crop up in old families whose blood is too blue to be wholesome.

This lad was taken as boarder in a flat which the student shared with another woman, and they soon began to be troubled with curious phenomena. About the same time every evening the dogs in a neighbouring mews began a furious outcry of barking and howling, and a few moments later the French window leading on to the verandah would open. It did not matter how often they got the locksmith to it, nor how they barricaded it, open it would come at the appointed time, and a cold draught sweep through the flat.

This phenomenon took place one evening when the adept, Z., was present, and he declared that an unpleasant invisible entity had entered. They lowered the lights, and were able to see a dull glow in the corner he indicated, and when they put their hands into this glow, felt a tingling sensation such as is experienced when the hands are put into electrically-charged water.

Then began a mighty spook-hunt up and down the flat, and the presence was finally cornered and dispatched in the bathroom. I have staged the incident somewhat more picturesquely in my story, but the essential facts are the same. The result of the dispatching of this entity was a marked improvement in the condition of the boy patient, and the elicitation of the following story.

The boy, whom we will call D., was in the habit of going to sit with a cousin who had been invalided home from France suffering from alleged shell-shock. This young man was another scion of a worn-out stock, and it transpired that he had been caught red-handed in that unpleasant perversion called necrophilia. According to the story elicited from the parents of D., this vice was not uncommon on certain sections of the Front, as were also attacks on wounded men. The authorities were taking drastic steps to put it down. Owing to family influence the cousin of D. was able to escape incarceration in a military prison, and was placed in the care of his family as a mental case, and they put him in the charge of a male nurse. It was while the male nurse was off duty that the unfortunate young D. was misguidedly employed to sit with him. It also came out that the relations between D. and his cousin were of a vicious nature, and on one occasion he bit the boy on the neck, just under the ear, actually drawing blood.

D. had always been under the impression that some "ghost" attacked him during his crises, but had not dared to say so for fear of being thought mad.

What may have been the exact percentage of neurotic taint, vice, and psychic attack, it is difficult to say, nor is it easy to decide which was the predisposing cause that opened the door to all the trouble, but one thing stood out clearly to all beholders, that with the dispatch of the psychic visitant, not only did D.'s condition clear up immediately, but after a short, sharp upheaval the cousin also recovered. The method of dispatch used by the adept, Z., was to pin the entity inside a magic circle, so that it could not get away, and then absorb it into himself through compassion. As he completed the operation, he fell over backwards unconscious. It was, in fact, the same method that I was instructed to use in dealing with my were-wolf, but it is a much more formidable task to absorb and transmute the projection of another person than to absorb one's own, and could only have been accomplished by an initiate of a very high grade, which Z. indubitably was.

His opinion concerning the case, though there was no means of obtaining independent confirmation of this, was that some Eastern European troops had been brought to the Western Front, and among these were individuals with the traditional knowledge of Black Magic for which South-Eastern Europe has always enjoyed a sinister reputation among occultists. These men, getting killed, knew how to avoid going to the Second Death, that is to say, the disintegration of the Astral Body, and maintained themselves in the etheric double by vampirising the wounded. Now vampirism is contagious; the person who is vampirised, being depleted of vitality, is a psychic vacuum, himself absorbing from anyone he comes across in order to refill his depleted resources of vitality. He soon learns by experience the tricks of a vampire without realising their significance, and before he knows where he is, he is a full blown vampire himself, vampirising others. The earth-bound soul of a vampire sometimes attaches itself permanently to one individual if it succeeds in making a functioning vampire of him, systematically drawing its etheric nutriment from him, for, since he in his turn is resupplying himself from others, he will not die from exhaustion as victims of vampires do in the ordinary way.

Z. was of the opinion that D.'s cousin was not the primary vampire in the case, but was himself a victim. Being a youth of unstable morale, he speedily acquired the vampire tricks, and the earth-bound soul of some Magyar magician exploited him. Through his act of biting and drawing blood from the neck of his cousin, this entity became transferred to young D., preferring pastures new to the depleted resources of its previous victim. Probably it alternated between the two, for it was not constantly with D.

Exactly what Z. did we do not know, for he was exceedingly secretive concerning his methods, but in the light of subsequent knowledge I should imagine that he absorbed the etheric energy of the earth-bound soul, and thus deprived it of its means of resisting the Second Death. Merely to drive the resisting soul out to the Judgment Hall of Osiris would have involved leaving behind an astral corpse, which for some time would have continued to give trouble.

It may be interesting to note in connection with this case that during the time that Miss L. was at the occult college in Hampshire we had some rather curious happenings. There was an outbreak among us of exceedingly bad "mosquito bites." The bites themselves were not poisonous, but the stabs were of such a nature that they bled freely. I remember waking up one morning to find a patch of blood the size of the palm of my hand on the pillow; it had apparently come from a small puncture just behind the angle of the jaw. Several others had similar experiences. I have never seen anything like it, either before or since, nor did it occur again after Miss L. left.

I did not tell the adept Z. about it at the time, and later, when I was reminded of the incident and mentioned it, the opportunity for investigation had gone by. He expressed the opinion that it was a vampire's work, and cited similar cases which he had met with in the course of his experience. He said he had seen cases in Africa where the victim had become so bloodless that it was with difficulty that a specimen of blood could be obtained for examination, for it could hardly be induced to flow from the debilitated tissue.

Nothing can be done for such cases by medical science. They are dying by inches and yet no organic disease can be demonstrated. Nevertheless, their appearance is that of a person sinking from repeated haemorrhages.

When vampirism is suspected the thing to do is to go over that person's body inch by inch with a powerful magnifying-glass, and the search will probably be rewarded by the discovery of numerous minute punctures, so minute that they are not discovered by the naked eye unless they reveal themselves by becoming infected and suppurating, when they are usually mistaken for insect bites. They are bites right enough, but not those of an insect. The places to look for them are around the neck; down the inner surface of the forearms; on the lobes of the ears; about the tips of the toes and in a woman, upon the breasts.

It is said that a person with vampire tendencies develops abnormally long and sharp canine teeth, and I have myself seen one such case, and a curious sight it was. The two canine teeth, the pair that come between the incisors and the double teeth, were half as long again as the others, and terminated in points of needle-like sharpness.

True Vampirism in Western Europe appears to be rare, but Z. was of the opinion that many obscure cases of tropical debility in which anaemia played a prominent part might be attributed to this cause.

6 HAUNTINGS

Interference by earth-bound souls ♦ Case of dead drunkard who over-shadowed his wife ♦ Case of dead lover who caused astral projection in his fiancee ♦ Thought-atmospheres ♦ Example of stage fright ♦ Case of haunting by the atmosphere left behind by a living drunkard ♦ How to distinguish between atmospheres and entities ♦ Haunting by a suicidal lunatic ♦ Phenomena connected with case of haunting by a Black Occultist ♦ Vampirism ♦ Poltergeist phenomena ♦ Outbreaks of fire ♦ Method of handling ♦ Subsequent elucidation ♦ Forces evoked by ritual magic ♦ Their effect on casual visitors ♦ Forces evoked by Christian rituals ♦ Hauntings of vicarages ♦ Objects magnetized by ceremonial ♦ Incident of the consecrated crosses ♦ Spurious curios ♦ Incident of the altar in the cast-room at the British Museum ♦ Types of atmosphere in the different rooms at the British Museum ♦ The mummy's curse ♦ Reverence for the sacred objects of another faith ♦ Dugpa Buddhas ♦ Incident in connection with a statue of the Buddha ♦ Evil thought forms returning to their sender ♦ Hallucinations of the insane are projected thought-forms.

THERE ARE TWO forms of "haunting" which have to be considered, the one which is due to a discarnate soul who interferes with a particular person, and the one which is due to the conditions prevailing in a particular place, and which affects any person sufficiently sensitive who happens to go there. Except in cases where the influence is exceptionally strong, the insensitive person is immune. To perceive a "haunting" one needs, as a general rule, to be slightly psychic; it is for this reason that children, Celts and the coloured races suffer severely from such interferences, and the stolid Nordic type is comparatively immune, and, to a lesser extent, the lively, materialistic and sceptical Latin.

Let us consider first of all the question of interference by a discarnate soul. It will be noted that I use the term "interference" and not "attack." The disturbance need not necessarily be an attack, any more than the drowning man who clings to his rescuer and drags him under is motived by malice. The entity that is causing the trouble may be a soul that is itself in distress on the Inner Planes, and is too ignorant of post-mortem conditions to know the harm it is doing by clinging so desperately to the living. It is for this reason that the wide dissemination of Spiritualistic teaching is of value, for it helps to relieve the tension between this world and the next.

As far as my experience goes, I am inclined to think that deliberate malevolence is rare; but this panic-stricken clinging is not uncommon, and explains why the survivor of a pair sometimes goes through very unpleasant experiences after the death of the partner. There are also cases, though rarer, wherein a soul who has some occult knowledge but is bound strongly to earth by sensual desires, uses a curious form of rapport in order to gratify those desires through the physical body of another.

There are innumerable instances of both these types of astral interference in occult and spiritualistic literature, but as I am confining myself to cases within my own experience, I will not cite them, but limit myself to listing the literature of the subject in the bibliography.

Someone of my acquaintance lost, after a long illness, her husband to whom she was much attached, but whom most people would have thought she was well rid of, as for many years he had been addicted to drink, and died finally after a long illness during which he was kept under morphia for prolonged periods, taking enormous quantities. He was a man of intensely malignant and selfish disposition, and died unrepentant. She, however, during the course of his last illness, when, being bedridden, he could do no more harm, elected to idolise him, and as soon as he was safely dead, canonised him into the family saint. She was interested in occultism and in the habit of practising meditation and invoking the Masters. In spite of all counsel to the contrary, she began to try and get into psychic touch with her husband, invoking him as her guide. Like many other men of a sensual disposition, he had clung desperately to life, remaining *in articulo mortis* for days. Fortunately for all concerned, it had been possible to persuade her to have his remains cremated, but despite all persuasion she brought all his belongings from the nursing-home where he had died and kept them in her bedroom, and made a little altar around his photograph and used it as the focus of her meditations.

The last illness had been a long and trying one, and she had been living at the end of a telephone wire, in a state of constant anxiety for weeks, but had had no physical strain, so there was nothing physical to account for the serious illness which ensued after the strain was over. It soon became noticeable that she, who had previously had a very lovable and gentle disposition, was gradually changing, so that not only in temperament, but in facial expression, she was growing like her late husband. Next a curious thing ensued. Her husband had died of an inflammatory spinal lesion which caused no pain at the site of the trouble, but intense pain in the nerves that issued from the spine at that point, so that the pain was referred to a particular distribution in the hands and arms, more upon one side than the other. The lady developed a severe neuritis that exactly corresponded in its distribution to her late husband's symptoms.

Another illustrative case is that of Miss E., whose fiancé was killed during the War. She says in a letter written to the person whom she consulted with regard to her problem;

"I was able to rise above the loss and separation at the time, but six months later I suffered nervous breakdown; from this time I have been troubled with weak nerves. For the last two months I have been having very extraordinary experiences which are causing me much perplexity and rendering me unfit for work. It is a night experience and has not once occurred during the day. After I have composed myself for sleep I find that gradually my body is losing all sensation; it feels as if I was being slowly frozen stiff. (I don't know how else to describe it.) At this stage I can sometimes rouse myself and overcome it, but I cannot always do this. My efforts to rouse myself are in vain, and although fully conscious I feel unable to move or call. Usually after this I sink into some kind of sleep. I have all kinds of experiences. Sometimes I visit strange places and talk with people I don't know. Sometimes my experiences are beautiful beyond description; sometimes I am threatened with danger of drowning or falling, but in these cases I always rise in the air and travel for miles, it seems to me. Sometimes I feel that I am just floating in the air. How long the dream lasts I cannot tell. When I wake up, however, I have great difficulty in moving for some time; but gradually I retain the power to move about, and after a lot of stinging sensation in the limbs I get up, usually feeling very tired and unrefreshed, but sometimes I feel none the worse for the strange experience. But it is undermining my health and happiness, and it cannot be good."

In conversation she amplified the statements in her letter, and said that during the experiences described, someone, she thought it was her fiance, was trying to prevent her from getting back into her body again after these nocturnal expeditions.

The case was entirely cleared up in one week by means of telepathic treatment. The notes on the manner in which the work was done are of considerable interest.

"The treatment was given to the entity that was causing the trouble, not merely to the patient, and it was the release of the obsessor from his plane of work and helping him Heavenward that gave freedom to his victim."

In the other type of haunting, that in which it is the place which is the focus of manifestation, not a special person, we must distinguish between the earth-bound entity which remains attached to a particular spot, and the thought-atmosphere which is left behind after violent emotions have been experienced there.

Let us consider first the question of thought-atmosphere, of which I can give a very illuminating example. A friend of mine who was a student at a school of dramatic art consulted me concerning an attack of stage fright she had had, which left her rather nervous as to its recurrence. She was an experienced student, in fact a pupil teacher, and she was having some extra tuition from the head of the school. Going for her lesson one afternoon, she found that her teacher had just finished taking the junior students for their end-of-term examination in elocution. She went on to the stage and stood beside the small table which had been placed there for the convenience of the examiner, and commenced to recite the piece on which she was to have her lesson. She herself had no occasion for nervousness; as had already been noted, she was an experienced speaker and teacher; moreover, nothing of importance hung upon this lesson, it was merely one of a series. Nor was she usually nervous or self-conscious. But as soon as she tried to start, she experienced a complete "dry-up," and stood paralysed, unable to utter a word. A little prompting soon started her off, however, but she had experienced a nasty attack of stage fright, and it shook her nerve.

From the psychic point of view, the explanation was not far to seek. She was standing in the mental atmosphere created by a series of girls who had gone on to that platform for an examination upon which a good deal depended for them, and who had all been correspondingly nervous. She herself, being sensitive, had been affected by this atmosphere, which induced in her a similar mental state by means of what is called "sympathetic induction," a phenomenon well known in electricity and in acoustics, but equally valid in psychology.

No doubt the unfortunate examinees themselves were infecting each other. It may well be that the "microphone panic," so well known to broadcasters, is caused by the thought-atmosphere generated by a succession of nervous people who have stood upon the same spot.

An experience of my own may be of interest in this connection. I took a bed-sitting-room in a hostel, and as soon as I came there, I found myself afflicted with the most intense depression. I am not usually subject to the blues, being normally a cheerful soul, but as soon as I entered this room, which was a sunny and pleasant, the cloud descended upon me, but lifted again as soon as I went out of it, whether into the dining room of the hostel, or out of doors. I soon recognised that here was something that needed to be dealt with, and enquired as to the history of the room. I was told that it had previously been the bedroom of the last owner of the house, who had been addicted to drink and had gone bankrupt. It is a curious fact that drunkards and drug addicts make very evil psychic atmospheres, whereas a person who is a common criminal, however bad, is not nearly so noxious and his atmosphere fades rapidly.

In these two cases there was no question of an entity, discarnate or incarnate, being concerned in the matter; there was merely an unpleasant mental atmosphere generated by some powerful and painful emotion that had been experienced over a considerable period at that spot.

Such a concentration, if very strong, will linger almost indefinitely. The structures that saw the concentration may have been pulled down and new ones built, nevertheless the forces remain, like a previous exposure on a photographic plate, and sensitive people are affected by them. The insensitive may escape comparatively scatheless.

It is not altogether an easy matter to determine whether the disturbance is due to atmosphere alone, or whether an earth-bound entity complicates the situation. Where an entity is present, it will usually be seen sooner or later. Moreover, it will usually be heard as well as felt. This latter sign, however, does not invariably indicate the presence of an organised entity, for I know of a case wherein a room that had been used as a lodge of ritual initiation was subsequently partitioned into an office and two bedrooms after the lodge was moved elsewhere, and the bedrooms were practically uninhabitable owing to the din of cracks, bangs and thumpings that went on at night. In such a case there was no reason to suspect the presence of any entity, for the rituals had not been of an evocative type, nor was the influence evil. It was merely force in a state of tension. It was sheer physical noise that made the disturbance, as I can testify, for I have slept, or rather, tried to sleep there.

Where a ghost is seen, it is usually also heard because for a form to be sufficiently substantial to be visible there must be a modicum at least of ectoplasm in its composition, and ectoplasm is capable of exercising force on the physical plane, in some degree at least. Where a ghost is both seen and heard, we may be sure there is an actual haunting. Where it is seen, but not heard, it may possibly be that a person with psychic tendencies is perceiving the images in the reflecting ether, the photographic plate of Nature, and there may be no actual entity present. Where the disturbance is heard, but not seen, it may be due to astral forces set in motion by ritual magic, and which continue for a while after the original impulse is withdrawn. These may be perfectly harmless, save that, they disturb the sleep in the same way that a rattling window would do. On the other hand, if powerful evocative rituals have been performed, and the clearing of the sphere has not been properly done, profound disturbances may result and the whole situation be exceedingly unpleasant.

Examples will again help to make the problem clear. As an instance of a non-ritual haunting, I may cite the case of a friend of mine who went to live in a block of modern mansions. From the first she was not happy there, and as time went by the oppression and distress strengthened. Coming into her drawing- room one evening at dusk, she saw in the half-light a man standing with his back to the room, gazing intently out of the window. She switched on the light, and found that there was no one there. On several occasions her maid saw someone walk down the passage leading to this room. Moreover, the hall door had a knack of coming open of its own accord.

My friend's depression deepened until finally, when standing herself at the drawing-room window one day, she had a sudden impulse to fling herself out. Then she realised that things were serious and that liver-pills and a weekend at the seaside would not put them right. Being an occultist, she understood the significance of the happenings that had been going on in her flat, and she made enquiries concerning the history of the square in which this block of modern mansions had been built. She learnt that it was the site of an old madhouse of sinister reputation. The form that she and her maid had seen was probably that of some unfortunate patient of suicidal tendencies who had succeeded in giving effect to his impulses on a spot corresponding to the situation of her room. The terrific emotional forces generated by his brooding and last desperate act were photographed on the atmosphere, as it were, and suggested to her mind thoughts of self-destruction just as the ill-temper or depression of a companion will induce a similar mood in ourselves without any word spoken.

Another example within the sphere of my experience, although it was not actually my case, is of much interest in that it combines an example of a very definite poltergeist haunting with vampirism.

I was once consulted by a mental healer to whom a very curious case had been brought. Some charitably disposed people had raised funds to found a home for unwanted babies, and a suitable house had been purchased on the outskirts of a village not far from London. The house had been a conspicuous bargain and they were very pleased with it.

Soon, however, they began to be disturbed by some curious phenomena, and also by inexplicable illness and seizures among the babies. One child, in fact, actually died and its death was not satisfactorily accounted for. Then one of the nurses, an Irish girl, began to be affected also; Celts are notoriously susceptible to psychic influences, and are always the first to be affected by them. It will be observed that the babies went down first under the attack, their resistance being low compared to that of an adult; and then the most sensitive of the adults was affected, the Irish Celt.

On several occasions the sound was heard of a cart and horse coming up the drive, but when the maid went to the door to open it, there was nothing to be seen. Soon the ghost became even more energetic, and took to shovelling the coal from side to side of an outhouse. It would shift several tons of coal in this way in a night, the occupants of the house lying shivering in their beds while lumps of coal thudded and rumbled against the sides of the bunkers. As to why or wherefore this particular manifestation should take place, I can offer no suggestion.

On several occasions different people saw a strange man crossing the hall, and immediately afterwards children were taken ill.

Finally, in addition to all other troubles, mysterious fires began to break out all over the house. A basket of clean linen in an empty room was found to be on fire. Curtains were found to be smouldering. Meanwhile, the unfortunate Irish nurse went from bad to worse, lying in bed too weak to stand up, and rapidly going off her head.

It will probably be suggested that some mischievous or demented person was at the bottom of the trouble, but it is difficult to know what human agency either could or would shovel a truck load of coal across a shed single-handed during the night.

The superintendent of the home was interested in mental healing and knew enough of the mind side of things to realise that something abnormal was happening in the house under her charge. She consulted a mental healer, who in her turn consulted me.

I made a psychic diagnosis of the case, and reported that in my opinion the house had at some time been occupied by someone who had a knowledge of occultism, and who, being upon the Left-hand Path, objected strongly to going to face his portion of Purgatory after the death of the physical body, and that he was maintaining himself in an intermediate state as an earth-bound spirit by drawing upon the vitality of the unfortunate children, and had accidentally drawn too much from one, thus killing it outright.

Working on this hypothesis, the healer undertook to give the case "absent treatment." Needless to say, the officials of the home were not taken into our confidence.

The result of this treatment was that the manifestations immediately ceased. No more children had seizures and the Irish nurse rapidly recovered. The superintendent was then told the hypothesis upon which we had worked. She was greatly interested, and made enquiries in the village as to the history of the house, and learned that it was notoriously haunted, which was the reason they had obtained it so cheaply. It appeared that no tenant could stop there long, and that there was a constant record of these exhausting and mysterious illnesses. It also transpired that about sixty years previously the house had been occupied for a long period by a man who was viewed askance by his neighbours as an eccentric and mysterious personage, and was reported to be engaged in some sort of research which necessitated the use of a laboratory into which no one was ever allowed to go, and in which he worked by night.

It is interesting to note that neither the mental healer nor myself ever visited the house or were within twenty miles of it; for it shows in what way these unseen forces can be manipulated from a distance.

A final example, taken from *The Confessions of Aleister Crowley* will serve to show the nature of a haunting produced by ceremonial magic in which the forces invoked are not adequately dispersed.

"The demons connected with Abramelin do not wait to be invoked, they come unsought. One night Jones and I went out to dinner. I noticed on leaving the White Temple that the latch of its Yale lock had not caught. Accordingly I pulled the door to and tested it. As we went out, we noticed semi-solid shadows on the stairs; the whole atmosphere was vibrating with the forces we had been using. (We were trying to condense them into sensible images.) When we came back, nothing had been disturbed in the flat; but the Temple door was wide open, the furniture disarranged, and some of the symbols flung about the room. We restored order, and then observed that semi-materialised beings were marching round the main room in almost unending procession.

"When I finally left the flat for Scotland, it was found that the mirrors were too big to take out save by the way of the Black Temple. This had, of course, been completely dismantled before the workmen arrived. But the atmosphere remained, and two of them were put out of action for several hours. It was almost a weekly experience, by the way, to hear of casual callers fainting, or being seized with dizziness, cramp or apoplexy on the staircase. It was a long time before these rooms were re-let. People felt instinctively the presence of something uncanny."

It is well known to all psychics that the sites of ancient temples where mystery-rituals have been worked, are always potently charged with psychic force. This force need not necessarily be evil, but it has a powerfully stimulating effect upon the psychic centres and stirs up the subconscious forces; and as the majority, of civilised people suffer in a greater or lesser degree from what Freud calls "repression," such a stirring of the subliminal mind produces a feeling of profound disturbance. We should not unquestioningly attribute evil influence to a place or a person that causes us discomfort; it may merely be that psychic force at a greater tension than we are accustomed to is disturbing our equilibrium.

The sites of monasteries that were disbanded with persecution at the time of the Reformation are also frequently badly "haunted" by psychic forces. The group-mind of a religious community is a very potent thing, and when it is disturbed by the corporate emotion of its members, the forces thus let loose are not readily dispersed. Moreover, the monks, initiates of the Mysteries of Jesus, would not be likely to hand over their sacred places to the despoilers with any good will. It has been reported again and again that a curse rests on those who profited by the spoliation of Church lands. This is too well known to require discussion in these pages.

There is another fact in connection with Church property, however, which may not be so well known, and that is the frequency with which psychic happenings are reported in connection with vicarages. In enquiring among friends and fellow-workers for data in connection with the research that has gone to the making of this book, I have been astonished how frequently a vicarage has been mentioned in connection with the phenomena of which I have been told.

The rituals of the Church are, of course, ceremonial magic, as is admitted by even such an orthodox authority as Evelyn Underhill. The average clergyman is not conversant with the technique of occultism, and has therefore little or no understanding of what he is doing. What influences he brings to the altar, and what forces he takes away therefrom, must therefore be an open question in each individual case. A man whose consciousness has been exalted by ritual, and who does not know how to seal his aura and return to normal is liable to psychic invasion.

Objects associated with any form of ceremonial operations are invariably highly charged with magnetism and intimately linked with the force whose uses they have served. I remember, many years ago, when I had but little knowledge of occultism and no pretensions at all to psychism, that two friends and myself were amusing ourselves by turning over each other's trinket-boxes. I picked up a handsome amethyst cross, from one of them, and immediately exclaimed:

"There is something extraordinary about this cross. It feels as if it were alive."

"That was the cross that was given me at my first communion," replied my friend, and it was originally a bishop's pectoral cross."

Her sister was greatly interested, and immediately brought her own jewel-case to me and asked me if I could pick out her first communion cross also, for, like her sister, she was a Roman Catholic, and these crosses that were given them as presents on the occasion of their first communion had been specially blessed by the priest. I was greatly interested to observe that from three or four ornamental crosses I was able to pick one which felt warm and living and electric to the hand, and pass it across to her, saying, "This is your communion cross," and it was.

I remember once as a small child, picking up a dying rook; the creature lay motionless on my knee for a few minutes and then gave a flutter and died. I had never seen death before but I needed no one to tell me that I saw it now. The "feel" of the creature, before and after that flutter, was different, I can only compare the feel of the magnetised and the unmagnetised cross to the difference between the living and the dead bird.

But the Christian is not the only religion that can magnetise its ceremonial instruments. There are other ritualistic religions, and some of these are debased. We ought to use much caution before we place about our rooms as ornaments objects which may have been associated with cults whose nature we do not understand. Many of them, of course belong to the Brummagem cult, and are dedicated to no more desperate deity than Mammon; but the genuine curio is a different matter.

I had an example of this once in the British Museum. I was visiting the room in the basement which contains a collection of plaster casts of the famous statues of antiquity, the originals being elsewhere. Suddenly I became aware of a sense of magnetic power. I turned towards it, and saw a small altar. Reading the label, I found that this was not a cast but the original. It is a very interesting test of psychism to sample the atmosphere of the different rooms of the British Museum. The benign and brooding peace of the Buddhist Room is a thing to be remembered. The flavour of the Ethnological Room is a thing to be got out of the mouth as quickly as possible. To me, at any rate, the Egyptian is disappointing; the mummies seem neither malignant nor benignant, but merely cynical. Perhaps I should feel differently, however, if I spent a night with them. Magnetism, which is dispersed during the day, charges up again in the silence and darkness of the night. I remember visiting Stonehenge amid a crowd of trippers and char-a-bancs, and thinking that the glory had departed; but it was a very different affair when I visited it in the desolation of a bleak spring day after its long winter solitude. It had charged up again and was as formidable as anyone could wish.

I should hesitate, therefore, to say that because the mummies and I have never struck sparks when we met in the British Museum, that their reputation is groundless. At the time that Tut-ankh-amen's tomb was being opened I said to myself, "If the mummy's curse does not work in this case, I shall lose my faith in occultism." We all know how it has worked, even unto the third and fourth generation. No novelist, deriving his ideas of ancient Egypt from an encyclopaedia article on Egyptology and some photographs, would have dared stretch the long arm of coincidence anything like as far.

The Egyptians attached great importance to the preservation of the physical body. The tombs of great men, as is well known, were protected by means of what are popularly called spells, and the power and scope of Egyptian magic are things that very few people realise. The modern student of occultism who reads Iamblichos on the Egyptian Mysteries, will have a surprise.

In most cases, however, the purchaser of Egyptian curios has nothing to fear; the worst that they will yield to psychic investigation is a vision of labour disputes in a mass-production factory. I have, however, heard of a very wonderful psychometric reading which was obtained from a mummy which, when subsequently unrolled, was found to consist entirely of French newspapers of recent date!

I have always been greatly amused by the indignation of Egyptologists against tomb robbers. After all, is there any distinction between the earlier and later visitors to a tomb save that one lot work by day and the other by night? In the view of the people who made the tomb, and spared nothing to render it inviolate and preserve the peace of their dead, the workers by night would probably be preferred, for they merely robbed, and did not strip and expose the nude bodies to the public gaze. There was a terrible outcry recently when some bodies were moved in a village churchyard to make room for the monument chosen to decorate the grave of a famous public man. Even the people whose religious feelings were not outraged by this act of sacrilege regarded it as in shocking bad taste. Yet nobody proposed to strip the gravecloths from the body of someone's wife or mother and photograph it stark naked. When it comes to the question of the mummy's curse, I am afraid that my sympathies are entirely with the mummy.

The initiate is strictly counselled that he should never blaspheme the name by which another knoweth his God, for it is the same force that he himself worships represented by another symbol. "The ways to God are as many as the breaths of the sons of men," says the old Arab proverb. We should have enough sympathy with the struggles of another soul towards the light not to desecrate the things that are sanctified by his hopes and endeavours, even if by nothing else. The Father of us all may understand their significance better than we do, and by His acceptance consecrate them for ever.

There are many Europeans who have a great affection for the Buddha, and have His statue in their rooms (though sometimes they confuse it with Chenresi, the stout and beaming god of good-luck). That the influence of that great Being, the Light of Asia, is noble and benignant, I would be the last to deny; but the statues of the Buddha are a different matter, and need to be approached with caution if genuine. Some of the worst black magic in the world is a debased form of Buddhism. To say this is not to insult that venerable faith, for it is only lack of opportunity that prevents the Black Mass from occupying that dubious eminence. In the Tibetan monasteries of the Dugpa sect there are temples each one of which contained literally thousands of statues of the Buddha. On various occasions one or another of these monasteries has been raided, either by rival religionists or Chinese troops, and its curios scattered. To be the possessor of one of these Buddhas, magnetised by Dugpa rites, is not a very pleasant thing.

I had a curious experience with a Buddha upon one occasion. It was an archaic soap-stone statuette, some nine inches high, and its owner had dug it up herself on the site of a Burmese city that had fallen in ruin and been swallowed by the jungle. It was placed on the floor in an angle of the stairs and served as a doorstop upon occasion. I had a flat on the top floor, and had to pass the melancholy little Buddha each time I came in or went out, and to me it seemed a desecration to see the sacred symbol of another faith treated thus. I tried to point this out to her, and asked her how she would feel if she saw a crucifix thus utilised, but without result. Meanwhile the little Buddha sat there patiently, getting the carpet-sweeper pushed in his face and receiving libations of slops.

One day, passing upstairs bearing a bunch of flowers, I was prompted to throw before him one of the traditional marigolds of Indian devotion. Immediately I was conscious that a link had been formed between myself and the little statue, and that it was sinister. A night or two afterwards I was returning home rather late, and as I passed the Buddha I had a feeling that there was something behind me, and looking over my shoulder, saw a ball of pale golden light about the size of a football separate itself from the Buddha and come rolling up the stairs after me. Thoroughly alarmed, and disliking this manifestation very much indeed, I immediately made a banishing gesture and the ball of light returned down the stairs and was reabsorbed into the Buddha, who, needless to say, got no more marigolds from me, and received a very wide berth until I left the flat shortly after. The experience was a singularly unpleasant one, and was a sharp lesson to me not to meddle with the sacred objects of another system unless I knew exactly what I was about. I learnt subsequently that some of these statues are consecrated with the blood of a human sacrifice.

I do not mean to imply by this that all Buddhist statues have been so treated; such consecrations are, I should imagine, comparatively rare; but I think no one who has a knowledge of the facts will deny that they occur, even as one might occasionally come across a Crucifix which had been used upside down at a Black Mass.

It is not every case of psychic disturbance, however, which originates externally. It is a well-known cosmic law that everything moves in circles, and whatever forces we send out, and whatever thought-forms we extrude from our auras, unless absorbed by the object to which they are directed, will return to us in due course. One of the most effective, and also one of the most widely practised methods of occult defence is to refuse to react to an attack, neither accepting nor neutralising the forces projected against one, and thus turning them back on their sender. We must never overlook the fact that a so-called occult attack may be evil thought-forms returning home to roost.

There are certain types of insanity in which the lunatic believes himself to be the victim of an attack by invisible beings, who threaten and abuse him and offer base or dangerous insinuations. He will describe his tormentors, or point to their position in the room. A psychic who investigates such a case can very often see the alleged entities just where the lunatic says they are. Nevertheless, the psychologist can come forward and prove beyond any reasonable doubt that the so-called "hallucinations" are due to repressed instincts giving rise to dissociated complexes of ideas in that patient's own subconscious mind. Does this mean that the psychic is mistaken in thinking he perceives an astral entity? In my opinion both psychic and psychologist are right, and their findings are mutually explanatory. What the psychic sees is the associated complex extruded from the aura as a thought-form. A great deal of relief can be given to lunatics by breaking up the thought-forms that are surrounding them, but unfortunately the relief is short-lived; for unless the cause of the illness can be dealt with, a fresh batch of thought-forms is built up as soon as the original ones are destroyed.

7 THE PATHOLOGY OF NONHUMAN CONTACTS

Other forms of life as well as ours ✦ Folklore and the Fairy Kingdom ✦
Nonhumans ✦ Esoteric data relating to conception ✦ Nonhuman souls in human
bodies ✦ The problems they present ✦ Their deleterious effect on humans ✦
Cause of their attractiveness to certain types of humans ✦ Problem of single-
element beings in a four-element universe ✦ Development of elementals through
association with magician ✦ Difficulties this may cause ✦
Distinction from Spiritualistic controls.

THERE ARE OTHER forms of life as well as ours whose sphere
evolution impinges upon the earth. In the realm of
folklore we constantly meet with the idea of intercourse
between the human and the fairy kingdoms; of the marriage
of a human being with a fairy spouse, or the theft of a child
by the fairies, an impish changeling being left in its place.
We shall be rash if we assume that an extensive body of folk-
belief is entirely without foundation in fact. Let us therefore
examine these old and crude beliefs and see whether we can
find any grounds for them, and if so, what the real nature of
the facts may be, and whether they throw any light upon
modern psychic phenomena of the kind we are considering in
these pages.

There are many of us who have met people who might well
be described as nonhuman, soulless, in that the ordinary
human motives are not operative with them, nor do the
ordinary human feelings prompt or inhibit them. We
cannot but love them, for they have great charm, but we
cannot but dread them as well, for they spread an infinitude
of suffering around them. Although seldom deliberately
evil, they are singularly detrimental to all with whom they

come in contact. They, for their part, are unhappy and lonely in our midst. They feel themselves to be alien and uncompanioned; every man's hand is against them, and in consequence it all too often happens that their hand is against everyone and they develop a puckish malevolence, though there is seldom calculated evil-doing. Gratitude, compassion, good faith, morality and common honesty are utterly foreign to their natures, as far beyond their conception as the differential calculus. They are not immoral, however, but simply non-moral. On the other hand, they possess the virtues of absolute sincerity and great courage. In terms of human ethics they are "undesirables," but they have an ethic of their own to which they are loyal, and that is the beauty which is truth, and this is all they know, and, as far as their life is concerned, all they need to know. In appearance they are usually small and slight, possessing unusual physical strength and endurance but very liable to nervous exhaustion and brain-storms. In social relations they take violent likes and dislikes; they show a facile and demonstrative affection towards those they like, but quickly forget them. Gratitude and pity are unknown to their nature. Towards those they dislike they are pettily malicious, and in all relations of life they are utterly irresponsible. One cannot describe them better than to say that they resemble nothing so much as a blend of Persian kitten and pet monkey. They have the beauty and aloofness and charm of the cat, and the amusing, mischievous destructiveness of the monkey. Many human beings hate them at sight; others are fascinated by them because they bring with them a sense of unearthly beauty and a quickening of the life-forces. I have been able to investigate the history of two such beings, and it is interesting to note that both of them were conceived while their mothers were under the influence of drink. There is a very great deal of information available concerning the occult aspect of the incarnation of souls, but not much of the knowledge concerning the actual facts of conception has ever found its way into print. I have given a little in my book *The Esoteric Philosophy of Love and Marriage.* I cannot enter into the subject deeply in these pages, for it would be too much of a digression. Some points, however, it is essential to touch upon for a comprehensive survey of our subject.

At the moment of sexual union a psychic vortex is formed resembling a waterspout, a funnel-shaped swirling that towers up into other dimensions. As body after body engages, the vortex goes up the planes. In all cases the physical, etheric and astral bodies are involved; the vortex therefore always reaches as far as the astral plane; a soul upon the astral plane may be drawn into this vortex if it is ripe for incarnation, and thus enter the sphere of the parents. If the vortex extends higher than the astral plane, souls of a different type may enter this sphere, but such extension is rare, and therefore it is said that man is born of desire, for few are born of anything else.

But this vortex may not only extend vertically up the planes (speaking metaphorically), but it may also, under certain conditions, be deflected, as it were, out of the normal human line of evolution, so that its open end extends into the sphere of evolution of another type of life. Under such circumstances it is theoretically possible for a being of a parallel evolution to be drawn into incarnation in a human body. Occultists hold that this occasionally occurs, and explains certain types of nonpathological abnormality which are occasionally met with.

These nonhumans are either adored or hated by their human associates. They have a peculiar fascination for certain types of temperament, the types that psychologists call the unstable. In these types the subconscious comes very near to the surface, deep calls to deep, and they are instinctively drawn towards the elemental kingdoms.

There is nothing more disastrous than marriage with a non-human, for they have nothing in their nature that can satisfy the normal human yearnings for affection and sympathy. The one saving feature in such a union is that grounds for divorce are invariably readily available, for the morals of the non-human are those of the barnyard.

The power of nonhumans to injure their enemies is comparatively small, for they are aliens in a strange land when incarnated in human form, and cannot avail themselves of any of the ordinary human resources of mischief. They are, in fact, singularly defenceless and helpless, and themselves suffer acutely, at the hands of society. It is otherwise, however, in their relations with their friends. They seem to have an infinite capacity for inflicting hurt on those who love them. Not deliberately or maliciously, but like a child pulling flies to pieces out of idleness not realising what it is doing. Obeying the laws of their own nature, they are destructive to beings of the human evolution. Yet what other laws can they obey? For them to submit to our standards is to deny their deepest instincts.

The effect they have upon those who love them constitutes such a well-marked syndrome among the psychic pathologies that we must consider it in detail. The person who forms a rapport with a nonhuman becomes deeply stirred by the elemental forces that find ingress to our sphere through the channel of this wandering and alien soul. He becomes, as it were, drawn away from normal human things and set wandering upon the confines of the fairy kingdom, and yet he can find there no rest for his foot and no sustenance for his soul. The story of the handsome fisher lad and the mermaid is indicative of this condition. She loves him, draws him to her and he drowns, for he cannot live in the element of water.

The explanation of the curious power, both of fascination and destruction, which is exercised by nonhumans may lie in the fact that they belong to one element only, whereas in man all four are combined. Any elemental contact is stimulating to us, because elemental beings pour forth in abundance the vitality of their own particular sphere, and this vitalises the corresponding element in ourselves. But if a four-element creature is drawn into the sphere of a single element he is poisoned by an overdose of the one element in which he finds himself, and starved of the other three. It is for this reason that mortals in the fairy kingdom are always said to be enchanted or asleep. They are never living normally in full possession of their faculties.

An equally difficult problem is set to the non-human who is drawn into our midst. A single-element creature is bidden to control and assimilate an additional three elements for which it has no equipment or experience, and the result is disastrous.

But it is not enough that we should merely describe the conditions and state the problems in these pages. Our aim is essentially practical. What then can be done when a non-human has to be faced and dealt with? It must be clearly realised that any mating between a human and a non-human is a hopeless proposition. In the first place, it can only be the preamble to a divorce, because non-humans are promiscuous in their sexual habits; and, secondly, there is nothing in the nature of a non-human that can satisfy the higher aspirations of the human. We must not allow the human form to mislead us as to the existence of a human soul. A nonhuman is a pet animal, not a fellow creature. That, frankly, is the only possible ground upon which they can be approached. If we expect no more of them than we should of a pet bird, if we manage them as we should manage a kitten, we have got as near to the solution of the problem as we are ever likely to get until the Dark Angel mercifully restores them to their own kingdom; a mercy seldom long delayed, for nonhumans do not make old bones.

Human beings may also come into touch with elemental beings by themselves venturing into the spheres of elemental life. Such contacts need not necessarily be harmful to either kingdom provided those who enter into them know what they are about. In fact, such associations are frequently entered into by occultists in the course of their work and researches, but it is an undertaking for the advanced initiate only, not for neophytes.

There are cases, however, where such an association may lead to harm. The human partner in the association may be ill-equipped or ill-adapted for the undertaking. He may have ventured out beyond his depth, having picked up a formula from some more experienced occultist and used it without proper preparation. Or again, it is not uncommon to find people who have brought through from previous incarnations a natural aptitude for getting into touch with the elemental kingdoms. In such cases it may occur that an elemental who has had experience of relations with human beings may deliberately get into touch with them. This is in every way undesirable, for the elemental has not got the knowledge of human conditions necessary to enable it to avoid injuring its new friend. In any case, elementals have got a one-way intelligence, and it is not well that they should be senior partners in any alliance with human beings. The whole question of elemental contacts, an exceedingly fascinating one, is too extensive and intricate to be entered upon in these pages. It has been necessary to refer to it, however, for certain cases of psychic difficulty may be due to inexpert operations on both sides of the Veil.

These elementals, or nature spirits, are quite different to the controls with whom Spiritualistic circles come into touch. The Spiritualistic movement is highly organised on the Inner Planes, and promiscuous controlling is not permitted. Controls have, in fact, to "sit" for development in just the same way that mediums do, and there is invariably some experienced entity within call who can come to the assistance of the circle if all is not going well. Western Occultism was thoroughly disorganised and broken up by centuries of persecution; its Inner Plane conditions, consequently, present many tangles and gaps even to this day. It is nothing like as well organised as the Spiritualistic sphere. The great Orders have their definite contacts and work strictly within them, keeping a firm hand on neophytes; outside the Orders there is a good deal of chaos and banditry, and it is unwise to venture far save in the company of an experienced occultist who understands the technique of the methods employed.

There are many people for whom the Deva Kingdom, as the sphere which the elementals share with the Nature Spirits is sometimes called, has a great fascination, and they try by meditation and ritual to get into touch with it. In my opinion it is decidedly risky for a person who is not an initiate to attempt this work. It is exceedingly apt to lead to mental unbalance, if not to actual obsession. Not that the nature contacts are evil, but they are profoundly disturbing to the human consciousness because they stir those atavistic depths which the psychoanalyst aims at laying bare by means of his technique. Anyone who is acquainted with the literature of practice of psychoanalysis knows that the abreaction is an important factor in this system; it is a crisis, and can, for the time being at any rate, upset the patient pretty thoroughly and exacerbate all his symptoms. When we touch the elemental contacts we get the same reaction that is caused by psychoanalysis when the censor is being penetrated.

Persons in whom the subconscious mind is near the surface, such as the artist, the crank, the unstable, and, for the matter of that, the genius in any walk of life, love the elemental contacts because they stimulate the elemental forces in their own nature which are to them the springs of their power and inspiration. But the average citizen, whose mental content is organised largely on a basis of repression and compromise in order that he may be a citizen at all and take his place in organised society, is upset by the elemental contacts according to the proportion of repression to compromise in his make-up. Compromise is the normal lot of humanity; repression is the pathology of compromise. The person who has managed to effect a working compromise between the different elements of his nature can afford to allow himself a holiday with the Devas without doing anybody any harm; but the person who is repressed will find that they disagree with him actively because they are having the same effect upon him that a drastic psychoanalysis would have. We hear sometimes of the tragedy that results from taking the last dose in a bottle of tonic of which arsenic is one of the ingredients. This is due to the fact that the bottle has not been thoroughly shaken up each time a dose has been taken, so that the arsenical sediment has all collected in the last dose and reached a poisonous concentration. So it is with the elemental contacts; they are a potent tonic, but they can reach a poisonous concentration under unsuitable circumstances.

I have never come across or heard of a case of pathology due to the fascination of the Element of Earth; it is not an element that usually attracts the amateur experimenter, though the initiate appreciates its value and importance. I have come across cases, however, of sensitive people dwelling in a mountainous country, especially in narrow gulches where there is a paucity of sunlight, who have become obsessed with the fear of the mountains. They do not fear so much that the mountains will fall upon them as that they will close over them, as the cave closed upon the children who followed the Pied Piper of Hamelin. The psychiatrist will, of course, recognise this symptom as belonging to the well-known psycho-neurosis of claustrophobia. This, however, does not invalidate my statement; for in my opinion we may find that in a more intimate knowledge of the elemental kingdoms we shall come upon the clue to both claustrophobia and agoraphobia.

Mountaineers also know this peculiar terror with which the great hills can obsess mankind. It is neither giddiness nor mountain sickness, but a curious oppression of the spirits by the overwhelming grandeur of nature. The same force, when not at a poisonous concentration, inspires the passionate love of the hills or of the sea that Kipling has celebrated so gloriously in one of his poems.

The pathologies of the Element of Water may be a fascination so great that a man will walk out into the sea until he drowns. Swinburne had this peculiarity, and has immortalised it in several of his poems, " Strike out as the heart in us bids and beseeches, athirst for the foam." On one occasion he was picked up in the open sea by a Breton fishing-smack, swimming tirelessly, many miles from land, borne on the sea by currents, but oblivious of his danger. Being rescued, he sat upon the deck with his mane of red hair drying in the wind, chanting sea-poems to his rescuers, a spectacle that one would have given much to witness.

Another curious case of water-pathology I knew personally. A very level-headed woman, a school teacher, was obsessed by a horror of rough waves. She always declared that if she went onthe sea-front to watch a storm, the waves made a "dead-set" at her. She lived at a seaside place, but so great was her dislike of the waves that she did not care to walk on the promenade when the tide was in. She was cured of her fear in a curious way. She took initiation into Co-Masonry, and found to her surprise that from that day forth she was free from her fear of the sea. I am not a Co-Mason, and speak subject to correction, but I believe I am right in saying that Co-Masonry differs from other forms of Masonry in that Elemental Invocations have been introduced into it.

The Element of Air, as all occultists know, is a very tricky element to deal with. More initiates turn off the Path in the Grade of Air than in any other, and it is rare to see a Ritual of Air worked without something being dropped or knocked over. It is a quarrelsome element; when it is being worked, the operators are apt to bicker and squabble. It is also intimately associated with sex, as is revealed by its symbolism. If an occultist is making a magic circle, and for any reason wishes to seal it with the Kerubim of the Elements instead of the Archangels, as is more commonly done, and feels himself unequal to the task of drawing a presentable eagle, the symbolic form of the Kerub of Air, he will use the Zodiacal sign for Scorpio. The evolutionary connection between the snake and the bird is well known to biologists; but long ages before Darwin, initiates used the Serpent and the Eagle to represent the unsublimated and sublimated aspects of the life-force. The Scorpion connects with the Serpent through the Dragon.

I had a very curious experience myself in connection with the Element of Air. I am betraying no secrets if I say that certain grades of initiation refer to the elements, for the fact is too generally known, and too obvious, for it to be any more mysterious than the Queen of Spain's legs.

To begin with, I have an exceptionally bad head for heights, and as the Abyss of Height belongs to the Element of Air, I obviously have no natural affinity with it. The ceremony went exceptionally badly even for an Air Ritual. Two of the principal officers, husband and wife, helped to maintain its reputation as a contentious element by having a family jar in the middle of the proceedings, and the usual upsets and smashings occurred on a generous scale.

For the next fortnight I lived in the midst of a cataclysm of crockery. I smashed my way through two entire tea-sets and all the mantelpiece ornaments. The ornaments just fell off the mantelpiece one by one of their own accord. I actually saw two of them do it. I did not know at the time that the Element of Air had this sinister reputation. I realised that something queer was afoot, however, and asked my teacher about it. She was much amused, but I was not, because it was my crockery that was supplying the raw material for the phenomena. She advised me to get into sympathetic touch with the Sylphs, as the initiation had evidently not been altogether successful. I tried to do this, but I was in London at the time and met with no success, for the elemental contacts, with the exception of Fire, cannot be worked successfully in a city. The smashing went on, and I was reduced to a tin mug and a tooth-glass, for I saw it was useless to get any more china until things had settled down.

Then I went away for my summer holiday and found myself on the summit of a high and isolated hill on a day of bright sun and high wind. I was very conscious of the nearness of the elemental kingdoms. The air seemed full of silver sparkles, which is always a sign that the veil is thin. There was no one present save some friends who were sympathetic. I faced into the wind and raised my arms in invocation. Suddenly we saw below us a figure bursting through hedges and leaping ditches and running wildly toward it. We presently recognised it as another of our friends, and when he joined us he told us that he had felt the sudden rush of power while in the valley and on an overpowering impulse started for the hill-top. Then all of us, without any suggestion of leadership, began the Dance of the Elements, whirling like dancing dervishes upon that hill-top. Fortunately nobody was about, but I do not know that it would have made very much difference if they had been, for we were caught up out of ourselves and the air seemed full of rushing golden flames, lying level in the wind. For days afterwards we seemed charged with elemental energy by that extraordinary dance.

It may be interesting to note that we danced with a circular movement, each revolving on our own axis at the same time, and that we both danced and revolved deosil, that is, with the sun. All this occurred spontaneously, the tide of the elements catching us up and away. I have never known a more glorious experience. It was indeed the divine inebriation of the Mysteries.

After this there were no more smashings of crockery.

I have already noted my exceptionally bad head for heights. I have found that it is considerably mitigated, temporarily at any rate, by the Invocation of Air. I am of the opinion that the curious impulse which causes people for no reason whatsoever to commit suicide by throwing themselves from heights may be due to the same impulse that causes people who are obsessed by the Element of Water to swim out to sea, as I have recorded of Swinburne.

These apparently causeless suicides by Water and Air are, in my opinion, a form of union with the god which is one of the ideas underlying human sacrifice. There are two types of human sacrifice, the willing and the unwilling. The unwilling sacrifice, the prisoner struggling or drugged into passivity, is used, not to propitiate the god, as is usually thought, but in order that his vital forces may serve as a basis of manifestation. The willing sacrifice, in which the victim will be either a priest or a devotee of the god has for its motive the idea of divine union, not altogether unknown to Christian mystics, who seek its achievement by a living death, whereas the adherents of juggernaut escape with one brief pang.

The European belief of one man, one life, has imbued us with the idea of death as the supreme evil. Therefore the European very often does not go to his death when he unites with the elements, but his higher self withdraws from incarnation, leaving his body ensouled by a curious kind of intelligent automaton, which deteriorates rapidly. Whatever may be the status of the soul that withdraws, that which is left behind is not nice. I feel, therefore, that it must seriously delay and distort the evolution of the human Monad if it turns aside into the sphere of the Deva evolution. It may well be that some of the creatures whom at first sight we might classify as nonhumans are really humans who have had a Deva phase in their Karmic record. There is a very interesting field of research awaiting the person who systematically investigates the past lives of the weak-minded and the mentally deranged.

The pathologies of the Element of Fire are also rare, though it may be that the aimless incendiary and pyromaniac belong to this class. I have never personally had any opportunities of investigating this type of case. Algernon Blackwood writes of one in his very interesting story, "The Regeneration of Lord Ernie," which is published in his volume of short stories entitled *Incredible Adventures*.

Indeed, this author is exceedingly fond of drawing his inspiration from the Deva kingdom, and has some most interesting studies of the subject scattered through his books.

Any organic geographical unit develops something of an oversoul, and where the differentiation is marked, the oversoul may become a very definite entity. If there are among the inhabitants of the district any who are sensitive to the Unseen, they may form either an affinity or a repulsion for this oversoul. A great forest has a very marked personality, and there are few white men who can resist its influence, becoming markedly changed and dehumanised if exposed to it for long periods without the companionship of others of their race. Natives, on the other hand, seem to enter into it and be part of it.

It is well known how often trees are objects of worship in all parts of the world. They have very marked personalities and strong magnetic fields. In the spring, when the sap is rising, even nonpsychics can often see the aura of a tree. It can best be seen by getting at a distance of a couple of hundred yards and looking at the sky beyond the top of the tree. The aura will then be perceived as a whitish cloud, like a patch of lighter-coloured sky, surrounding the top of the tree, and usually swaying gently from side to side.

There is a curious antagonism between elms and humanity, and about orchids all sensitive persons agree there is something sinister. Tropical vegetation, as a whole, is over powerful for humanity. Under the tremendous stimulation of the solar fire the elemental forces are concentrated to a poisonous strength. I am not personally acquainted with the West Coast of Africa, but from what I can gather I am of the opinion that the elemental forces and the atmosphere made by Juju rites are between them more responsible than the climate for earning that part of the world its sinister reputation as the White Man's Grave. There are other spots where the climate is equally hot and humid, Burmah, for instance, but there is no other spot that produces the same loosening of moral fibre. The only place that is at all comparable to it is the Caribbean Sea, which produces, not so much a demoralisation, as a fierceness and violence quite alien to the racial characteristics of the people who go there.

8 THE RISKS INCIDENTAL TO CEREMONIAL MAGIC

Esoteric theory of the nature of evil ◆ Qabalistic system ◆ Negative Evil ◆
Positive Evil ◆ The Qlippoth ◆ Unfortunate experiment with geomancy ◆
Case of obsession by the Abramelin demons ◆ Sources of danger in practical
occultism ◆ Accidents occurring in ceremonial workings ◆ Accident due to the
breaking of the circle during an exorcism ◆ Strange death in island of Iona ◆
Difference between ceremonial magic and initiatory ceremonie ◆
Mme. Blavatsky's prejudice against ceremonial ◆
Necessity of ceremonial in the West.

IF THE PROBLEM of psychic self-defence is to be adequately dealt with, we must have an understanding of a subject upon which very little has been written - the nature of the forces of intelligent and organised evil.

The great faiths of the ancient world all had their evil gods as well as their beneficent deities, and they did not call these evil gods devils. In Hinduism we have Shiva and Kali; in the Egyptian system we have Set and Besz and Typhon; in the Grecian pantheon there are Pluto and Hecate.

All the other faiths, also, have their angelic choirs, their Archons, or builders, and all the hierarchy of heaven. Protestant Christianity alone has forgotten its angelology, the Creator has to be both Architect of the Universe and Bricklayer, forming man from dust of the ground without assistance.

If we refer to *Paradise Lost*, however, we shall find that Milton was familiar with both divine and infernal hierarchies, and that these were graded and charted according to a definite system. Anyone who is acquainted with the Qabalah will recognise that in Milton he meets a fellow-Qabalist.

In the Qabalah we find the esotericism of the Old Testament. I propose to use the Qabalistic terminology to explain the esoteric theory of evil because, firstly, it is the one I am most familiar with; secondly, it forms the basis of Western occult thought and all mediaeval magic is based upon it, together with much modern magic; thirdly, it is, in my opinion, singularly lucid, coherent and comprehensive; and being a system consecrated by antiquity, I cannot be accused of romancing, or fabricating my own system.

In order to render my concepts clear, a brief explanation of Qabalistic doctrine must be given. As it is not possible to enter into an exposition of this vast system, I will state certain axioms dogmatically, and explain them by illustration instead of argument, thus obtaining the maximum clarity for the minimum expenditure of space.

The initiate recognises two kinds of evil, Negative Evil and Positive Evil. Negative Evil is the polarising opposite of Good. Let us try and make this clear by an illustration. Every action gives rise to a reaction. The forward drive of the bullet is equated by the recoil of the gun. Everything which moves has to have the equivalent of a thrust-block against which to push, something firm under its feet from which to take off. It is difficult to walk on a slippery surface because it offers no resistance. We must have something for the foot to grip, to push against, and give us the forward impulse at each step.

Negative Evil is the thrust-block of Good; the principle of resistance, of inertia, that enables Good to "get a purchase."

But Negative Evil is more than this. We might call the principle of resistance the "negative" aspect of Negative Evil. For it has also a "positive" aspect, the Principle of Destruction.

We can best explain the cosmic function of the Principle of Destruction by calling it by its esoteric name of the Scavenger of the Gods. Its function is to clear up behind the advancing tide of evolution, removing that which has become effete so that it may not choke and clog evolving life.

We now find the answer to the eternal riddle as to why God tolerates the Devil. The Devil is the cosmic thrust-block and Scavenger of the Gods. It is this aspect of evil which is given a more detailed symbolism in the pantheons of other faiths, having its Shiva and Kali, or its Pluto and Hecate aspects. We can now see why these resistive and destructive forces are classed as gods and not as demons, for they are reactions according to cosmic law, not anarchical and chaotic forces.

We now come to the consideration of Positive Evil. This again has a "negative" and "positive" aspect. Its "negative" aspect is pure chaos, unformed substance and uncoordinated force. It has been aptly called the Cosmic Abortion. To drift into the sphere of "negative" Positive Evil is like being caught in a psychic quicksand.

We are now ready to consider the sphere of "positive" Positive Evil, the demons themselves, or the Qlippoth, as they are called in the Qabalah. In order to understand their significance we must make a further excursion into Qabalistic philosophy.

The Creator is conceived of as bringing the universe into manifestation through a series of Divine Emanations, ten in number. These are called the Ten Holy Sephiroth, and are represented in a diagram as arranged in a particular pattern. This is the famous Tree of Life, the key to all symbolism.

The Sephiroth were not emanated independently, each from the Divine Source; but overflowed, the one from the other. As soon as one Sephira has emanated another, these two are said to be in equilibrium, compensating each other. But there is a period during the emanation of a Sephira when the force is not yet in equilibrium, but is pushing out unsupported, like an incomplete arch. It is the uncompensated force emanated during this epoch of unbalance, and never subsequently absorbed after the establishment of the new sphere, which constitutes Positive Evil. There are, therefore, ten kinds of Positive Evil, just as there are ten Divine Emanations.

To these spheres go, according to their kind, all the evil imaginings of the heart of man that are not neutralised by repentance or compensated by the overplus of good in other members of the same group-soul. There is a deep occult doctrine here which we cannot enter upon now; it must suffice to state it dogmatically in explanation of the Qabalistic conception of the Qlippoth. When we consider all that must have been poured into these ten sinks of iniquity since the days of Atlantean Magic, through the decadence of Babylon and Rome, down to the Great War, we can guess what rises up from them when their seals are broken.

Not only do influences emanate from them which tempt and corrupt souls, each according to its susceptibility, but time has served for the formulation of evil intelligences. These probably originated through the workings of Black Magic, which took the essential evil essence and organised it for purposes of its own. The beings thus formulated assumed an independent existence, developed, and multiplied their kind. They appear as dreams and hallucinations, and may produce a considerable degree of objective phenomena, such as noise, deposit of slime or blood, balls of light, and, above all, stenches of an amazing pungency.

The Ten Divine Emanations are personified as Archangels and the Ten Infernal Emanations are personified is Archdemons. It is these which are the Names of Power in Magic. Each Sephira, then, has its obverse side in the corresponding Qlippottic demon. The initiated adept always gains control over the demonic force before he attempts to utilise the angelic force which, by the appropriate means, can be contacted in each Sephira. If he does not do so, he contacts them both simultaneously. Moreover, the planets, the elements and the Signs of the Zodiac are all intimately connected with the Sephiroth, being arranged upon the Tree of Life in a pattern known only to initiates.

The initiated adept is exceedingly careful what he does when he is working with these potencies because he knows that he has always got the Qlippoth in the background. The uninitiated occultist goes ahead gaily, juggling with such Names of Power as he has picked up from the innumerable books on the subject now available for the general reader, thinking that if he does not invoke the demons he will not get them. He forgets that every planet is a Jekyll and Hyde. Consequently, ceremonial magic has got a bad name owing to the unpleasant frequency of untoward results, just as surgery got a bad name before the days of Lister. It is the imperfect technique that is the trouble.

I was once doing some experimental work with geomancy, which is a method of divination belonging to the Element of Earth. Now all divinations, when performed according to their esoteric formulae, always begin with an evocation of the genius that presides over that particular operation. The genii of geomancy are not of a very high type. I was imperfectly familiar with the method, and was trying to set up my prick-figure on a piece of paper instead of using a tray of wet sand as I should have done. Things began to go wrong, and the room was filled with the most terrible stench of drains. The appropriate banishing ritual was immediately performed, and the air cleared; but there was not much doubt about the objectivity of this phenomenon while it lasted.

A very interesting case is given in the *Occult Review* for December 1929, in a letter to the editor signed H. Campell.

"Desiring some information which I could not get in any ordinary way, I resorted to the System of Abramelin, and to this end prepared a copy of the necessary Talisman, perfecting it to the best of my ability with my little stock of knowledge. The ritual performed, I proceeded to clear my place of working.' A little knowledge is a dangerous thing;

my ritual was imperfect and I only rendered the Talisman useless without in any way impairing the activities of the entity invoked. This looks like nothing else than gross carelessness on my part; and to a certain extent this is true - but the point I wish to make is this, that my knowledge of this particular system, and therefore my ritual, were imperfect; and in any case, I had been shown no method of combating this particular entity when once aroused. Now note the results.

"Unfortunately I have no account of the date when these occurrences began, but the first hint of trouble must have come on or about March 3, 1927. I can guess the date with fair accuracy because, as I was to learn, the manifestations were always strongest about the new moon, and after I had gone to sleep. Upon this occasion I can remember waking up suddenly with a vague feeling of terror oppressing me; yet it was no ordinary nightmare terror, but an imposed emotion that could be thrown off by an effort of the will. This passed almost as soon as I stood up, and I thought no more about it.

"Again on April 2, or thereabouts, I was troubled by the same feeling, but regarded it as nothing more than a severe nightmare, though the fact that my sleep was distorted towards the time of the new moon had occurred to me; while as full moon drew on, the nights were peaceful again.

The new moon of May 1 brought a recurrence of the trouble. This time very much more powerful, and necessitated an almost intolerable effort of will to cast it off. Also it was about this time that I first saw the entity which was rapidly obsessing me. It was not altogether unlovely to look at. Its eyes were closed and it was bearded, with long flowing hair. It seemed a blind force slowly waking to activity.

"Now there are three points which I must make quite clear before I proceed. In the first place, I was never attacked twice in the same night. Secondly, when I speak of physical happenings, the smashing of glass and voices, they were never, with one absolutely inexplicable exception, actual, but pure obsessions; and this leads to the third point. Not one of these incidents happened while I was asleep. Always I found myself awake with the terror upon me and struggling violently to cast off the spell. I have had nightmares before, but no nightmare that I have ever had could hold my mind in its grip for minutes at a time as this thing did, or send me plunging through a ten-foot-high window to the ground below.

"The first indication I had that these visitations were absolutely out of the ordinary course of events came on May 30. About midnight I was suddenly awakened by a voice calling loudly, 'Look out,' and at once I became aware of a red serpent coiling and uncoiling itself under my bed, and reaching out onto the floor with its head. Just at it was about to attack me I jumped through my window, and came to earth among the roses bushes below, fortunately with no more damage than a badly bruised arm.

"After this there was absolute peace until June 30, when the real climax came. I had seen the thing again on the night of the new moon, and had noticed considerable changes in its appearance. Especially it seemed far more active, while its long hair had changed into serpent heads. The night after I was awakened by a violent noise and jumped out of bed. I then saw the noise was caused by a great red obelisk which crashed through the west wall of my room and leaned against the wall at the east end, smashing both that and the window to pieces but missing my bed, which was in an alcove to the left of its path. In its transit it had smashed all the mirrors, and the floor and top of my bed were strewn with broken glass and fragments of wood. This time the obsession must have lasted some minutes, I dared not move for fear of cutting myself, and to reach the matches - wherein, I knew, lay safety - I had to lean across the bed and again risk the glass. Yet in my heart I knew that all this was false, but had no power to move. I could only stand there, incapable, looking at the shattered room in a state of hopeless terror.

"And now comes the most extraordinary part of the whole business. When I had finally mastered the obsession, I went to bed again dead tired, and I know that the only sound I made that night was jumping to the floor, also my room is at least a hundred yards from the rest of my family, yet next morning at breakfast I was asked what was the terrible noise in my room during the night.

After that I realised that the game was up. I had not taken these occurrences lying down, but I knew that it was impossible for me to try and control the force which I had set in motion. In desperation I turned to a good friend, who, I was aware, knew much of these things. She did not hesitate, but came at once to my assistance, and from that day to the present the trouble has absolutely gone from me.

"Such is the case; and I only hope it may warn those who are contemplating my folly to treat with the greatest of care any printed systems of magic, and not to use them at all unless they have the fullest control over the entities invoked."

Among the general public, who do not dabble in occultism, the results of a magical mishap are never seen, and the only doctors, who ever see them are fellow-initiates who happen to be medical men, and they, naturally, keep silence. The catastrophes are of varying degrees of severity, ranging from a bad fright to a fatality.

I cannot say much upon these subjects, for they are among the most secret paths of occult lore. Enough must be hinted, however, to reveal what, under certain circumstances, may be experienced. I do not think it in the least likely, however, that the Qlippotic demons will be encountered save through the use of ceremonial magic. They are rare as anthrax in England, but it is as well to know the manner of their manifestation so that, when encountered, they may be recognised.

The great majority of dabblers in occultism are protected by their own inaptitude. They fail to get results, and consequently come to no harm; but if they should succeed in getting results they would find that they had their hands full. The serious student, unless he is working under skilled guidance, may also find himself in difficulties, and for various reasons.

He may be insufficiently experienced in the operation he has undertaken, for in magic theory is one thing and practice is another. A student of occult science will often take a formula out of a book and try to use it. He might just as well study the instructions in a book on surgery and try to operate. Most formulae are incomplete, there is always unwritten work. Some of the "barbarous names of evocation" which the uninitiated use as Words of Power, are really the initial letters of a mantric sentence or formula. I came across an invocation once in which the Word of Power was Tegatoo. On investigation this turned out to be the battered remains of The Great Architect Of The Universe.

Even an experienced occultist may get into difficulties if he attempts magical work when he is in bad health, over-tired, or has had even a moderate amount of alcohol, for very little is too much when the Invisible Forces are being handled. Equally does this apply to each of his assistants. A chain is no stronger than its weakest link, and if one of the team cannot handle the forces, everybody is going to suffer. A ritual lodge is no place for the well-meaning ineffectual.

There is an immense amount of dabbling in occultism going on today. Most of it is innocuous because it is totally ineffective; but there is never any knowing when one is going to strike a live wire. Take, for instance, the advertisers in various occult papers who offer to supply "charms that work." One of two things is certain. Either they do not work at all, in which case one is wasting one's money on them; or they work by means of some power with which they have been charged. What is the nature of that power, and did the persons who made the charm or talisman really know what they were about? Did they take the precaution to bind the baser aspect before magnetising with the higher aspect?

These are the elementary precautions of the practical occultist who has been properly trained. Did the maker of the talisman know them?

Again, one buys second-hand books on magic. Who was the previous owner and for what purposes were these books used? Or one buys a new book which has been brought out by some occult school for propaganda purposes. Those books are often magnetised before they are sent out, and so form a magnetic link between the purchaser and the Order which caused them to be issued.

Or someone may join a group who has previously been associated with another occult group whose contacts were debased. Unless the proper precautions are taken, that person will bring the psychic contagion in with him, and his fellow-members may have unpleasant experiences.

I well remember it being said to me by an occultist of great experience that two things are necessary for safety in occultism, right motives and right associates. We lull ourselves into a false security if we believe that good intentions are sufficient protection. My advice to the would-be student is to invoke the Master to send him an initiator, and to refuse to attempt any practical work until he is fully satisfied that the initiator has been found.

I cannot here enter into either the precautions to be taken against untoward happenings in practical occult work, nor the remedies to apply if they take place; I will merely indicate the signs by which such an eventuality may be recognised. This is all that can be done, and all that is necessary in a book of this type; the initiate knows what to do without need of guidance from me; the non-initiate cannot do anything, and must seek assistance. It is enough for him if he knows when such assistance is needed.

If things go wrong in the course of a magical ceremonial, the power "shorts," and someone, it may be the operator, or it may be the weakest person in the team, gets "knocked out" as if he had received a punch from an invisible pugilist. When picked up, he will be very dazed and badly shaken, and will certainly be some days, possibly weeks, before he gets over it. He will be in a state of complete prostration and considerable mental confusion, which will gradually wear off. Unless there is some organic defect, such as hereditary mental instability, a bad heart, or hardened arteries, there will be a complete recovery, given time but naturally it is a bad outlook should one of these conditions be present, and those who have them should not take part in occult experiments. Personally, I do not believe that the invisible forces alone will ever actually cause the loss of life or permanent disability in the absence of any physical lesion. The person who goes out of his mind as the result of a psychic shock would have gone out of his mind if he had been in a railway disaster or any other drastic emotional experience.

Unless the psychic atmosphere indicates otherwise, it is not necessary to do any banishings, or take precautions against obsession, because the power has dispersed itself in the very act of inflicting the shock.

During my early days of occultism I developed my powers very rapidly because I recovered the memories of previous incarnations en bloc, and with them the capacities acquired in previous lives, and I shook myself up severely on numerous occasions before I learnt the technique of handling the invisible forces. I never experienced any permanent ill-effects from my mishaps, though I admit that upon occasion I have been extricated by my friends from a considerable amount of debris.

During the early days of my occult career a girl was brought to me by a mutual friend, who told me that the mother of this girl, an ardent student of occultism, seemed to have a terrible effect upon her daughter. The mother was a widow, and mother and daughter lived together under very comfortable material circumstances; but whenever the girl made a friend, or showed any desire to leave home, the mother performed extraordinary antics, coming to the daughter's room at night and drawing signs in the air about her bed. The effect of all this upon the girl was most peculiar. She felt unable to free herself from the mental domination the mother had obtained over her, and she was wasting away in a most curious fashion. When I saw her, although able to get about, she looked like nothing I have ever seen save a famine victim.

I made a psychic investigation, and formed the opinion that the mother was working by means of an entity of which she had obtained possession. How this had been accomplished in the present instance, I do not know, but such things are common in occultism. I determined to take on the case, and to chase and, if possible, break up this artificial elemental. I was away from the group I was accustomed to work with, but among people keenly interested in occultism of every sort, size and description, and I had no difficulty in picking up a team to help me with the undertaking.

I had no qualms about the undertaking. A second-hand elemental, directed by a woman with only a rule-of-thumb knowledge of magic, did not appear to me to be a formidable opponent. I had seen a good deal of practical occultism, had lent a hand at similar operations and possessed the necessary formulae. So I went round the town, asked certain friends to lend a hand, and others to come and see the fun. To be frank, our attitude was that of a party of small boys going ratting.

We met at the appointed time and place. Formed our circle, and went to work. The method I meant to use made it necessary for me to leave my body, and the group were really there to look after it while I was out of it, and see it came to no harm. I got out on to the astral readily enough, did my job, and returned, feeling very pleased with myself, for it was the first time I had operated entirely on my own, without the supervision by my teacher.

As I began to recover physical consciousness, which is just like coming round from an anaesthetic, I had a sensation as of machinery running, and felt as if I were lying on something very lumpy. I opened my eyes, and saw something brown towering above me to an enormous height. As I gathered my senses together, I discovered that I was lying on the floor, close to the skirting, across the feet of an unfortunate man, who was thus securely pinned against the wall, and it was he, shaking in his shoes, that had felt to me like the vibration of machinery. Various other members of the circle slowly and reluctantly reappeared from behind the piano and sofa and other heavy articles of furniture. They had seen some practical occultism for once in their lives, but they did not appear to like it.

It appears that, after I had gone out and left them with my unconscious body, they got a good deal of phenomena in the way of bells and voices outside the circle. If they had kept quiet, it would have been quite all right, but they lost their heads and scattered. Then, the circle being broken, I began to perform antics, arching up on my head and my heels and, in some way that has never been explained, arriving at the far side of the room at the feet of one of the circle, which, of course, did not improve matters.

Then an extraordinary thing happened. We were just gathering ourselves together, thinking that everything was over, when a force of what nature I have never known suddenly rushed round the circle, and one member seemed to take the brunt of it. He went flying across the room and landed, fortunately for him, face downwards in an arm-chair, and was ill in bed for three weeks.

While all this was going on, the father of one of the people taking part became uneasy about her, and walked across from where he lived at the far side of the little town, to see what was happening. Like most little country towns, this one usually went to bed early, but he told us that as he came along he saw that innumerable windows were lit up, and he heard the sounds of children crying all down the street.

When I think of the risks I took and the conditions under which I worked in those early days, I wonder that I or any of my friends are alive to tell the tale. It is said that there is a special Providence to look after fools, drunkards and little children. I think there must be another that looks after inexperienced occultists and their friends.

It may be interesting to note that as a result of this operation which I so rashly undertook, the girl was entirely freed from the domination of her mother, and began forthwith to put on flesh and rapidly became normal. That end of it, at least, was entirely successful.

Another very curious case is that referred to in the *Occult Review* of January, 1930.

"The mysterious death of a student of occultism, Miss N. Fornario, is receiving the attention of the authorities at the present time. Miss Fornario was found lying nude on the bleak hill-side in the lonely island of Iona. Round her neck was a cross secured by a silver chain, and near at hand lay a large knife which had been used to cut a large cross in the turf. On this cross her body was lying. A resident of London, Miss Fornario seems to have made her way to Iona for some purpose connected with occultism. One of the servants at her house in London stated that a letter had been received saying she had a 'terrible case of healing on.' One newspaper report alludes to 'mysterious stories on the island about blue lights having been seen in the vicinity of where her body was found, and there is also a story of a cloaked man.' Occultists no less than the general public will await with interest any disclosures that may be forthcoming concerning this occurrence."

No disclosures ever were forthcoming, however, and conjecture alone can work upon the case. One detail only can I add to the brief but comprehensive report of the *Occult Review*. The body bore marks of scratches.

I knew Miss Fornario intimately, and at one time we did a good deal of work together, but some three years before her death we went our separate ways and lost sight of each other.

She was half Italian and half English, of unusual intellectual calibre, and was especially interested in the Green Ray elemental contacts; too much interested in them for my peace of mind, and I became nervous and refused to cooperate with her. I do not object to reasonable risks, in fact one cannot expect to achieve anything worth while in life if one will not take risks, but it appeared to me that "Mac," as we called her, was going into very deep waters, even when I knew her, and that there was certain to be trouble sooner or later.

She had evidently been on an astral expedition from which she never returned - She was not a good subject for such experiments, for she suffered from some defect of the pituitary body. Whether she was the victim of psychic attack, whether she merely stopped out on the astral too long and her body, of poor vitality in any case, became chilled lying thus exposed in mid-winter, or whether she slipped into one of the elemental kingdoms that she loved, even as Swinburne swam out to sea, who shall say ? The information at our disposal is insufficient for an opinion to be formed. The facts, however, cannot be questioned, and remain to give sceptics food for thought.

It may be as well to say in concluding this chapter, that when I speak of the experiments of ceremonial magic, I do not mean ritual initiation. Now a ritual initiation is of course ceremonial magic, and so, for the matter of that, are the sacraments of the Church. But the occultist, using his terms perhaps somewhat loosely, does not include the initiatory rituals when he speaks of ceremonial magic.

There are many varieties of initiatory ceremonies, but these are all designed to work upon the soul of the candidate only. Ceremonial magic, on the other hand, in the technical sense of the term, is designed to work upon the soul of nature. The two operations, although there are innumerable forms of each, are entirely different in type, and aim at, and achieve, entirely different results.

There is a strong prejudice against ritual magic among those interested in popular occultism owing to the strictures passed upon it by Mme. Blavatsky. Now Mme. Blavatsky was trained in the Eastern School and had very little, if any, practical acquaintance with the inner aspects of Western Occultism, nor was she a master of its methods. She spoke from an Eastern standpoint and judged Western esoteric conditions by those she had seen in the East, where Tantric magic has become depraved in the hands of Dugpas and similar sects.

In the dense and materialistic atmosphere of the West it is exceedingly difficult to get any results worth mentioning without the use of some form of ceremonial. Even the Theosophical Society, of which she was the foundress, has unconsciously drifted into Western methods, adopting the Catholic ceremonial and the Masonic initiations as side chapels to its main temple, and the mixture is giving trouble. The "Back to Blavatsky" movement within its ranks may be able to produce a much purer ethical and metaphysical teaching, but I think we may safely prophesy it will produce no practical results, in Europe at any rate.

Ought we to eschew ceremonial methods because occasionally, in inexpert hands or under unsuitable conditions, they lead to disastrous results? Ought we to eschew motor racing, or mountaineering, or flying, or research into the nature of radioactive substances? All these take their toll of life each year. There is an unjustifiable risk which no level-headed person will run if they can help it, and there is a justifiable risk which everybody must be prepared to take who wants to come out of the ruck. It is not every follower of the Inner Way who is suitable for ceremonial work, just as it is not every individual who is fitted to handle the controls of an aeroplane; but there are some people, both men and women, to whom a spice of danger is a spur which brings out the mettle of their pasture, and these will always be found in the van of great adventure.

PART II

DIFFERENTIAL DIAGNOSIS

9 DISTINCTION BETWEEN OBJECTIVE PSYCHIC ATTACK AND SUBJECTIVE PSYCHIC DISTURBANCE

Psychism a frequent cause of self-delusion ♦ Unexpectedly rapid development of
students sometimes leads to emotional disturbance ♦ Recovery of distressing
memories of a previous incarnation ♦ Findings of inexperienced psychics to be
accepted with caution ♦ "Old maid's insanity" ♦ Reactions to fixations ♦
Magnetism of an adept too potent for many people ♦ The fraudulent ♦
The insane ♦ The sex-cycle in relation to mental unbalance ♦ Case of cyclic
insanity ♦ The best test for genuineness is to be found in an examination of
motives ♦ Case of delusions of persecution ♦ Examples of genuine psychic
attacks for comparison with bogus ones ♦ Need for caution
in making a diagnosis.

PSYCHISM, HOWEVER genuine, is a fruitful cause of self-
delusion. A psychic is invariably highly sensitive and
suggestible. This is the basis of his gifts. Psychism not being
a normal development, among Europeans at any rate, the
psychic is, in the language of nautical engineers "over-
engined for his hull." He is consequently unstable, liable to
violent emotional reactions, and in general exhibits those
aberrations of conduct we are accustomed to associate with
artistic genius. Unless a psychic is trained, disciplined,
protected and watched over by those who understand his
condition, his psychism is never reliable because he is blown
about by every wind of influence. The psychic and the
neurotic are closely akin in their reactions to life, but the
neurotic differs from the psychic in that, instead of being
over-engined for his hull, he is under-hulled for his engines.
The result is the same, however, a discrepancy between the
force and form with the consequent inability to maintain a
central, reasoned, directing control. The technique of the
occult discipline is largely directed towards maintaining

control of the, disparate forces, compensating the
sensitiveness of the psychic, and protecting him from
unwanted impressions. It is never well to learn how to open
the door of the Unseen unless at the same time one learns how
to close and latch it.

As was noted in the Introduction, it is comparatively seldom
that the Unseen comes in search of human beings. As the
Caterpillar told Alice concerning the Puppy-dog, "You let it
alone, and it will let you alone." But if we begin to study
occultism, or even to dabble in it, sooner or later we are liable
to obtain results, provided, of course, that the system we are
using contains the germs of efficacy.

In the case of a person who is coming on to the Path for the
first time, progress is necessarily slow and laborious; but a
soul that has taken initiation in previous incarnations may re-
open the latent psychic faculties so rapidly that the problem
of maintaining the harmonised coordination of the
personality becomes a serious one. It is exceedingly common
for a person who is making his first contact with the occult
movement to experience psychic disturbance. This is
sometimes attributed to evil influences, sometimes to evil
entities. Neither of these inferences may be just. There is a
third possibility, which is responsible for by far the greater
percentage of victims - the mere fact that consciousness is
being disturbed by an unaccustomed force. How common a
thing it is to see a child feverish and fretful during the first
few days of a seaside holiday. It is not necessarily sickening for
an illness. The strong air and unaccustomed food and the
excitement of its new surroundings are disturbing its
sensitive physical equilibrium. So it is when the neophyte is
disturbed at the outset of his occult career. The unaccustomed
vibrations are upsetting him, and he is having an attack of
occult indigestion. In both cases the treatment is the same -
temporary restriction of the diet which has caused the
disturbance.

Another cause of psychic upset may lie in the partial recovery
of the memories of past incarnations if these include any

painful episodes, especially such as are connected with esoteric studies. The entry of occult concepts into the conscious mind tends to awaken the subconscious memory of similar experiences in past lives. The emotion surrounding a memory is invariably recovered before the actual image of the incident. (This is one of the best tests for the accuracy of memories of past lives.) This foreshadowing emotion may hang about for a long time on the threshold of consciousness before the images clarify sufficiently to become tangible. If the emotion that is rising over the horizon is of a painful nature it may cause considerable disturbance, and in the absence of an experienced adviser may be attributed to an occult attack, or to the psychic perception of evil influences in the occult group to which the neophyte is affiliated. It is necessary to use very great caution in drawing conclusions from the psychic impressions of an inexperienced student, who is apt to be as full of alarms as a two-year-old thoroughbred.

On the other hand, the instinctive reactions of a pure and sensitive soul are not to be ignored. There are such things as Black Lodges and evil entities. We must not allow the cry of "Wolf! Wolf!" to make us either callous or careless. In any case, the victim is suffering remediable discomfort.

It is an exceedingly difficult thing to determine psychically whether the complainant has reasonable grounds for his feelings, for his own imagination will have filled his atmosphere with menacing thought-forms. It is no simple matter to decide whether these thought-forms are subjective or objective. The wisest way is to rely on such evidence as is capable of objective examination, and enquire into the record of the particular group or occultist against whom the charges are being brought. But it is equally necessary to enquire into the record of the person who is bringing the charges. That that person is filled with the loftiest ideals is no proof that he has a level head, a clear and unbiassed judgment, or appreciation of the nature of evidence. A person need not be a deliberate liar to make statements that are very far from the truth.

Another factor which has to be reckoned with is the vagaries of the sex instinct in a person in whom that instinct is repressed. Consider the case of a woman, perhaps no longer young, whose circumstances for the first time permit her to follow her own inclinations; a very common case with home-keeping women, who have to wait for dead men's shoes before they can set out on life's journey. She takes up occultism, towards which she may always have had a leaning, and joins some circle for study and possible ritual initiation. The leader of that circle will in all probability be a person of strong individuality. The inexperienced, love-starved new-comer is glamoured. Ritual is a very stimulating thing, as Anglo-Catholic clergy have found to their cost. The woman, possibly quite ignorant of the facts of life, finds herself strangely stirred. She is frightened, she senses that something of the Kingdom of Pan is approaching. Her instincts will usually guide her truly enough in divining the source from which the disturbing influence proceeds. She will point an unerring finger at the magnetic male. She will seldom take into account the reactions of the female in the presence of the male.

If she is a woman ignorant of the facts of life, the charge she brings will usually take the form of an accusation of hypnotic influence. She does not realise that nature is the hypnotist. If she is a woman who knows something of the world, the charge may be of improper advances. One glance at the woman is usually enough to tell us whether there is likely to be any foundation in this charge or not. It is seldom the young and pretty girl, who might reasonably be apprehensive, who is the teller of these stories. It is a curious fact that it never seems to occur to the complainants either to take refuge in flight or put the matter in the hands of a solicitor. If, at the end of a long tale full of dark hints and unspeakable innuendos, the question is asked, "What exactly did he *do*?" the answer usually is, "He looked at me in a meaning way."

When one of these stories is being told we should be wise to give more attention to the bearing of the person who is telling it than to the facts alleged. This will usually yield the more valuable information. It is the most difficult thing in the world to get a genuine victim to speak. A woman who is broadcasting the tale of her own shame is usually a woman scorned, and the reliability of her testimony in the matter is in inverse ratio to her loquacity. Do not let us forget that it takes two to make a scandal as well as a quarrel, and the person who admits a mistake and asks for help to retrace wandering footsteps is much more likely to be worth helping than the one who claims to be even as the angels in heaven, where there is neither marrying nor giving in marriage.

So great is the need for caution in assessing the facts in a charge of immorality that the law courts will not accept the evidence of the victim, even on oath and under cross-examination, unless it is supported by additional testimony. Equally well does the doctor know the same type of mentality, and a common form of mental derangement is called Old Maid's Insanity, even in the textbooks.

I could cite cases by the dozen in exemplification of the preceding statements, but they have not sufficient occult interest to justify their inclusion in these pages.

If the leader of the group is a woman, a different set of reactions come into play though the same causes are at work. It is not generally realised that the fixation, or "crush" of one woman for another is really a substitute love affair, as is proved by the fact that the girl who has plenty of admirers, or the woman who is happily married is never given to them. In this case, just as much as in the normal, heterosexual attraction, "hell knows no fury like a woman scorned"; it is not, for obvious reasons, possible to bring charges of improper behaviour. (Though in one accusation this was alleged against me, and I was accused of being a man in disguise and attempting to seduce the complainant, and the charge found believers.) The charge brought in such cases usually takes one of two forms, the mechanism being either, "You don't love me, therefore you are cruel. I have been badly treated"; and the most far-fetched instances are raked up in support of this charge. Or, "You don't love me, therefore I hate you. The attraction you have for me is hypnotic."

It must be borne in mind in assessing these charges that a trained occultist, especially if of high grade, has an exceedingly magnetic personality, and this is apt to prove disturbing to those who are unaccustomed to high-tension psychic forces. For whereas the person who is ripe for development will unfold the higher consciousness rapidly in the atmosphere of a high-grade initiate, the person who is not ready may find these influences profoundly disturbing. An adept who allows unsuitable persons to enter his magnetic field is blameworthy for his lack of discrimination and discretion, but he cannot justly be charged with abuse of occult powers. He emanates force involuntarily and cannot help himself. The greater adepts always live in seclusion, for not only do they need solitude for their work, but their influence upon unprepared souls produces too violent a reaction, and it ends in the Cross or the hemlock cup.

We must not be unmindful of the fact that the person who comes to us with a long tale of occult attack and asks for assistance, especially financial assistance, may simply be "pitching a yarn," and should use the same discrimination that we would in listening to any other "hard-luck story," trying to differentiate between the deserving and the undeserving. I knew a man who allowed an alleged adept who was undergoing an alleged occult attack to take refuge in his studio, and returned after a short absence to find that the alleged one had been selling the furniture to buy drink; and there was every reason to believe that the only spirits who were in any way concerned with his troubles had entered the studio in bottles.

The complaints of occult attack may have their source in nothing more or less than the delusions of the insane, and it does not necessarily invalidate this fact that a second person can be found to give supporting evidence. There is a curious form of insanity known to alienists called *folie de deux*, in which two people intimately associated together share the same delusions. It is usually found in such cases that one is definitely insane, and that the other is of a hysterical type and has become imbued with the delusions of her associate by means of suggestion. I use the feminine pronoun because this form of insanity is rare with males. It usually occurs with two sisters, or with two women living together.

There is another pitfall for which the inexperienced do well to watch out in their dealings with the person who complains of an occult attack. Insanity may be periodic in its manifestation, outbreaks of acute mania alternating with periods of complete sanity. This periodic aspect should always be watched for in the case of women, in whom any temperamental instability becomes greatly exaggerated during the times of monthly periods, at the change of life, during pregnancy, and, in fact, at any period when the sex life is stirred to activity, whether emotionally or physically. It is also well to bear in mind that in pathological cases the periodicity of a woman's function may be greatly disturbed.

I had a sharp lesson in this respect upon one occasion, which exemplifies the need of caution. We had, at the introduction of one of our members, received into one of our community houses a woman whose husband, a well-known man in public life, refused to live with her, so I was told, and had made several attempts to do away with her, and threatened to have her certified insane if she in any way resisted him. These facts were vouched for by a circle of friends to whom both husband and wife were known. I kept this lady under observation for a month in order to see whether there was anything to justify the charge of insanity, and seeing nothing, took up her case. At the seventh week, however, trouble ensued. She got into a great state of excitement, declared that she was being starved, and ill-treated by the person who, in my absence, was responsible for the house. Seven weeks later we had another bout, in which she said that evil influences were proceeding from a certain cupboard in her room, wandered about the house in exceedingly inadequate apparel, and lost all self-control. This attack also passed off in a few days. It came out in the end that she suffered from chronic appendicitis which involved the right ovary, and whenever her exceedingly irregular menstruation occurred, she went right off her head for a few days. The position was greatly complicated by the fact that in the interregnum she was to all outward appearances perfectly sane. After she left our community house she told exactly the same stories about us that she had previously been telling about her husband. The out-and-out lunatic is a much less serious problem to society than these border-line cases. They need dealing with extremely cautiously, for they can cause an immense amount of trouble.

When an insanity has once become well developed anyone who has had experience of lunatics has little difficulty in recognising it. Each type of insanity has its characteristic facial expression and even gait. But it is not so simple a matter for even the expert to recognise an insanity in its incipient stages. Lunatics are exceedingly plausible, and if they have picked up something of the jargon of the occultist or spiritualist, can make out an extraordinarily good case for themselves. Even the experienced alienist often has to keep a case under observation in order to ascertain whether it is an actual insanity or not.

In a field where experts are frequently in doubt, what is the layman to do who finds himself confronted by a case which rouses his suspicions? He cannot be expected to recognise insanity when he sees it, but his own common sense ought to be sufficient to enable him to recognise sanity. In other words, let him suspend judgment upon the alleged facts and concentrate upon the question of motive. It is here he will find his best indication. If a person can offer no valid explanation as to the reasons for the attack that is being made upon him, nor as to its cause or origin, we can probably rest assured that it originates in his own imagination.

In one case which came into my hands for help, the victim declared that he was being persecuted by telepathic suggestion. I enquired as to the origin of this persecution, and he said that some people who lived in the next flat used to sit in a circle and concentrate upon him. I asked him why they did this. He did not know. I asked him how he knew they did it, and he could not tell me. He merely reiterated that they did it, although he admitted that he had never been inside their flat, never, in fact, even spoken to them except to exchange a good morning on the stairs. It was immediately apparent that there was no conceivable motive that could cause these people to go to the trouble of persecuting him. If anyone has ever tried any experiments with telepathic suggestion, they will know what intense concentration it requires, and, in fact, what hard work it is, and one cannot possibly imagine anybody putting themselves to the trouble of doing it over long periods of time without a very definite motive. I have, however, heard of a well-authenticated case of a woman, who had a liaison with a married man, attacking his wife in this way. I have also myself known of two cases in which a certain individual, at one time prominent in transcendental circles, in connection with what the newspapers impolitely called his "Prayer Shop," and equally well known in the City in connection with his efforts to obtain gold from sea-water, used telepathic suggestion in order to induce the signing of cheques and documents. Before a visitor was expected for an interview, he would sit down and concentrate upon him. So strong was the influence thus exerted that a man of my acquaintance threw up a post he held under him because of the undue mental influence he felt was being exerted over himself, and another resigned off the board of one of his companies for the same reason.

In both these cases an adequate motive for the mental attack is not far to seek. Compare these two cases with the previous one, and the difference can readily be perceived. We should, however, be just as cautious in deciding there is nothing wrong as in accepting at their face value any statements that may be made to us. Moreover, we should always bear in mind when dealing with a person who is obviously mentally unbalanced and who alleges a psychic attack, that the mental unbalance may have been induced by the psychic attack. Life is a strange thing at best, and many things that are stranger than usual can happen to those who move in occult circles.

10 NON-OCCULT DANGERS OF THE BLACK LODGE

Black Lodges connect with the underworld ◆ Kinds of crime usually associated
with Black Lodges ◆ Necessary precautions ◆ Character and record of
occult teachers ◆ *Truth* periodical - Blackmail ◆ Undue influence ◆
Drugs ◆ Immorality ◆ Danger to boys - Human sacrifice ◆
Revolutionary politics ◆ Signs of a Black Lodge.

THE FACTS CONSIDERED in the previous chapter, though they should make us exceedingly careful in weighing evidence, must not blind us to the fact that there are black sheep in every fold and that a fraternity which started out with the best intentions may quite inadvertently, through the ignorance or imperfections of its leaders, begin to drift on to the Left-hand Path. Perfectly innocent people enter it when it is in process of drifting but not yet avowedly black and may find themselves in waters that are unpleasantly dirty, even if not actually dangerous.

The esoteric dangers will be studied in detail in the next chapter, but we may very well consider in this place the exoteric dangers which may occur behind the Veil of the Temple, for human nature is much the same wherever we meet it, and shows little originality in choosing its road to the Pit. It might be thought that in such a book as this there were no need to touch upon these matters, but if this book is to serve the purpose for which it is intended, it is necessary to do so for three reasons; firstly, because the greater proportion of the students of esotericism are women, and even in these enlightened days they are usually ignorant of the life of the underworld, and a Black Lodge leads by a straight and narrow way into the land of apaches and demi-mondaines, quite apart from its other drawbacks. Secondly, a knowledge of these facts is essential for differential diagnosis. Thirdly, occult powers are not infrequently used to obtain purely mundane ends, therefore when the question of ordinary criminality occurs in connection with an occult organisation, the issue may be complicated by an admixture of methods that belong to another plane.

We must always remember that a lodge may not necessarily have been formed for the express purpose of evading the law; it may have started with a perfectly legitimate end in view, and have been exploited by evil-doers for their own purposes, for, owing to the secretive nature of its proceedings, the fraternity form of organisation lends itself to various forms of law-breaking.

One occult organisation is well known to have been involved in the drug traffic, another is riddled with unnatural vice. A third degenerated into what was little better than a house of ill-fame, and its head was an expert abortionist. Others have been involved in subversive politics. Those who join fraternities without properly investigating them and the credentials of those who are running them may find themselves involved in any or all of these things.

Behind the veil of secrecy, guarded by impressive oaths, many things may happen, and it is therefore essential to inform oneself most carefully concerning the character, credentials and record of the leaders of an organisation.

If these are not readily accessible, something is wrong. The Mysterious Stranger, who has just arrived from the East or the Continent, both rather vague addresses, is probably a fraud.

If difficulty is experienced in discovering the antecedents of an alleged adept, enquiries could be made of the well-known periodical (However, *Truth*, formerly of Carteret Street, S.W.1. stopped publishing many years ago.) *Truth* was originally founded to expose abuses in financial and public life, and for this purpose keeps a 'Black List' of individuals who are better avoided. It is fair and fearless in its methods, neither a persecutor nor a respecter of persons. It keeps a watchful eye upon the occult field and pillories charlatans, a task for which it should have the gratitude and support of all who have the cause of the Wisdom Religion at heart.

The commonest danger to which a person who gets into the company of undesirables is exposed, is to be induced to part with more money than is convenient by the time-honoured expedients of either swindling or blackmailing, the latter being by far the commonest form of unpleasantness in Black Lodges. The one and only remedy in all such cases is to place the matter in the hands of the police. Firstly, it is your duty as a citizen in order that others may not be victimised as you have been. Secondly, if you don't, your persecutors will not leave you until they have sucked you absolutely dry, and not even then if they can still find a use for you as a cat's-paw. A blackmailer is never got rid of by giving him money. It is merely an invitation to call again. Act quickly and firmly at the outset and you will soon be at the end of your troubles.

To demand money with threats is blackmail, and to coerce to any course of action by threats is also a crime. Any arrangements entered into, or documents signed in consequence of threats are not binding. Threats need not necessarily be gross and open, such as the pointing of a revolver; anything which coerces you against your inclinations may be interpreted as a threat. For instance, supposing it were intimated to you, however tactfully, that if you did not subscribe to the funds of an organisation, your interest in occultism would be gossiped about and possibly involve you in unpleasantness with your relatives or your employers, this, in the eyes of the law would be blackmail. Anything, in fact, which plays upon a person's fears is a threat.

Let us now consider what is the best thing to do if you are being threatened. It is seldom wise to answer threat with threat. The best thing is to reply that you will think it over and see what can be done, and then go straight to the nearest police-station and tell the whole story. You can be sure of the utmost courtesy, even kindness, and that every effort will be made to help you even if you have to admit that you have not been wholly blameless yourself. In coming to the police and telling them frankly the position of affairs you have, in popular language, "turned King's evidence," and the authorities will go a long way to protect anyone who does this.

Do not be deterred by the fact that you cannot bring forward any additional testimony in support of your statement. The police may tell you that there is not sufficient evidence for them to apply for a warrant; nevertheless, they will make enquiries, and the very fact that the police are making enquiries will be sufficient to frighten blackmailers out of their wits and probably out of the country, nor will they usually stop to make the threatened disclosures *en route*, but will "go while the going is good." Moreover your complaint will go on to the police records, and a watch will be kept; in due course another complaint may be made, or, for all you know, may already have been made, and then the net begins to tighten.

Always remember that the blackmailer has a great deal more to fear from exposure than you have; for whatever unpleasantness may be in store for you, he has to look forward to a long term of penal servitude, and possibly the dreaded " cat " if the case is a bad one.* A timely reminder of this fact works wonders with prospective blackmailers.

Nor need the fear of exposure of your own shortcomings deter you. The nature of the charges brought against you by the blackmailer will never be mentioned. It is not you who are being tried. Neither will your identity be disclosed. You will be referred to as Mr. A. or Mrs. B. Far from being treated as an evil-doer or having the finger of scorn pointed at you, you will find that you are looked upon as a person who is

---

* See "Note" at beginning of book.

performing a public service and every effort will be made by those in authority to smooth your path. A determined effort is being made at the present time to stamp out this abominable crime, and judges are giving exemplary sentences and protecting prosecutors in every way in order to encourage them to come forward.

But quite apart from any form of coercion, unwary persons may, while filled with enthusiasm or glamoured by the new revelation, part with considerably more money than they can comfortably spare; they may even literally lay their all upon the altar, and then, disillusioned by subsequent events, greatly regret having done so. In many such cases a competent solicitor can secure a refund. The courts do not look with favour on excessive contributions to "movements."

It goes without saying, that no rightly conducted organisation would consent to augment its funds at the expense of the ruin of one of its members. It must, of course, equally protect itself against capriciousness and spite and the machinations of the kind of mentality that tries to buy influence by subscriptions. It has always been our custom, in the Fraternity of the Inner Light, to insist that any woman who proposes to give a large donation should consult her financial adviser before doing so. For one reason or another we have refused upwards of twenty-five thousand pounds during the last seven years. Nor have we had any reason to regret having done so. The strength of an occult organisation does not lie upon the physical plane.

It is well known that there are various drugs which can be used to exalt consciousness and induce a temporary psychism. It may not be equally well known that most of these substances come under the regulations of the Dangerous Drugs Act, and that to obtain them from irregular sources, or even to be found in possession of them save for a legitimate purpose, is to render oneself liable to prosecution, and in this case too the authorities are exceedingly alert and the magistrates exceedingly drastic.

All initiates of the Right-hand Path agree in declaring that to exalt consciousness by means of drugs is a dangerous and undesirable proceeding. There may be research workers who for legitimate reasons wish to undertake experiments, but I cannot conceive of any legitimate reason for introducing a neophyte to the drug habit. In any case, if such experiments are undertaken, they should be conducted under the supervision of a qualified medical practitioner who will be in a position to prevent catastrophe or deal with it should it arise. The drugs that alter consciousness also affect the heart, and hearts are not always all they should be. Moreover, the composition of rare drugs is not standardised and varies enormously; they are liable to contain various impurities, and samples may turn out to be unusually toxic. The unpleasantness of having upon one's hands an unexpected and unaccountable corpse is only exceeded by the unpleasantness of becoming the corpse oneself, either of which eventualities may happen when people begin to experiment with the drugs that "unloose the girders of the mind."

The morals of mankind in general leave much to be desired from the point of view of the purist, and the occult organisations, occupying as they do, the sea-coast of Bohemia, leave more than usual. A few of the best, maintaining that occultism is essentially a religion, uphold a high standard; the remainder are blest with a kaleidoscopic collection of soul-mates. This need not concern us here. If people choose to kick over Mrs. Grundy's apron-strings, that is their affair. Nor need we at the moment consider the occult abuses of sex-force, which will require detailed consideration in their proper place. All we need consider in this chapter is the purely normal form of loose living which is camouflaged under a pretence of occultism. Of this I have seen numerous cases. The head of one group systematically seduced his pupils under the pretext that it was part of their initiation, and the group accepted the situation in a spirit of the purest self-sacrifice. Several others sailed unpleasantly near the wind, with the result that "crushes" and the subsequent nervous breakdowns were very prevalent. It ought hardly to be necessary to say that such methods form no part of the Right-hand Path.

It is amazing to what an extent women of the highest ideals and of good family and wide culture can be induced to accept such theories and practices. The danger of membership of such a group to young girls or unsophisticated women can readily be imagined.

I have often been accused of being narrow-minded in my attitude towards groups in which such happenings are allowed to go on, but the cost in human suffering is so great and the general demoralisation so sordid that tolerance comes perilously near to cynicism.

It may not generally be realised, but there is just as much danger of corruption in a Black Lodge for boys and youths as there is for women. There have been a number of cases so flagrant that the police have intervened, both here and abroad.

In ancient times, and among primitive peoples, human sacrifice was a common incident in connection with occult practices. It is not unknown in Eastern Europe even at the present day. The nursery story of Bluebeard has its origin in the practices of the infamous Gilles de Rais, Marshal of France and comrade of Joan of Arc, who slaughtered innumerable children and youths in connection with his magical experiments. I have never heard of a case in England, but there have been at various times some curious killings reported from the United States which look suspiciously like ritual murders, but in the absence of adequate information it is impossible to come to a final conclusion upon them. There recently came into my hands, however, a book upon magic published for private circulation, in which the statement is made that the ideal blood sacrifice is a male child.

The charge of revolutionary activities is one that has been frequently made against the occult movement. There are certain things, however, which must be borne in mind when assessing the truth of this charge. Firstly, the occult movement is not a homogeneous whole. It is totally unorganised and unregulated, and may best be likened to the state of England before the Norman Conquest. Conditions in the various groups and associations vary widely, and what is true of one may not be true of another. There can be no doubt whatsoever that various organisations at various times have been implicated in politics, as witness the Theosophical Society's association with Indian political movements; but we must bear in mind that one generation's revolutionaries are the next generation's reactionaries. After all, politics are a matter of opinion, and even the people we disagree with may turn out to be right in the end. I, personally, am of the opinion that an occult fraternity is extremely ill-advised to concern itself with politics for reasons which I have stated in another of my books, *Sane Occultism*, and which I will not enter upon now, as they are not relevant to these pages. But as folk from time immemorial have banded themselves together for political action we cannot very well take exception to what the law permits. People who join an organisation established for political work join it with their eyes open and presumably for the purposes for which it was founded. Grounds for objection arise, however, when an organisation is founded for non-political pursuits and subsequently the leaders, without consulting, or even informing their supporters, take up political activities on their own account and use their organisation for the purpose, thus involving their followers without their consent in whatever complications may arise, and using money contributed for a specific purpose for ends other than the donors had in view.

It may be wondered what use, at the present day, revolutionaries could make of the occult organisations. Within my personal knowledge they have used, or attempted to use them, for the purpose of getting letters to people whose correspondence is being watched, and I myself once received a request to allow a person who had been deported to return to the country under an assumed name and reside in one of our community houses as a member, and was offered some hundreds of pounds for so doing.

Needless to say, the correspondence was sent straight to the authorities.

The problems which we have considered in this chapter are not peculiar to occult fraternities, but are common to any organisation which does not discriminate as to its members. The organisations which advertise must perforce take all comers and sort them out in the light of subsequent experience, and some of these experiences can be very queer indeed. One cannot blame an organisation that picks up an occasional black sheep, one only takes exception if it retains an accumulation of them.

A lodge of dubious whiteness can be readily recognised by the type of people who belong to it, who may best be described as the seedy adventurer type with a sprinkling of smart society folk, who often have a taste for crude flavours in the way of sensation. The really Black Lodges are as carefully guarded as the high-grade White Lodges, and no outsider can gain entrance to them. The serious student of Black Occultism is out for knowledge and magical experiment and he is not going to waste his time on a tyro. Those who choose to graduate into a Black Lodge after serving their apprenticeship in the Outer Court of a White Lodge do so with their eyes open, and experience must be their teacher. One cannot feel that they deserve much sympathy if the experience is a painful one. The person I am out to help is the person who is a victim, not the one who is hoist with his own petard. The man or woman who, rejecting the steady grade of the Way of Initiation, chooses to go up with a rocket had better come down with the stick.

Any request for a large sum of money should always be regarded as a danger signal. It is one of the strictest conditions of initiation that occult knowledge may never be sold or used for gain. I know of an occultist who charges £300 for one of the initiations he confers; and he will give it to anyone who has got £300. In my opinion, the person who pays out £300 for such a purpose deserves the kind of initiation he is going to get.

It is also a bad sign when an occultist makes free with signs and wonders before the uninitiated. No genuine adept ever does this. The person who reads your past incarnations, describes your aura, rolls up his eyes, twitches, and gives you a message from your Master as soon as he is introduced, is a person to be avoided.

The more I see of the occult movement, the more I am amazed at the things people can say and do and "get away with." The average person is out of his depth when he deals with psychic matters. He usually goes through three phases. Firstly, he thinks it is all superstition and fraud. Secondly, his scepticism being breached, he will believe anything. Thirdly, if he ever gets as far as thirdly, he learns discrimination, and distinguishes between the Black Fraternities, the White Fraternities and Fatuous Fraternities.

11 THE PSYCHIC ELEMENT IN MENTAL DISTURBANCE

Personality, individuality and reincarnation ♦ The three great instincts ♦ Hysteria ♦ The neurotic ♦ Organic insanities ♦ The endocrines ♦ The blood ♦ Contacting the Unseen ♦ Qabalistic concept of the Invisible Kingdoms ♦ The Qlippoth in relation to insanity ♦ Consciousness in relation to the Spheres ♦ The Psychism of the psychopath ♦ Common ground of psychology and occultism ♦ Occult methods of dealing with insanity ♦ Obsession.

WE HAVE SEEN in a previous chapter that nervous and mental disorders can stimulate a psychic attack, especially if the subject is familiar with the terminology of occultism. We must also consider the part played by psychic attack in nervous and mental disorders. But before we can embark upon this section of our studies, we must give a brief explanation of the nature of nervous and mental disturbances and the distinction between them. We will not go into academic considerations, for these pages are not written for the orthodox professional psychologist, who has an abundance of textbooks at his disposal, but for the person whose interest is primarily in occult matters, and who comes to the study of the subject unequipped with the technicalities of psychology and psycho-physiology, two sciences of which at least a working knowledge is exceedingly necessary in the pursuit of practical occultism.

In the course of an incarnation the mind is built up on the foundations of the traits of the Higher Self or Individuality, which is the immortal soul that develops in the course of an evolution. The mind, therefore, is part of the personality - the unit of incarnation - commencing at birth and dissolving at death, its essence being absorbed by the individuality, which evolves thereby.

The mind is essentially the organ of adaptation to the environment, and it is when that adaptation fails that neurotic and hysterical troubles begin. Each living creature is the channel for a current of life-force which proceeds from the Logos, the Creator of this universe. This current is divided into three main channels represented to us as the three great natural instincts, Self-preservation, Reproduction, and the Social Instinct. These are the mainsprings of our lives. The pressure of life itself is behind them, and if they are thwarted beyond their power of compensation (considerable as that is) they are like streams whose channels are blocked, and which in consequence overflow and make a morass of the adjacent land.

Emotion is the subjective aspect of an instinct. That is to say, when an instinct is at work, we feel emotion. Every emotion we feel can be referred to one or other of the instincts. Our resentment of a slur upon our dignity has its roots in the instinct of Self-preservation. Our love of art has its roots in the instinct of love, beauty and creative expression which, upon its lowest arc, is called sex. Each of these instincts has its high spiritual aspect and its elemental physical aspect, and transmutation from one plane to another takes place freely, so that unless we understand the significance of these manifestations we shall be misled. In their understanding is the key to the science of life.

If one of these great instincts is so thwarted that all attempts at compensation break down; or if the temperament is so inelastic and unaccommodating that it will not modify its demands, the ego makes a final desperate attempt at adjustment which goes outside the limits within which harmonious relations with the environment can be maintained. Communications with the environment break down, and the mind has, in part at least, quitted the sphere of reality for the sphere of imagination. The sense of fixed values is lost, and things assume a symbolic importance. This breakdown may be partial, relating to certain aspects of the life only, or it may be total.

In hysteria, the damned-up forces of life remain in the channel, but spurt with concentrated force through any sluice that may be opened to them. Consequently, instead of the river below the obstruction being a smooth-flowing body of water, it descends in rapids and whirlpools difficult and dangerous to navigate, so that the barque of life makes shipwreck therein. The surrounding country, too, is reduced to a morass, neither land nor water. In other words, the temperament becomes tempestuous and unduly emotional, and the non-emotional factors of the mind, such as judgment and self-control, are demoralised. Such a temperament must of necessity be perpetually in difficulties with life, and periodically the repressed emotions boil over in fits of screaming, crying and convulsive muscular movements, which act as safety valves and relieve the pressure temporarily.

The neurotic differs from the hysteric in certain well-marked ways which need to be carefully borne in mind, as they are very important from the practical standpoint. The troubles of the neurotic start in the same way as those of the hysteric, being due to repressed emotion and failure to adapt to environment; but in his case, the life-forces set to work to cut fresh channels for themselves that shall circumvent the obstacle which blocks their path. Consequently we get what the psychologist calls displacement of emotion. Some comparatively innocuous matter becomes the object of an outpouring of emotion which in no way concerns it, for it has been made a substitute for something else. It is this curious underground tracking of emotion in the mind which causes so much trouble, for the sufferer is not insane, and yet certain sections of his values and reactions to life are perverted. He is an extremely tricky person to deal with because he is given to unexpected and quite irrational loves and hates and fears, and acts accordingly.

Similar conditions prevail in the organic insanities; the psychological results are the same, but because the origin is physical, not mental, they are but little amenable to psychotherapy. Certain things can be done to alleviate them, however, even if they are not entirely curable; therefore let us consider them from both the psycho-physical and occult standpoints.

The body is the vehicle of the mind. If the vehicle be faulty, the mind cannot express itself accurately; its reactions will be distorted. Orthodox science says that the brain is the organ of the mind, but esoteric science says the brain is the organ of perception of sense impressions and coordination of efferent impulses. It is the telephone exchange of the nervous system. It is only one of the points where mind touches body, the others being the ductless glands of the endocrine system, the pineal, pituitary, thyroid, adrenals, thymus and gonads; to which may be added the Solar Plexus and Sacral Plexus. The student of Tantric physiology will be very dull if he has not observed that the Chakras coincide in their physical location with the endocrine organs.

Now the endocrines have for their task the maintenance of the chemical composition of the blood. They pour into it their secretions, called hormones, in certain balanced proportions. If the balance is in any way upset, either by an overplus of one secretion or shortage of another, profound changes in metabolism take place. The whole of the life processes are regulated by the endocrines, and can be speeded up or slowed down in their different aspects as the balance of the endocrines alters. This endocrine balance is known by physiologists to be intimately associated with emotional states, and especially with the alertness or stolidity of the temperament. Psychologists do not sufficiently appreciate the importance of the recent work upon the endocrines, but occultists have a knowledge of this aspect of psycho-physiology as part of their traditional teaching. The breathing exercises of the yoga system are based upon this knowledge, and are exceedingly potent, as are all occult practices which are brought through correctly to the physical plane. In fact, we may say that no occult process is really potent, nor can it be said to have completed its circuit, unless it has its point of contact with dense matter; a point which many occultists leave out of their calculations. Occultism, though primarily a mental process, is not a purely mental process. It is both spiritual and material.

In the great majority of cases of insanity, organic brain changes cannot be demonstrated, but alienists are more and more coming to recognise that they may look for the clues of Hecate in the blood. Its chemical composition may depart from normal, whether owing to a change in the hormone balance or to the by-products of disease. This change in the blood chemistry is immediately followed by a change in the emotional tone. It may become over-emotional or depressed, apathetic or irritable. The ancients described these conditions admirably as the four humours, the sanguine, the bilious, the lymphatic and the choleric.

It has been abundantly demonstrated by physiologists that emotional states affect the chemical composition of the blood. It is gradually being realised that these changes are brought about through the mediation of the ductless glands, which may be called the emotional brain, just as the grey matter within the skull may be called the sensory-motor brain. It follows, therefore, that if through some interference with their functioning the glands produce a blood-composition corresponding to that produced by them when a particular emotional state is giving its special stimulus, the individual will experience the physical sensations associated with the corresponding emotional state. His mind will proceed to adjust itself to these conditions by accounting for them through the imagination as best it may. So that if there is a state of the blood characteristic of the condition of fear, fear-images will arise in the mind. It is upon this basis that the organic insanities produce their characteristic mental states.

Whether the emotional state be due to a mental cause or a physical cause, the result is the same for the patient. Organic insanities are distinguished from functional ones solely by their origin. An organic insanity tends to depart further from the normal than a functional nervous disorder, because in the latter a considerable degree of compensation takes place, for the patient can to a great extent pull himself together and keep himself from going to disastrous extremes. This is not the case with an organic insanity, which proceeds to its logical conclusion. It is for this reason that a neurotic, although he may suffer severely, seldom has a complete breakdown unless he is sure of the necessities of life. The self-preservation instinct keeps him on his feet.

Having considered the physical and subjective bases of mental disturbances, we are now in a position to assess accurately the part played by the Unseen. What happens when a neurotic takes up occultism? We can best answer this question by considering what happens when a normal person takes up occultism. He learns for the first time of the existence of the Invisible Worlds and begins to think about them. Immediately he does this he comes into touch with them. At first he may not be able to perceive them consciously; nevertheless he is feeling them subconsciously and they are affecting him. His life shows this to the close observer in a thousand ways.

There are great forces moving like currents in the Unseen, and we are drawn into these according to our temperamental affinity for them. The violent personality is drawn into the Current of Mars, the emotional, suggestible one into the sphere of Luna. The influences of these spheres play upon them. Now the occultist working under a proper system, knowing that he has got to meet these forces sooner or later, picks them up one by one voluntarily and by means of the appropriate rituals, and synthesises them within his own nature. He knows too that each aspect has its obverse. The Virgin Mary is reflected in Lilith. The older faiths knew this, but popular Christianity, which has no roots in tradition, has forgotten it. Protestant Christianity threw away its occult aspect at the Reformation. All the pagan pantheons have gross aspects of divinities as well as etherial ones. We need to search the refuse-heap of history for the lost parts of our own tradition if our faith is to be complete, and the most profitable line of search is in the Qabalah and the Gnostic literature. The literature of the Gnosis has been largely destroyed by systematic persecution, but in the Qabalah there is still left for us a complete system. The Jews, being strictly monotheistic, did not speak of gods, but they recognised a hierarchy of angels and archangels which is the equivalent of the pagan pantheons. It is through these ethereal messengers that the All-Father formed the worlds.

Let us consider once more the Qabalistic doctrine of the Qlippoth, for it has an intimate bearing upon the problem of insanity. The doctrine of the Ten Holy Sephiroth, arranged in their correct pattern to form the Tree of Life, is invaluable in enabling us to conceive the Invisible. The First Sephira is concentrated out of the Unmanifest, the Point within the Circle. This emanates the Second, which in its turn emanates the Third. As soon as one has emanated another, these two are said to be equilibrated; but when emanation is in process, there is a period of unbalanced force. This, as it were, goes off by itself in the Cosmos and establishes a sphere of its own, unconnected with the Cosmic system. Consequently, each sphere of the Cosmos has its counterpart in Chaos, in miniature, it is true, but nevertheless potent and functional.

Each sphere, in the course of its evolution, builds up an Over-soul which is called by different names in different systems. In the Qabalistic system we call them the Archangels, the Spirits before the Throne. The Sphere of the Sun is represented by Raphael, the Sphere of the Moon by Gabriel. The Obverse Sephiroth, or Qlippoth, build up in exactly the same way. In the Habitations of Hell these two are known as the Disputers and the Obscene Ones, whose names sufficiently indicate their characters. The Sphere of the Sun is also the point of manifestation of the Messiah or Saviour upon earth. The Prince of Peace has His obverse in the Disputers. Who that has had the Vision Beautiful does not know the reaction that follows it, and the need of wisdom, self-control and patience to deal with the forces that are released not only in the soul but in the environment? It is for this reason that periods of purgation and discipline precede all revelations. We must keep the vigil before we can sit at the feast.

Consciousness, released from the Sphere of Earth, rises straight upwards to the Sphere of the Moon. This is the negative, feminine, receptive, psychic sphere. From thence it passes onwards to the Sphere of the Sun. This is the positive, masculine sphere of the higher consciousness, the vision of the seer as distinguished from the psychic. Upon either hand the path is flanked by the Spheres of Hermetic Wisdom and Elemental Beauty.

These Spheres, which have to do with the grades of initiation, need not concern us in the present pages. We shall only have to do with the Sphere of the Moon, Luna, the Mistress of the Luna-tic. Now Luna was represented by the ancients under diverse forms as Diana the chaste huntress, symbol of sublimation, and Hecate, patroness of witchcraft and childbirth. We have already noted that the Qlippoth of the Sphere of Luna are called the Obscene Ones. Hence it is that when the unstable soul advances by the Path of Saturn that bridges the Astral and enters the Sphere of Luna, he touches her Hecate aspect and finds himself *en rapport* with the Obscene Ones, whose chief is Lilith, she who giveth lustful dreams. Need we then wonder that Freud finds the dreams of the neurotic filled with sexual images in their most perverted and debased forms? The Rabbis knew their psychology just as well as he does.

As has already been noted, the neurotic is very often psychic, and the psychic is very often neurotic. What may we expect to happen to the soul that has taken initiation in a past life, retains subconsciously the psychic development thus conferred, and finds itself incarnated in a neurotic personality in this life? He will come under the dark dominion of the Moon, and Lilith will be his mistress. Through the ill-fitting doors of the neurotic temperament the forces of the Abyss find ingress. The dissociated complexes of the Microcosm are reinforced by the dissociated complexes of the Macrocosm, for that is precisely what the Qlippoth are.

Occultists and their ignorant admirers, the superstitious, have always held that insanity had to do with demonic possession. Modern medicine disputes this, and declares the various manifestations of the diseased mind to be due entirely to subjective psychological processes. At present these two schools of thought are like two armed camps, drawn up for battle and shaking their weapons at each other. Each is too sure of his own ground to be willing to give the other a hearing. It is my belief that a common ground can be found for the meeting of these two opposing viewpoints. Psychology demonstrates the mechanism of the mind and can explain the mental processes whereby the ideas of the deranged assume their ultimate form. It can show the connection between these ideas and the dreams of the normal mentality. What it cannot explain is the fundamental difference between these subjective states and the normal waking consciousness. It is here that the occultist can tell the psychologist something that it is worth his while to hear, for he can show how these visions can be produced experimentally and at will by means of ceremonial magic. And still more important, the occultist can show him how these visions can be dispersed and the psychic faculties closed down and sealed.

This brings us to the practical part of our considerations: How far can the methods of ritual magic be applied to the relief of mental disease? They are undoubtedly palliative, but they will not produce a permanent cure unless the origin of the disturbed mental condition is found and cleared up. Unless this be done, as fast as we disperse the phantoms, they will re-form, because the mental state of the patient is invoking them. Under such circumstances, no magic circle can be kept intact. As fast as we break the rapport with the Abyss, the patient renews it.

But such conditions constitute a vicious circle. The Qlippotic forces with which a contact has been established will actively develop it, and will hold on to their victim when attempts are made to dislodge them. In this rationalistic age we are apt to forget that there is such a thing as organised and intelligent evil. If the physical causes of this disturbance have been cleared up, the septic focus eradicated, or the tumour pressing upon the ductless gland excised, and still the mentality does not return to normal, an exorcism will often produce immediate and marked results.

In the case of the neurotic, whose trouble is entirely in the sphere of the mind, an exorcism is of enormous value as a preliminary to the appropriate psycho-therapeutic treatment because it clears the ground and prevents re-infection, giving the patient a chance to make a fresh start. It is possible for the Qlippotic demons to gain so powerful a hypnotic influence over a victim that he is powerless to break it by any effort of his own will, nor can the orthodox type of psycho-therapy touch the root of the trouble. The exorcism may have to be repeated two or three times in the course of the treatment, because the rapports may be renewed after they have been broken. But once the patient's complexes have been cleared up, they will not return. In any case, an exorcism produces marked temporary benefit; during the lull the patient gets a chance to pull himself together and the evil influences are undermined. A courageous patient, who is cooperating intelligently, will seldom have to be exorcised more than three times provided material conditions are favourable. I have seen cases cleared by a single exorcism, and remaining well indefinitely so long as ihe patient obeyed instructions and had nothing whatever to do with the Unseen, neither reading books upon occultism nor associating with people who were interested in such subjects; and I have also seen the Abyss re-establish its influence when the patient disobeyed instructions and re-awakened the old vibrations.

We need to realise that the human consciousness is not a closed vessel, but like the body, has a continual intake and output. The cosmic forces are circulating through it all the time, like sea-water through a living sponge. Whatever emotional state may arise within us is reinforced from outside. The subjective self only has the kindling, the Cosmos supplies the fuel. Once the fire is started, the cosmic forces of the appropriate type will stoke it. Just as the devout Catholic is inspired by the influences of his patron saint, invoked by prayer, so the neurotic is hag-ridden by his obsessive demon, invoked by the morbid broodings of the dissociated subconsciousness. The occultist maintains that the generalised principle of evil has its intelligent channels, just as the organised Principle of Good has Its ministering spirits. Any observer who considers the phenomena of mental disturbance will find much to support this hypothesis.

The question of obsession is an exceedingly important one. The word is used very freely in occult circles, and is held to mean the withdrawal of a soul from its body and its replacement by another soul, but I doubt whether this is a true representation of what happens. It has always appeared to me that in obsession we have not got the actual replacement of one soul by another, but the complete domination of one soul by another. It is hypnotic domination, and we can explain it in terms of the known psychology of hypnosis, the hypnotist in the case being an astral entity.

There is an operation in magic known as "assuming the god-form," in which the operator identifies himself in imagination with the god and so becomes a channel for its power. It is one of the special modes of Egyptian magic wherein the priest always wore a mask to represent the animal head symbolically attributed to the god he represented. This imaginative identification is a method well known in occultism and is often employed in order to enter into the inner life of a plant or a crystal as a mental exercise. The effects of it are very marked and very peculiar. I am inclined to think that it is this method, combined with hypnosis, which is used by the obsessing entity, which first identifies itself with its victim and then superimposes its own personality upon his, thus obtaining a vehicle of manifestation. I am also of the opinion, however, that it is only in certain abnormal states, whether induced by disease of mind or body, or by some of the more drastic operations of black magic, that this imposition can take place.

PART III

THE DIAGNOSIS OF
A PSYCHIC ATTACK

12 METHODS EMPLOYED IN MAKING A PSYCHIC ATTACK

Witchcraft, ancient and modern ◆ Knowledge of drugs ◆ Factors concerned in making a Psychic attack ◆ Mental concentration ◆ Invocation of a Cosmic force ◆ Example of a ceremonial invocation ◆ The magician himself the channel of evocation ◆ Method of contacting the victim ◆ Substitution ◆ Talismans ◆ Magnetised objects ◆ Motives for psychic attack ◆ Case of the concert singer ◆ Case of the Oriental Adept ◆ Mental trespassing.

ANYONE WHO READS the old books on witchcraft, usually compiled by the professional witch-finders from the confessions of alleged witches extorted under torture, will find that the phenomena described fall into certain broad categories which are so constant in different ages and in different parts of the world that we are left with the impression that there must be some fire behind so much smoke. The State records of witch trials in Scotland, the reports of a priest charged with the task of extirpating witchcraft in Northern Italy, the archives of Brittany, the stories of magic in classical literature, and finally, travellers' accounts of the practices of primitive people all over the world, all corroborate each other, agreeing as to the phenomena described, the explanations given by the witches of their methods, and the broad divisions into which the phenomena fall.

We must first take account of the use of drugs, of which the Black Fraternity in all ages have possessed a remarkable knowledge. Potions, unguents and fumigations were used extensively and among all the weird and wonderful ingredients of which they were composed we now and again find substances which are known to be medicinally potent.

The poppy which gives sleep and dreams, hemp which gives visions, datura which produces loss of memory, blighted grains which produce abortion, certain insects which are powerfully aphrodisiac, certain barks which are effectually anaphrodasiac, and in the New World, the buds of a certain cactus - all these and many others play their part in the witch brews. Paracelsus earned fame by turning some of the traditional magical brews to medicinal purposes. The Borgias earned infamy by employing them as subtle poisons which destroyed the mind without necessarily destroying the body. It is related that the Roman philosopher Lucretius was driven insane by a magical draught given him by his wife in order to restore to her his lost affections. There exist old recipes for witch unguents which contain opium and cantharides. It is not difficult to imagine what manner of dreams would come in the sleep thus induced. C. S. Ollivier, in his recent book, *Analysis of Magic and Witchcraft*, gives it as his opinion that attendance at the Sabbat was often achieved by means of drug-induced dreams.

Subtle poisons also undoubtedly play a part in the effectiveness of curses, a favourite method being to make a talisman of brass, copper or lead, and fasten it inconspicuously at the bottom of a drinking vessel or cooking pot. What effect the talisman had is conjectural, but there is no doubt at all about the effect of the steady dissolving of small quantities of lead and verdigris in the food.

But while all these things were a part, and a considerable part, of the witch-cult, they cannot, strictly speaking, be considered a psychic method of attack, and we only refer to them in these pages in order that their effects may be excluded from the diagnosis.

There are three factors in a psychic attack, any or all of which may be employed in a given instance. The first of these is telepathic hypnotic suggestion. The second is the reinforcement of the suggestion by the invocation of certain invisible agencies. The third is the employment of some physical substance as a *point d'appui,* point of contact, or magnetic link. The force employed may be used as direct current, transmitted by the mental concentration of the operator, or it may be reserved in a kind of psychic storage battery, which may be either an artificial elemental or a talisman.

In chapter 11 we have considered in some detail the psychology of suggestion, and need not repeat what has already been said, save to remind the reader that the essence of telepathy consists in the sympathetic induction of vibration. Experimental psychologists are already suspecting that emotion is closely akin to electricity; they have proved conclusively that emotional states alter the electrical conductivity of the body. The occultist believes that emotion is a force of an electrical type, and that in the case of the ordinary man it radiates out from him in all directions, forming a magnetic field; but in the case of the trained occultist it can be concentrated into a beam and directed. Supposing you are able to concentrate your whole attention upon a single feeling, inhibiting all else, you will have achieved a pure emotional state, unadulterated and undiluted. All the life-force coming into your soul will therefore flow in this single subdivision of a single channel instead of in the many ramifications of the usual three channels previously referred to. The concentration will be terrific, but it will only be achieved at a terrific price. It is in order to achieve this terrible concentration that the saints of the West and the yogis of the East practise a torturing asceticism. You must sell all that you possess in order to purchase this pearl of great price, and an echo of the method lingers in the fairy-tale tradition that the person who finds the lucky stone can only have one wish. Such a concentration is good for one purpose, and one purpose only. We can concentrate on a healing, or on a destruction, but we cannot work at both simultaneously; neither can we readily change over from one to the other. We cannot combine incompatibles within the limits of a single life. That is to say, if we have concentrated on a work of malediction and death in order to achieve an act of revenge, our rage being satiated, we cannot immediately reverse the spin of the soul and reconcentrate upon works of wisdom and redemption. We may liken the soul moving with the tide of evolution to a wheel spinning clockwise, or deosil; and a soul moving against the tide of evolution to a wheel spinning counter-clockwise, or widdershins. The position of the axle can be altered so that the wheel revolves at any angle without the direction of its revolution being effected, but the flywheel has to be stopped before the engine can be reversed, and a big flywheel takes a great deal of stopping. Moreover, in order to reverse the flywheel, we have to stop the engine. The normal movement of the soul is deosil, forward with the current of evolution. We need to think many times before we undertake to reverse that spin even momentarily, in order to undertake a work of malediction and death. The old saying, "There is the devil to pay," is a true one. Indeed, it is questionable whether there is such a thing as momentary reversal of spin. Momentum has to be checked and worked up again before reversal of spin can take place.

Very great forces can be developed by this subjective concentration of the mind itself, but even greater forces can be rendered available if we apply the mechanical equivalent of gearing; if, in other words, while this tremendous concentration is being held, we pick up the contacts of the corresponding cosmic force. We use the powers of the human mind as a self-starter, and as soon as its lesser driving-wheel is flying round merrily, we throw in the clutch of the main engine. There is a brief period of struggle as the little machine forces over the reluctant levers of the great machine, then the vapour fires and then the engine takes up its work. After that it is only a matter of engaging the gears and driving - if you can! So it is with ceremonial magic.

Let us consider a concrete case of someone who wants to avail himself of a fighting force. He would have recourse to a ceremony of the planet Mars. He would therefore gather together in his temple all that was appropriate to Mars. He would drape his altar with a scarlet cloth; he would himself wear a scarlet robe. All his magical implements would be of iron and his rod of power would be a naked sword. Upon his altar he would place five lights, five being the number of Mars. Upon his breast would be the symbol of Mars engraved upon a steel pentagon. On his hand would be a ruby ring. He would burn sulphur and saltpetre in his thurible. Then, according to the work in hand, he would call upon the angelic or demonic aspect of the Fifth Sephira, Geburah, the sphere of Mars. He would invoke either the deity-name in Geburah, calling upon the God of Battles to hear him, or the arch-devil of the Fifth Infernal Habitation. Having performed this mighty invocation, he would then offer himself upon the altar as the channel for the manifestation of the force.

There are many formulae extant designed to enable a force to be brought through without the necessity of the magician himself being the channel. In my opinion they are one and all ineffectual; the only possible substitute for the magician himself being a trance medium. It is for this reason that ritual magic so often fails to come off. You cannot make custards without breaking eggs, and if you mean to be a magician you have got to "go the whole hog." When it is a question of bringing through the angelic aspect of a force, the matter is on a clear footing. To be the channel of such a force is a great privilege and is an initiation in itself. The operator has simply to eliminate from his nature all incompatibles and maintain his concentration without wavering. The worst that can happen is that he should fail to obtain his results. But when it comes to bringing through the demonic aspect of a sphere, the matter is on an entirely different footing. Very few people care to offer themselves for the manifestation of such a force as Asmodeus. I do not believe that there is any reliable device for invoking the devils without being obsessed by them save the method of Abramelin, which involves six months' preparation and is only operated after the knowledge and conversation of the Holy Guardian Angel have been attained. The edge of the Abyss is well fenced. It is not possible to fire a gun and avoid the recoil.

Having invoked and concentrated his force, our sorcerer has next to consider his target. He has to get into astral contact with his victim. In order to do this, he must form a rapport, not quite as easy as might be imagined. First he has to find his victim and establish a point of contact in his sphere, and then, working from this base, succeed in piercing his aura. An unfocussed force is not very much use. A focus has to be achieved. The usual method is to obtain some object which is impregnated with the intended victim's magnetism, a lock of hair, nail-paring, or something habitually worn or handled. Such an object is magnetically connected with its owner, and the sorcerer can work up the trail and thus enter the sphere of his victim and establish a rapport. He then proceeds as does any other practitioner of suggestion who has succeeded in getting his victim into the first stages of hypnosis. By means of the magnetic link he has gained the psychic ear of his victim, who will hear his suggestions subconsciously. It now remains to be seen whether the thought-seeds thus planted will strike root or be cast out from the mind. In any case the victim is rendered disturbed and uneasy.

If a magnetic link cannot be obtained, the practitioner of black magic has to fall back upon other devices. One of the most common is that of Substitution. Something is chosen and by means of ceremonial is identified with the intended victim. For instance, a small animal may be baptised with the victim's name, and then immolated, usually with torture, the operator meanwhile concentrating upon the personality of the original. The old device of making a wax image and melting it before a fire, or driving nails into a wooden statue, baptised with the name of the victim, are frequently met with in the records of witch-trials. The actual driving of the nail has no conceivable effect upon the victim, but it helps the concentration of the operator.

The talismanic method in various forms is also employed. A talisman is a symbol representing a certain force, or combination of forces, depicted upon a suitable substance and magnetised by ritual. It can be made from anything which will retain magnetism; metals, precious stones or parchment are usually employed; paper is less effective unless it be enclosed in a metal case. Water and oil can be effectually magnetised but soon lose their potency. A talisman is made by invoking the requisite force, as already described, and then concentrating it upon the prepared object, which is placed ready upon the altar before the evocation begins.

A talisman thus made has next to be brought into the magnetic sphere of the victim. It is related that Lady Burton, anxious to convert her free-thinking husband, the famous Sir Richard Burton, the great explorer, used to get her priest to bless little statues of the saints and put them in the pockets of his clothes. A similar device is used by the workers of black occultism. Magnetised objects are placed in the rooms habitually occupied by the victim, or buried in his path, so that he must pass over them frequently.

These talismans of evil not only work by their own power, but also serve the sorcerer as a point of concentration for his meditations. Harmful effects are also produced by objects which have been used in black magic and have become impregnated with the forces they were employed in generating. Odds and ends of magical equipment turn up in some queer places. I was present at an auction in a country town when the twelve signs of the Zodiac, neatly painted on a blackboard, came up for sale. Various of my friends have picked up magical treasures, such as altar lamps and incense burners that obviously came out of ritual lodges, but the prize of the collection was a magical rod that was put up to auction along with a bundle of fire-irons. Large crystals for scrying are frequently seen in antique shops. All such things need carefully de-magnetising before they are brought into one's psychic sphere.

I was taking part at one time in a series of psychic experiments which had been going on very well, when, for no apparent reason, things went wrong and there was a considerable upheaval. We did not know at the time, but we learnt later, that the owner of the flat where they were being held had obtained possession of a floor-cloth that had been used in ritual magic by an occultist whom only the utmost leniency could call doubtful.

The artificial elemental is really the basis of the efficacy of curses. In this case no physical substance is employed, but a portion of the Akasha is moulded into a definite form and held thus by the will of the operator until, as it were, it "sets." Into this mould is poured the concentrated energy of the operator, something of his own self goes into it. This is its soul, and it is like a self-steering torpedo which is set to move in a curve towards a chosen mark. Or the operator, if an expert magician, may deliberately ensoul this thought-form with elemental essence, which is the raw, undifferentiated substance of life drawn from one or another of the elemental kingdoms. It is in order to do this that the curse is invoked in the name of some being. The curser declares, "I curse you by so and so." This is the form of evocation which calls the ensouling essence into the thought-form, thus making an artificial elemental which is endowed with an independent life of its own.

If we want to know something of the efficacy of curses, we have only to consider the record of the men who were connected with the opening of the famous Tut-ankh-amen tomb. There are many other cases equally well authenticated.

One can become exposed to occult unpleasantness either by thwarting or in some other way falling foul of an unscrupulous occultist, or by getting oneself involved with a dubious occult fraternity. In the case of a quarrel with an occultist, in addition to the ordinary human motives for an abuse of power, one has to reckon with the fact that an adept who is not of the whitest nearly always suffers from that unpleasant psychic disease of "hypertrophied ego." He will love power for its own sake, and take any defection on the part of an erstwhile follower, or any resistance to his imperious will as a personal insult or even injury. With a trained mind, an angry thought will do damage, and I have known cases of occultists who, out of pure pique, went to extraordinary lengths of spite. One can only hope that they did not really believe in the efficacy of what they did, and were merely playing to the gallery "pour encourager les autres" and ensure loyalty among their supporters.

Another thing which is particularly disliked by this type of adept is any attempt on the part of a pupil who has broken with him to make use of what he has been taught. There seem to be no lengths to which a jealous guru will not go in order to smash his chela psychically.

In one case which came to my knowledge a concert singer had had "treatment" for the improvement of her voice from an adept of sorts. She finally decided that she would spend no more money on this enterprise, and told him so at the visit which she had decided should be the last. He concentrated his gaze upon her and told her that if she broke with him, as soon as she went on the concert platform she would see his face in the air in front of her, and her throat would close and she would be unable to utter a sound, and that this horrible experience would occur every time she tried to sing until she returned to him and continued to have "treatment" (at a guinea a time). This potent hypnotic suggestion proved effective, and her career was at an end until the spell was broken.

The following letter contains a very illuminating experience, and is of value, not only for its account of a psychic attack, but also for its description of the manner in which the attack was combated.

"In the winter of 1921–1922 I was told (from the Inner Planes), 'We see your initiation into the Order of the Christ.' I did not understand very clearly and I waited."

In June, 1922, an Oriental, the head of a great religious Order, came to see me. (I was living in Switzerland.) We will call him Z. I expected great things from him and looked on him as a sort of Master. Knowing that he had met Abdul

Baha, I thought to please him by putting A.B.'s photo on my walls, but when Z. entered my room I saw at once that he did not quite like it. We conversed for a while and he asked me several questions. Suddenly he offered me initiation into his Order. I was taken aback and did not feel the *inner* consent. I said I must reflect. Later on an inspiration(?) came to me and I said, 'Is your Order the Order of the Christ?' He answered, 'It is.' I told him of my experience (related above) and accepted initiation; but I had the inner conviction that all was not right.

"I felt no inner response to several incidents during the initiation, and I began to call mentally and earnestly upon the Christ, and kept on doing so until the end of the ceremony. (I learned afterwards that he had told one of his disciples that I had accepted initiation *but not the Master.*)

"It would take too long to relate other less important details so I go on to our second interview during which he asked me several times to leave the town where I was and to join him in active work. This time I heard the inner voice clearly ; it said, 'No.' Suddenly he said, 'Sit in front of me; I will heal you.' (I was in very bad health at the time.) He fixed his eyes on mine with a strong commanding gaze. Mentally I called on the Christ and I felt form all round me a sort of shell. 'There,' he said, 'I have healed you.' The inner voice said, 'No.'

"Well, he went away and I had a "bad time" for I had the feeling that all was not right, though I had no suspicion of evil. (Nor have I now.)

"I wrote an account of this interview to a friend, and a letter from her crossed mine. She told me that about the time of my interview with Z., of which she was unaware, she was told to join our spiritual teacher in helping me. She withdrew from the Outer Planes, and then she realised that strong hypnotic forces were playing upon me in waves. Again and again she had to use all her spiritual power to help me withstand them, but finally we stood on a rock, bathed in light and free.' My letter gave her the key to it; but she replied, 'Take care, Z. will try again. He realised that he was baffled; he will try on the Inner Planes next time.'

"Now comes the great experience. A few weeks later, at night, I had a very vivid vision, it seemed; but it was a real experience. I was in the middle of a group of seven or eight persons of whom I saw two clearly. On my left was a woman entirely veiled in black, but she made a startlingly clear figure for all that. On the right was Z. He said, 'Now I will give her the second, the higher initiation.' And he seized my right arm with force. But I disengaged myself, and standing straight and calm I said (I can hear myself now). Before this ceremony proceeds I wish to make a statement. I can allow nothing and no one to come between me and the Christ.' There was a howl, a tossing of hands and everything disappeared.

"Soon after I tore up my initiation card, put Z. out of my mind and have had no conscious personal experience of him since. But I had introduced him to a young French musician of high social standing, whom he found much to his taste. (We will call him F.) There is a close friendship between F. and me, and at that time he needed some Oriental music for one of his compositions - on the other hand, he might have been extremely useful to Z., towards whom he felt strongly attracted. After my own experience I began to be much alarmed, but felt that I was not big enough to deal with the situation, so I said nothing to F. but prayed that he might be protected from all evil. Shortly afterwards F. told me in his letters of various astral experiences. In his dreams he was going through all sorts of disagreeable things and voices kept saying to him, 'Ask Z. to help you. He will help you.' Then he became conscious of my presence and began calling on the Christ (all this in his dream) and everything vanished. This happened more than once. Only when I met him again did I tell him of my own experience.

"I must add that a friend with psychic power came to see me at this time and said, 'This last week, at night, I have seen you three times. You asked me to help you save a young man who was in danger. What did it mean?"

The above case indicates clearly the deliberate use of mental power by Z. His pretence of "spiritual healing" being an obvious attempt at hypnosis. My correspondent says definitely that she has never suspected him of deliberate evil; rather was he acting rightly according to his lights. I maintain, however, that any attempt to dominate others, or in any way to manipulate their minds without their consent, is an unwarrantable intrusion upon their freewill and a crime against the integrity of the soul. How can we judge the intimate spiritual needs of another, especially if that other has not elected to confide in us? What right have we to invade his spiritual privacy and thrust our tampering fingers into the wheels of his innermost being? It is so common a practice to send the names of people to healing circles with a request that they should be concentrated upon, without taking the preliminary precaution of asking their permission, that I have heard it announced from the platform of a large Spiritualist public meeting that only those cases could be taken up which gave their written consent.

Fortunately for all concerned, the proceedings at such "healing circles" are usually so futile that nobody need mind being concentrated upon by them even if they were attempting murder.

The principle, however, remains, and I can only record my opinion once more, as I have already recorded it many times, that such a proceeding is an outrageous breach of good manners and good faith, and contrary to all occult tradition. I think I can honestly say that I have never wished to direct the great currents of destruction upon my fellow-occultists, but there are some of them I would like to get face downwards across my knee!

13 THE MOTIVES OF PSYCHIC ATTACK: PART I

Love-philtres ◆ Psychic pressures ◆ *Congressus subtilis* ◆ Lilith of the Qabalists ◆ "Counterparts" ◆ The sons of God and the daughters of men ◆ Incident of astral projection in a liaison ◆ Curious case of substitution ◆ Fairy matings ◆ Etheric aspect of sex-congress ◆ Incubi and succubi ◆ Magical experiments of Mr. X: (a) with an unmarried girl; (b) with a married woman ◆ Unnatural vice.

WE HAVE NOTED in a previous chapter that the simplest way to find out whether the victim of an alleged psychic attack is romancing or not, is to seek for motives, and if they are not discernible, to give imagination the benefit of the doubt. The commonplace motives of greed, lust, revenge and fear of betrayal do not need psychic discernment for their discovery but are perceptible to the naked eye. There are other motives, however, that may be operative in occult circles but which would be passed by unsuspected by the ordinary investigator.

The old charm-books that have come down to us, mostly via the servants' hall, are replete with recipes for securing the love of the opposite sex. The ancient grimoires supply more elaborate ritual prescriptions, and the reports of witch-trials contain frequent indictments of the wise woman who, for a consideration, undertook to direct people's affections towards persons for whom they apparently had no natural predilection. Are such operations to be taken seriously, or should we class them with the anti-fat pills that reduce without dieting ?

We have already referred to the old love-philtres. The ancients were well acquainted with the aphrodisiac drugs which excited sexual passion. Nor are the moderns altogether ignorant of them, as carefully-worded advertisements in certain astrological publications reveal. There are firms in France which specialise in the manufacture of chocolates which contain masked doses of these drugs. Publicity was given to their production recently owing to the death of two girls and a man through taking overdoses. There are cocktails in use in this country containing so-called "tonic" ingredients whose effect is well known. If these are not "love philtres," what are they?

We are not concerned in these pages with methods that belong solely to the physical plane, but these matters call for mention because there are grounds for belief that upon more than one occasion, even in this country, aphrodisiacs have been employed as an adjuvant to occult practices. There was a certain firm which began to advertise extensively and was building up a nice business in what might be called "occultist's sundries." Among other preparations which they supplied was "Incense for the operation of Venus." However, the firm came to an untimely end through the intervention of the police, both partners going to jail.

But apart from the use of purely material means, it is not difficult to see what uses could be made of mental influence in this direction. I have seen several cases that looked extremely, suspicious, but in these matters it is very difficult to get at the facts. The manner of attack is intangible and leaves no trace, and the victim may be unsuspicious and entirely ignorant not only of the psychic side of sex, but also of its physical and subtler emotional aspects. Moreover, those who have suffered most usually talk least. One may occasionally hear of the attempt which was frustrated. The attempt which was successful very rarely comes to light because the victim has just as much motive for concealing it as the aggressor.

When we come to purely occult practices, there are two ways in which the desired end can be achieved; psychic pressure may be brought to bear upon the desired person so that he or she shall come under the influence of the operator; or the psychic operation known as *congressus subtilis* may take place.

What exactly is *congressus subtilis*? We shall have to know a good deal more than we do at present about the occult side of sex before we can answer that question. In the first place, what are the facts, or alleged facts, of the matter? The ancients held very definite beliefs upon the subject, and these beliefs can very often afford us a clue, even if we do not accept the very anthropomorphic explanations by which they are accompanied.

It was believed that the arch-demon Lilith had a very great deal to do with these matters. According to the Qabalists, Lilith was the first wife of Adam, who used to visit him in his dreams while he was as yet alone in the Garden of Eden, and the Lord God became so perturbed at these goings-on that He created Eve as a counter-attraction. Witches were the recipients of similar attentions from the Devil. St. Theresa of Avila records that the Godhead Itself visited her. The Virgin Mary received the Holy Ghost. St. Anthony was tempted by apparitions of beautiful female demons. There are many cases on record of whole nunneries being attacked by the Devil, who visited their members. George Moore, in his exceedingly interesting study of convent life, *Sister Theresa*, gives an account of an outbreak of "Counterparts" among the younger nuns, in which they formed liaisons with angelic lovers, who were supposed to be the souls of those who were drowned in the Flood. We read in Genesis and in the Book of Enoch that the Sons of God mated with the daughters of men, and the demonic race was the result. The folk-lore of every country contains instances of the mating of humans with elementals, usually with disastrous consequences. Classical literature is full of stories of the visits of gods and goddesses to human kind. What shall we say of all such stories? Is there any element in them beyond fairy-tale and wish-fulfilment? We can readily understand the motive of the nun who, wishing to conceal the identity of her paramour, declares herself to be with child by the Devil. We can equally understand the psychology of the rest of the convent that take up the story and see the Devil in every corner.

Let me cite certain cases which have come within my personal knowledge and see whether in the light of these we can sift fact from phantasy. There came to visit me once a young man who was in love with a married woman. He told me that upon several occasions he had had a very vivid dream of visiting her, and she had simultaneously dreamed of receiving his visit. He was anxious to perfect the technique of this operation, hence the visit to me. I am afraid I was unsympathetic, consequently I did not obtain any further information concerning this curious experiment.

An even more curious case came to my knowledge some years ago. A woman told me that in the days of her youth she had been engaged to marry a man to whom she was very deeply attached, and who was murdered while working as a missionary in West Africa. Having lost the only man she felt she could love, she consented to marry a second cousin who had long been in love with her, and who was a semi-invalid. Whenever she had relations with her husband, she always visualised the form of her first lover. She herself was short, dark and petite. Her husband, a blood relation, was similar in type to herself, and a weed into the bargain. But her three sons were tall, upstanding blond men of the nordic type, bearing a strong resemblance to the dead man. The truth of this story was vouched for to me by a friend of the family.

I have known personally two alleged "changelings." The male had the pointed ears of Pan, and if anyone was ever a son of the Devil, he was. The female was a curious and fascinating creature, essentially non-human, and when her child was born it came into the world with no more trouble than a kitten. Both these beings were conceived when their mothers were under the influence of drink, and both of them were characterised by a marked callousness, which in one case developed into deliberate cruelty. Although very peculiar to look at, neither of them was in the least defective, both being, in fact, possessed of considerably more than the average share of brains.

Anyone who has any knowledge of the esoteric aspect of sex knows that union is as much etheric as physical. It is this fact which constitutes the real difference between normal union and self-abuse, and explains why the former is vitalising and harmonising, and the latter is exhausting and nerve-wrecking. May we not conceive it possible for anyone who can project the etheric body, or a being whose densest vehicle is etheric, to play a part in unions under certain conditions? And if we accept the theory of mediumship, or of obsession, which is a pathological form of mediumship, what shall we say concerning the possibility of a union while one or other of the partners is under control? What manner of soul might come through into incarnation under such conditions?

Mediaeval tradition recognised two classes of demons which invade sleep, and called them Incubi and Succubi. These were held to be responsible for lascivious dreams. Modern psychology discounts their services and looks nearer home. The psychic, however, is of the opinion that there is something in the old belief, and that the lustful imaginings of men's hearts (and women's too, for that matter) do indeed produce artificial elementals according to the method described in a previous chapter, and that these elementals are something more than subjective images, and have an objective etheric existence and play their part in the genesis of certain experiences. For instance, a person may have dreams and phantasies of a lascivious nature, and these may give rise to their characteristic thought-forms; these thought-forms, now existing independently of the mind that originally conceived them, and being in the aura of that person, give him suggestion just as any other thought-forms projected telepathically from the mind of another person might do. We little realise the extent to which we give ourselves telepathic suggestion by means of extruded thought-forms. We are, in fact, ensphered by our own atmospheres, emanated by ourselves. I remember being told as a child that if a bird-cage were hung immediately under the canopy of an old-fashioned four poster bed, the bird would be found dead in the morning, poisoned by the carbonic acid gas exhaled by the sleeper lying below. We little realise the extent to which we are psychically poisoned by our own emanations of unguarded and unpurified thoughts.

It is well known that orgasm takes place in dreams, accompanied by appropriate dream-pictures. The ancients believed that such an experience was due to the action of demons. Moderns believe it to be due to physical tension. It is not so generally known that there are people, both male and female, who can produce the same reaction at will solely by means of day-dreams. May we not ask ourselves whether it cannot also be produced by means of telepathic suggestion, and whether this may not have played a part in the operations of many covens?

There is another curious phase of this aspect of the Left-hand Path, which was brought to my knowledge through a case which came into my hands. A young girl, simple-minded and unsophisticated, living a very isolated life with a widowed mother, went to consult a well-known psychic, whom we will call Mr. X. In the circle in which both Miss Y. and Mr. X. moved there was another, and prominent figure, whom we will call Mr. Z., who had a reputation for a knowledge of magic. Mr. X. told Miss Y. that he had read the records of her past lives, and that there was a karmic tie between herself and Mr. Z., and that she could help him in his work by pouring out upon him her love and magnetism. She was instructed to meditate upon Mr. Z. every night as she lay in bed, until she fell asleep. This poor girl, lonely and unsuspicious, gave herself up unreservedly to this task. Presently, however, she began to grow uneasy. Her common sense asserted itself, for she found the meditations she was required to perform were having a very disturbing effect upon her; but Mr. X. allayed her fears and recalled her to her allegiance by assuring her that he had looked into the future and seen that eventually Mr. Z. would marry her. By now she had upon her hands a heart-breaking love affair which was making her very unhappy and unfitting her for work. A number of letters upon the subject were exchanged between Miss Y. and Mr. X., which I have seen. I did my best to persuade her to drop the whole affair. Mr. X. succeeded in persuading her to go on with it, playing upon her feelings and telling her how terrible would be the plight of Mr. Z. if she withdrew her psychic support, and renewing his assurance of a karmic tie which would result in an ultimate marriage if she were faithful. Miss Y., pitifully distressed and bewildered, betook herself to certain of the leaders of the organisation to which all three of them belonged. These people seconded my advice that she should discontinue these practices, but persuaded her to surrender the very compromising letters which were in her possession. Having secured these, they declared that the whole transaction was imagination on her part, and instead of turning this choice pair of scoundrels out of their ranks, let them continue to function as usual.

This would be a strange enough case if it were an isolated one, but it is not. Another woman came to me about this time in a state bordering on insanity, and told me that she too had been consulting Mr. X., who had told her that she had already received initiation on the Inner Planes, though she might not be conscious of it, and that her psychic faculties were on the point of opening (a stock remark of his), but if she wanted to make real progress on the Path she must cease to live with her husband and he (Mr. X.) would put her in touch with her astral soul-mate. The consequence of this precious advice was to break up her home and send her out of her mind. One day, walking in the Park, she met Mr. Z., and declared him to be her astral lover, a statement which Mr. X. confirmed, and embellished with the information that Mr. Z. was also the Master who would initiate her.

I tried to persuade her to bring the whole transaction to a summary conclusion and return to her husband, but she replied that she could never do this after the astral experiences she had had. Mr. X. re-established his influence over her, she left the address at which I had known her, and I have never heard what became of her. Her condition when I last saw her was deplorably emaciated, wild-eyed and twitching with convulsive movements.

Would anyone believe the story of such a woman? Obviously no one, *unless they had seen the letters that I had seen*. Nor is this the only case; a fellow-worker of mine told me of two precisely similar ones which had come to her knowledge in connection with Mr. X. It is cases such as these which make the honest investigator of occult phenomena thankful that there is upon our statute-book a law which enables magistrates to deal effectually with occultists who prostitute their powers. It is so generally known that no initiate may use the occult arts for gain that it is difficult to sympathise with people who pay some advertising occultist his half-crowm or half-guinea and then find themselves let in for unpleasantness.

What conclusions may we draw from the incidents that I have related, for the facts of which I can vouch from personal knowledge? Four women are persuaded to embark upon a meditation process whose aim is to pour out force. The nature of the force that is to be poured out is indicated by the fact that the married women are instructed not to live with their husbands and the unmarried girl is encouraged to fall in love with the man who is made the focus of the operation. This man is the head of a group of people known to be occupied with practical occultism and ceremonial. The conclusion I draw is that an occult experiment was afoot, and that, regardless of the consequences to them, these women were being made use of in order to carry it out, the procurer being the well-known psychic, Mr. X., and the operator the notorious Mr. Z.

The same group have to their credit a recurring series of scandals in connection with unnatural vice. If this were merely vice as such it would not come within the purview of these pages, but it appears to be used systematically as a means of obtaining occult power. Those who have any knowledge of the deeper aspects of occultism know that sex force is one of the manifestations of kundalini, the serpent-fire that according to Tantric philosophy lies coiled at the base of the spine, or in the terms of Western occultism, the sacral plexus. The control and concentration of the kundalini force is an important part of the technique of practical occultism. There is a right way of directing it through thought-control, the technique of which I have explained in my little book, *The Problem of Purity* (Rider); but there is also another method, which consists in stimulating this force, and then directing it into abnormal channels where it will not be absorbed, but remain available for magical purposes. It is for this reason that in certain forms of the Black Mass the altar is the naked body of a woman who may either be still living, or have been slain sacrificially. A. E. W. Mason gives an account of such a transaction in his book, *The Prisoner in the Opal.*

Less expert operators, however, cannot control this form of force; as soon as they generate it, it has to go to its logical conclusion. They therefore employ another type of stimulus, not the woman, but the boy or youth. The practice of paederasty in connection with occultism is very old, and was one of the causes of the degeneration of the Greek Mysteries.

I have dealt with these subjects in some detail in another book of mine, *Sane Occultism.** Particulars of the actual cases can be found by reference to the files of *Truth*, the journal already referred to.

---

*Republished in 2001 by Samuel Weiser as *What Is Occultism?*

14 THE MOTIVES OF PSYCHIC ATTACK: PART II

Disputes with occult fraternities ♦ Powers of the penalty clause in
initiation oaths ♦ Incident in initiation ceremony ♦ The Adept who defied his
Order ♦ The cat attack ♦ An astral skirmish ♦ The Iona case again.

IT IS A MATTER of general knowledge among occultists that
it is not a pleasant thing to fall foul of an occult fraternity
of which one has been made a member by means of a
ceremonial initiation and to which one is bound by oaths. As
we have already seen, the malignant mind of a trained
occultist is a nasty weapon; how much more so the group-
mind formed out of a number of trained minds, especially if
concentrated by means of ritual?

But in addition to the individual mental force of the
members of a fraternity, and in addition to the collective
force of its group mind, there is another factor to be
reckoned with when a genuine occult organisation is
concerned in operations of either protection or destruction.
Every occult organisation depends for its power to initiate
upon what are called its " contacts," that is to say, upon one
or more of its leaders being psychically in touch with
certain forces. If, in addition to this, the organisation has a
long line of tradition behind it, a very potent collection of
thought forms will be built up in its atmosphere. Every
initiation ceremony contains in some form or other the
Oath of the Mysteries, which binds the candidate neither to
reveal the secrets of the Mysteries nor to abuse the
knowledge they bestow. This oath always contains a Penalty
Clause and an Invocation wherein the candidate submits
himself to a penalty in the event of a breach of faith, and
calls upon some Being to exact the penalty. Some of these

oaths are most formidable affairs, and they are administered with every circumstance of solemnity that stage management can devise. The way in which the occult fraternities have succeeded in preserving their secrets shows how seldom these oaths are broken.

In the event of a dispute with an occult fraternity, the force invoked in this oath may come into action automatically. If the recalcitrant brother is in the spirit of the tradition and it is his chiefs who are at fault, the power invoked in the oath will be a potent protective influence with which the chiefs themselves will collide. If, on the other hand, he breaks faith with the Mysteries, this avenging punitive current will come into action although his defection may pass undiscovered. I was informed by an eyewitness of an incident which took place at an initiation, in which the candidate, a man to all appearances normal in every way, after taking the oath in the usual manner, suddenly screamed most terribly, startling everyone, and was ill for some weeks as if from a severe nervous shock, and never had anything more to do with occultism. No explanation of the incident was ever forthcoming. I was present myself upon one occasion when a batch of three candidates was being "done," and it was suddenly noticed in the course of the ceremony that the number of the candidates had become reduced to two. Enquiry elicited the fact that the third had taken fright and fled.

What happened in these two cases, I do not know; whether there had been a breach of good faith, or whether one was intended, no one can say; but something put the fear of the Lord into these two individuals pretty effectually. That no such shock is inherent in the ceremony is proved by the fact that these are the only two cases in my experience, and I have seen a very large number of ceremonies. Personally, when I took my own initiation I felt as it I had come into harbour after a stormy voyage.

Another man who was intimately known to me as an advanced occultist was turned out of the Order to which he belonged, why, I do not know, but from what I saw of him I should imagine there were plenty of reasons. In defiance of his initiation oath he began to work an independent lodge. He was warned to desist, and did so, dismantling his temple. But he immediately began to get together another temple in a carefully concealed place; and this time he was more ambitious, for he made ready to attempt the Greater Mysteries. He was an exceedingly clever craftsman and made all the equipment of the temple with his own hands so that no one should know what was afoot. Concealed behind Nottingham lace curtains in a mean street in West London was a beautiful little temple of the Greater Mysteries. He completed this work after some months of arduous toil, no one knowing of it save those in his immediate confidence. But before commencing the actual ritual work he went away for a short holiday at the seaside, and there he was seized with a heart attack while sitting on the beach and died in four hours. The Order secrets were not betrayed.

Another man who had had a dispute with the same famous Order, printed and published their secrets as an act of revenge. He was a man of good social position, considerable wealth and brilliant literary abilities, already making a name for himself as a writer. From that moment he began to go downhill, and came to poverty and disgrace. The curse of Ahasuerus seemed to be upon him, and he was hounded from country to country, finding no abiding place. No publisher will handle his books, no paper will review them.

Let me finally tell of my own experiences in an astral skirmish. I wrote a series of articles on the abuses prevalent in occult fraternities, and these were published in the *Occult Review*.* My writing is largely inspirational, a great deal "coming through" of which I have no previous knowledge, and in this particular case I evidently shot a great deal better than I knew, and got myself into serious trouble. My first intimation of it was a sense of uneasiness and restlessness.

---

*Reprinted in *What Is Occultism?* (Weiser, 2001) Formerly published as *Sane Occultism*.

Next came a feeling as if the barriers between the Seen and the Unseen were full of rifts and I kept on getting glimpses of the Astral mingling with my waking consciousness. This, for me, is unaccustomed, for I am not naturally psychic, and in the technique in which I was trained we are taught to keep the different levels of consciousness strictly separate and to use a specific method for opening and closing the gates. Consequently one seldom gets spontaneous psychism. One's vision resembles the use of a microscope in which one examines prepared material.

The general sense of vague uneasiness gradually matured into a definite sense of menace and antagonism, and presently I began to see demon faces in flashes, resembling those picture-images which psychologists call by the unpleasing name of hypnagogics, flashes of dream which appear upon the threshold of sleep. I was quite unsuspicious of any particular individual, though I realised that my articles had probably stirred somebody up pretty thoroughly; what was my surprise, then, to receive from a person whom I looked upon as a friend and for whom I had the greatest respect, a letter which left me in no doubt whatever as to the source of the attack and what I might expect if any more articles were published. I can honestly say that until I received this letter I had not the slightest suspicion that this person was implicated in the scandals I was attacking.

I was in a somewhat difficult position; I had fired off a charge of shrapnel on general principles, and had apparently "bagged" a number of my friends and associates and fluttered the dove-cote generally. My position was rather complicated by the fact that I did not know nearly as much as they apparently suspected me of doing; I had, of course, known that these abuses existed sporadically about the occult field as everybody in the movement knows; but to know in this vague way is one thing, and to put one's finger on specific cases is another. I had evidently blundered into something much more considerable than I had bargained for. I felt like the small boy who, fishing for minnows, has hooked a pike. I had to decide whether I would try and get my articles back from the *Occult Review*, or whether I would let them run their natural course and take the consequences. I had had a very strong impulse to write those articles, and now I began to see why I had had it. I shall have something to say in another chapter concerning the Watchers, that curious section of the Occult Hierarchy which is concerned with the welfare of nations. A certain section of their work is apparently concerned with the policing of the Astral Plane. Very little is actually known about them. One comes across their work sporadically and pieces the bits together. I have crossed their trail on several occasions, as I will tell later. Whenever black magic is afoot, they set to work to put a spoke in its wheels. Be that as it may, I came to the conclusion that, in view of what had now transpired, the impulse I had had to take in hand this piece of work might have emanated from the Watchers. At any rate, the work obviously needed doing. Someone had to tackle these plague spots if they were to be cleared up, so I determined to stick to my guns and see the matter through, and so left the articles in question to run their course.

Very soon some curious things began to happen. We became most desperately afflicted with black cats. They were not hallucinatory cats, for our neighbours shared in the affliction, and we exchanged commiserations with the caretaker next door who was engaged in pushing bunches of black cats off doorstep and window-sill with a broom, and declared he had never in his life seen so many, or such dreadful specimens. The whole house was filled with the horrible stench of the brutes. Two members of our community at that time went out to business every day, and at their offices, in different parts of London, they found the same penetrating reek of the tom-cat.

At first we attributed this persecution to natural causes, and concluded that we were near neighbours of some fascinating

---

*Reprinted in *What Is Occultism?* (Weiser, 2001) Formerly published as *Sane Occultism*.

feline female, but incidents succeeded each other which made us feel that things were not quite in the ordinary course of nature. We were getting near to the Vernal Equinox, which is always a difficult time for occultists; there was a sense of strain and tension in the atmosphere, and we were all feeling decidedly uncomfortable. Coming upstairs after breakfast one morning, I suddenly saw, coming down the stairs towards me, a gigantic tabby cat, twice the size of a tiger. It appeared absolutely solid and tangible. I stared at it petrified for a second, and then it vanished. I instantly realised that it was a simulacrum, or thought-form that was being projected by someone with occult powers. Not that the realisation was any too comforting, but it was better than an actual tiger. Feeling decidedly uncomfortable, I asked one of my household to join me, and as we sat in my room meditating we heard the cry of a cat from without. It was answered by another, and another. We looked out of the window, and the street as far as we could see was dotted with black cats and they were wailing and howling in broad daylight as they do on the roofs at night.

I rose up, gathered together my paraphernalia, and did an exorcism then and there. At the end we looked out of the window again. There was not a cat in sight, and we never saw them again. The visitation was at an end. Only our normal population of local mousers remained to us.

The Vernal Equinox was now upon us. I must explain that this is the most important season of the year for occultists. Great power-tides are flowing on the Inner Planes, and these are very difficult to handle. If there is going to be astral trouble, it usually blows up for a storm at this season. There are also certain meetings which take place on the Astral Plane, and many occultists attend them out of the body. In order to do this, one has to throw oneself into a trance and then the mind is free to travel. It is usual to get someone who understands these methods of work to watch beside the body while it is vacated to see that it comes to no harm.

In the ordinary way, when an occult attack is afoot, one clings to waking consciousness at all costs, sleeping by day and keeping awake and meditating while the sun is below the horizon. As ill-luck would have it, however, I was obliged to make one of these astral journeys at this season. My attacker knew this as well as I did. I therefore made my preparations with all the precautions I could think of; gathered together a carefully chosen group to form the watching circle, and sealed up the place of operation with the usual ceremonial. I had not much faith in this operation under the circumstances, for my attacker was of much higher grade than I was, and could come through any seals I might set. However, it afforded protection against minor unpleasantness.

The method of making these astral journeys is highly technical, and I cannot enter upon it here. In the language of psychology, it is auto-hypnosis by means of a symbol. The symbol acts as a door to the Unseen. According to the symbol chosen will be the section of the Unseen to which access is obtained. The trained initiate, therefore, does not wander on the astral like an uneasy ghost, but comes and goes by well-known corridors.

My enemy's task was therefore not a difficult one; for she knew about the time I must make this journey and the symbol I must use in order to get out of the body. I was therefore prepared for opposition, though I did not know what form it would take.

These astral journeys are really lucid dreams in which one retains all one's faculties of choice, will-power and judgment. Mine always begin with a curtain of the symbolic colour through whose folds I pass. No sooner was I through the curtain on this occasion than I saw my enemy waiting for me, or, if another terminology is preferred, I began to dream about her. She appeared to me in the full robes of her grade, which were very magnificent, and barred my entry, telling me that by virtue of her authority she forbade me to make use of these astral pathways. I replied that I did not admit her right to close the astral paths to me because she was personally offended, and that I appealed to the Inner Chiefs, to whom both she and I were responsible. Then ensured a battle of wills in which I experienced the sensation of being whirled through the air and falling from a great height and found myself back in my body. But my body was not where I had left it, but in a heap in the far corner of the room, which looked as if it had been bombed. By means of the well-known phenomenon of repercussion the astral struggle had apparently communicated itself to the body, which had somersaulted round the room while an agitated group had rescued the furniture from its path.

I was somewhat shaken by this experience, which had not been a pleasant one. I recognised that I had had the worst of it and had been effectually ejected from the astral paths; but I also realised that if I accepted this defeat my occult career was at an end. Just as a child who has been thrown by his pony must immediately get up and remount if he is ever to ride again, so I knew that at all costs I must make that astral journey if I were to retain my powers. So I told my group to pull themselves together and re-form the circle because we must make another attempt; I invoked the Inner Chiefs, and went out once more. This time there was a short sharp struggle, and I was through. I had the Vision of the Inner Chiefs, and returned. The fight was over. I have never had any trouble since.

But when I took off my clothes in order to go to bed my back felt very sore, and taking a hand-glass I examined it in the mirror, and I found that from neck to waist I was scored with scratches as if I had been clawed by a gigantic cat.

I told this story to some friends of mine, experienced occultists, who at one time had been closely associated with the person with whom I had had this trouble, and they told me that she was well-known for these astral attacks, and that a friend of theirs after a quarrel with her had had an exactly similar experience, and she too had been covered with claw-marks. In her case, however, she had been ill for six months and had never touched occultism again.

There is a curious epilogue to this story, which may or may not have any bearing upon it. I have already told the story of the mysterious death that took place on Iona. How the body of this unfortunate girl was found lying naked on a cross cut out of the turf. No cause of death could be found, and the verdict was that she died of exposure. But if she were lost, how did she come to lie down to die in this ritual manner, instead of wandering about? Why had she taken off all her clothes before leaving her house, covering herself only with a black cloak? And why did she take with her the large knife with which she cut the cross in the turf? I do not know her later history, for I had lost sight of her during the last two or three years of her life, but at the time I knew her she was associated with the woman I have referred to. The only marks found upon her dead body were scratches.

PART IV

Methods of Defence Against Psychic Attack

15 PHYSICAL ASPECT OF PSYCHIC ATTACK AND DEFENCE

WE HAVE DISTINGUISHED the various types of psychic attack, we have described the methods that can be employed in carrying them out, and we have also noted the various forms of delusion, fraud and auto-suggestion that may complicate the issue. We are now in a position to discuss the question of diagnosis. Let us consider the whole matter from the practical point of view. Supposing a stranger comes with a story of psychic attack, what should be our procedure?

We must first of all bear in mind that there is great need of caution in presuming that a psychic attack is being made. Psychic attacks are comparatively rare things. We must not assume we are dealing with one until we have excluded all the other things it can possibly be. Not so long ago I came across a ease of alleged obsession which turned out to be neglected constipation, and which was effectually exorcised with castor oil. If there are any physical symptoms at all, even if they are no more than a bad colour or a bad breath, a diagnosis ought to be made by a qualified medical practitioner, for even if the trouble have a predominating psychic element, its origin may be physical. Septic foci are really centres of decomposition, and as such they open the door to low forms of elemental life whose function is to assist in the return of dust to dust. Impurities in the blood-stream may poison the brain. New growths or abscesses may derange its functions. These things can only be recognised by the man who understands the body; other things being equal, the trained man is the better man, and the man with the best training is the best man, and the only place where an adequate training in diagnosis can be obtained is a general hospital. Moreover, should things turn out badly, the only person who can pull the chestnuts out of the fire is the person whose signature the authorities will accept on a certificate. Supposing the patient turns out to be a lunatic, what is the unqualified practitioner going to do with him? A very large proportion of the cases of alleged psychic attack turn out to be lunatics and hysterics. Incipient lunacy is a very hard thing to detect; hysteria is very cunning and plausible; a doctor who is handling human nature in bulk every day of his life will detect either of these two conditions much quicker than the layman who has never met them before.

It may be objected that it is a very difficult thing to find a doctor who will have a sympathetic attitude towards occultism. To argue thus is to misunderstand the position. The doctor is not being asked to cooperate with any occult operation, but to examine for physical disease, and if he finds it, to treat it. He is no more concerned in the occult measures that are taken for the benefit of his patient than he is in the church his patient attends.

If the doctor finds no evidence of organic disease, or some complaint such as varicose veins which can obviously have no bearing on the mental condition, the case may be held to have passed the first test, and we may feel that it is worth while to proceed to the psychic investigation. If the case is a bad one, or the trouble is of long standing, the doctor will probably find that the patient is debilitated, even if there is nothing definitely amiss, and will proceed to treat the condition accordingly. This is all to the good, for the better the physical condition of the patient the more mental control and stamina he will have. Sleeping-draughts, however, should be avoided if possible, and if they have to be administered, then the patient should be watched while he sleeps by someone who knows how to keep an occult guard, and the room in which he sleeps should be purified and sealed. In the ordinary way, if a person who is out on the astral meets with an occult attack, he bolts back to his body like a rabbit to its burrow and wakes up as if from a nightmare; but if the sleep is made unnaturally deep by a sleeping-draught, he cannot wake up, and is locked out on the astral, as it were, which is the last thing one wants in the case of a psychic attack. If a sleeping-drought is considered essential, for it is impossible to go without sleep indefinitely, the person who is watching beside the sleeper should observe carefully any signs that the sleep is being disturbed by dreams, and if he observes muttering or twitching, should immediately perform the necessary banishings and whisper into the ear of the sleeper soothing and reassuring suggestions such as Coué recommends should be done in the case of young children. One of the most distressing features of a psychic attack is that the victim fears to sleep because he feels that in sleep he is defenceless. Those who have read Kipling's terrible story, *The End of the Passage*, may remember that the victim of the occult attack therein described always went to bed wearing spurs in order that he might rowel himself and so wake himself up if he were struggling with his invisible enemy during sleep.

There is a great deal that can be done upon the physical plane to help the person who is suffering from an occult attack, and we may as well consider these physical methods while we are upon the subject of the part that can be played by a doctor in dealing with the case. Sunlight is exceedingly valuable because it strengthens the aura and makes it much more resistant. People are often advised to go away into the country on this account, but for the victim of an occult attack to go into the depths of the country may not be the wisest thing, because elemental forces are much more potent away from towns, and if he is threatened by an uprush of atavistic forces, he had better cling to the haunts of men. The sea, too, is an elemental force that is best avoided, for water is an element intimately associated with psychism. Large bodies of water and high mountains should be avoided in choosing a health resort for a person suffering from psychic trouble. The best place is an inland spa. Games, physical training, massage, anything that improves the bodily condition, are invaluable, but long solitary walks should be avoided because there is often a risk of suicide. The person who is the victim of an occult attack should at all costs avoid solitude.

There is another very simple measure which, gives immense relief in cases of psychic interference. It is obvious that the attack is made through the psychic centres, therefore anything which closes those centres will render the victim comparatively immune. It is well known how the stolid, materialistic type of person can live with impunity in haunted houses that drive the sensitive to madness and suicide. It is also well known that psychic work cannot be performed if there is food in the stomach; the best results are always obtained when fasting. The obvious corollary of these facts is that if we want to keep the psychic centres closed, we should not allow the stomach to become empty. The person who is facing a psychic attack should not go more than two hours without food.

Certain important psychic centres are in the head. One of the simplest ways of checking their activity is by drawing the blood down from the head. This can be done effectually by a hot bath or putting the feet in hot mustard and water. Another important centre is the solar plexus; during a psychic attack this is often felt to be tense and distressing. A large hot-water bottle, well filled so that it is heavy as well as hot, laid upon the solar plexus, which is the hand-breadth between the pit of the stomach and the ribs, will effectually relieve tension in that spot. Indeed, pressure without heat will give relief, and I have known cases where a firm pad held in place by a belt or corsets gave much comfort.

Above all things, the bowels should be kept freely open while facing a psychic attack, because there is nothing that puts one at so great a disadvantage as the accumulation of effete matter within the body.

All these simple physical remedies are readily available. They will not afford a cure for psychic pathologies, nor a complete defence from psychic attack, but they can give great relief from distress; they enable the victim to put up a much more effectual resistance, and by relieving the strain they increase his endurance. In many cases of psychic attack, he who endures longest wins; psychic attacks by human beings are not things which can be maintained indefinitely because they use up too much energy.

There is an old adage, "Never use a big spade if a little spade will do." Physical methods of defence involve much less outlay of energy that psychic ones, therefore it is psychically economical to make as much use of them as possible. Why trouble to exorcise the earth elements with a ritual if you can do it with a pill?

The question of diet also requires to be considered in this connection. The widespread propaganda of the Theosophical Society has caused vegetarianism to be regarded as a *sine qua non* of occult training. This, however, is not the case. The Western Esoteric Tradition does not make vegetarianism any part of its system, but teaches that a man should partake sparingly and temperately of the food of the land in which he finds himself. Personally I am inclined to think that occultism and vegetarianism are apt to be an injudicious mixture for an European, the result being a hypersensitiveness that makes life very difficult in our hard-driving civilisation.

Vegetarianism has to be thoroughly understood and exceedingly well done if it is to be successful, and even so, there is a goodly proportion of people who are incapable of digesting vegetable proteins, which are not nearly so easily dealt with as animal substances. Nothing but experience and experimentation can show whether a vegetarian diet suits a given person. Indigestion is not the only indication that all is not well. Loss of appetite, loss of energy, loss of weight, or a flabby stoutness are all danger signals which if disregarded will cause chronic ill-health. Vegetarianism may agree with a person well enough at first, but after a considerable period, possibly years, they may find that they are becoming subject to neuritis, neuralgia, sciatica, or one or another of the nerve pains. This is a sure indication that a vegetarian diet is affording insufficient nourishment, not because it does not contain the necessary food units, but because the digestion is unable to assimilate them and they are passing out of the body unchanged. Wherever there is a history of neuralgic pains complicating a case of psychic disturbance, I should be inclined to suspect chronic malnutrition as the cause of a hypertrophied psychism. In such cases it will probably be found that a gradual return to nourishing mixed diet will bring about a reduction of the hypersensitiveness, the undesirable contacts that have been formed will fade, and the condition return to normal. The change of diet, however, should always be made gradually lest the digestion be upset.

Anyone who is having trouble with psychic disturbance should immediately discontinue all occult practices and should exchange his habitual meditations for the prayers of his childhood, or New Thought methods. It is no time to open up the psychic centres when there is astral trouble. The thing to do in such cases is to get back on to the physical plane and stop there resolutely. There was a picture in an old number of *Punch* which to my way of thinking exactly expresses the correct attitude for the person afflicted by psychic trouble. In front of an old-fashioned four poster bedstead stands a ferocious female armed with a rolling-pin, and from under the valance protrudes the head of her spouse, who says, "Ye may whack me, and ye may thwack me, but ye canna break my manly spirit, for I'll no cam' oot."

If the victim of an occult attack concentrates on mundane things he is a heart-breaking proposition for any sorcerer. What is the sorcerer to do if, at the time when he is operating the Black art, his victim is at the local cinema roaring at the antics of Charlie Chaplin? There is an old saying that one nail drives out another. If in fear of invisible dangers, take up a sport with an element of risk in it.

16 DIAGNOSIS OF THE NATURE OF AN ATTACK

Physical condition may cause psychic centres to open ✦ Delirium ✦ Problem of diagnosis ✦ Method of approach ✦ Use of psychometery ✦ How to take a psychometric specimen ✦ Value of astrology ✦ How to take a history ✦ How to detect a liar ✦ Indirect approach ✦ Points of correlation ✦ Influence of places ✦ Influence of persons ✦ Need of caution in apportioning the blame ✦ The investigator should make an independent diagnosis and check it by the psychic's report ✦ Limitations of psychometry.

HAVING CONSIDERED the purely physical factors in a psychic disturbance, we may now come to the consideration of its genuinely psychic factors. We must always bear in mind, however, that because physical disease is found, it does not necessarily eliminate the psychic factor. A physical condition, such as an abnormal state of the blood, may cause a low form of psychism and put its victim in touch with evil astral conditions. Science may call it delirium or hallucination, but the occultist calls it pathological psychism and can do a great deal to relieve it, either by closing down the psychic centres, or by excluding evil psychic influences from the environment of the patient so that the spirits he sees shall be angelic instead of demonic, and cause him happiness instead of distress. The psychic centres forced open by a diseased blood-stream perceive anything that comes within their range of vision. Therefore let us ensure that nothing save what is pleasant shall come near them. We may not be able entirely to keep him off the Astral, but at least we can ensure that his wanderings shall be in a safe and pleasant part of the Astral. People do not realise the extent to which the wanderings of delirium can be directed and controlled by suggestions whispered into the ear of a sick person. We can companion the sick man in his astral wanderings and make our voice heard among his visions, by our knowledge driving away the evil presences that threaten him and guiding his dreams into the way of peace.

At the commencement of our diagnosis we must distinguish between three broad classes of psychic disturbance: those which are a by-product of physical disease, those which are due to malicious human action, and those which are due to non-human interference. The first type should be readily picked out by the doctor if, as has already been advised, recourse has been had to him as the essential preliminary. Moreover, he will also be effective in eliminating the frauds, for people moving in psychic circles and familiar with their terminology may simulate a psychic attack either in order to borrow money or obtain hospitality, or out of pure love of notoriety, a far commoner motive for human aberrations than is generally realised. Frauds usually either fade away or recover quickly when threatened with a physical overhaul. Those who decide to chance their luck are pretty quickly caught out by the man who has served his time in the out-patient department of a general hospital.

The diagnosis which the occultist has to make therefore lies in distinguishing between the attack of an incarnate mind and the attack of a discarnate mind. There are two ways in which he can do this, and he ought to use them both, so that they countercheck each other. He ought to get at least two independent psychics to psychometrise the case, and he himself ought to make his own diagnosis entirely from the case-history interpreted in the light of first principles. It is a great mistake to mix the psychic and the scientific. They are apt to neutralise each other. Let one person do the psychism and another the observation, and let proper precautions be taken to prevent the results of the clairvoyant investigation being vitiated by suggestion, or by the thought-reading of previously conceived opinions held in the mind of any of the persons concerned. It is therefore a good thing to send off the specimens for psychometrising at the commencement of an occult investigation, before any opinions have been formed.

It is not the simplest matter in the world to take psychometric specimens properly. I have seen a man bring a lock of hair belonging to someone else out of his pocket, where he had carried it about for a couple of days, and hand it over for psychometry. It was of course so thoroughly impregnated with his own emanations as to be useless. A psychometrical specimen should be some object thoroughly impregnated with the vibrations of a person. A garment recently and habitually worn, a lock of hair, a piece of jewellery, all these can be made to serve provided they are properly preserved. Crystalline substances, such as precious stones, hold magnetism better than anything else; metals are also good, whether precious or otherwise. A pocket-knife, for instance, will hold magnetism well. Wood holds it badly and so do paper, wool, cotton and artificial silk, especially the latter. Silk and linen are good. India-rubber is useless. Glass depends for its holding powers upon its form. If it is cut so that it will refract light it can be very good; if it is flat and purely transparent, like window-pane, it is almost useless. Stone is fair. Earthenware poor. An elaborate article is not as good as a simple article. For instance, a marquise ring is not as good as a signet ring. Letters are apt to be misleading because they often contain nearly as much of the magnetism of the recipient as of the writer. Some psychics can work from a photograph, but this method is not, strictly speaking, psychometry, for the mental image evoked by the photograph is used to pick up the corresponding image in the reflecting ether.

Great care should be used in taking a psychometric specimen, for it is readily contaminated by the magnetism of anyone who handles it, who is in proximity to it, or who even thinks about it concentratedly. For instance, if while packing up such a specimen for sending off you are brooding over the problem it presents and working out your own theory, the psychometrist may pick up your thought-form instead of reading the conditions of the person to whom the object belongs. The materials which are used for packing should also be free from magnetism. I knew of a case wherein the psychic said that a certain trinket belonged either to a nurse or to someone who had to do with hospitals. As a matter of fact, it belonged to neither, but had been packed in surgical cotton-wool.

When packing up a psychometric specimen, do it as expeditiously and with as little handling as possible. Take a piece of "virgin" black or white silk (not coloured), large enough to serve as a wrapper. Throw it over the article and bundle it up rapidly, handling it through the silk. In the occult sense, "virgin" means something that has never been used for any other purpose. For instance, you should not use part of an old dress or a cushion-cover. An article which does not lend itself to handling by this method can be picked up with sugar-tongs or the points of a pair of scissors and laid on the square of silk in which it is to be wrapped. Pack the wrapped article in a wooden box, being sure that any padding which is used is also virgin. The report of a single psychometrist should not be relied upon. Specimens should be sent to two at least. It is also well when sending specimens, and especially when sending a birth-hour for a horoscope, not to allow the name to be known lest gossip should be spread about. Astrologers are much too fond of handing round charts and discussing them. I have known some very unfortunate things come about in this way.

A horoscope from someone who understands the nature of the work in hand is of great value, for the position of the planets in the heavenly houses not only serves as an aid to diagnosis but is a very important guide to treatment. It is best therefore to explain to the astrologer the nature of the case, and the kind of information that is wanted, so that he can examine the chart accordingly. A horoscope is to an occult therapist what an X-ray photograph is to a doctor.

While awaiting these returns, and while his mind is still uninfluenced by them, the occultist should make his own independent diagnosis. In order to do this he should have at least two interviews with his patient. In the first he should hear the case-history, allowing the patient to present the facts in his own way, without guidance or leading questions.

Immediately the patient has left, the operator should write out the case-history with as much detail as he can recall. It is exceedingly undesirable to take notes in the presence of a patient, because it makes him nervous, for he feels that, in the words of the police-court; "everything he is saying will be taken down and used as evidence against them."

In preparation for the second interview the occultist should study his record carefully and have its points and sequence clear in his mind. Now is the time to question the patients concerning any discrepancies or hiatuses. This proceeding will reveal the liar, whether deliberate or hysterical, quicker than anything else, for the discrepancies of his second statement will be clearly revealed against the written record of his first. If he is telling the truth, the two statements will be in agreement. If he is distorting the facts, he will soon contradict himself.

Remember that you are dealing with a person who has something of either the psychic or the neurotic, or very likely both, in his disposition, and that your attitude towards him, and even your unspoken thoughts, will influence him profoundly. If he feels that you are doubting his veracity, he will lose his self-confidence and begin to think that his experiences may, after all, be the fruits of his own imagination. Consequently, he will suppress things which may be all-important from the diagnostic standpoint. It is in this outpouring of relevant and irrelevant detail that you are going to find your clues.

There are certain landmarks which you want to look out for in taking this case-history, but you do not want to let your patient realise what you are looking for, because if you have won his confidence, he will be very apt to take on your view-point, and if he sees you have formed any opinion, he will unconsciously twist incidents so that they fit in with that opinion. Do not allow him to guess the bearing of your questions, and then you will obtain from him an unbiassed response. In order to prevent his guessing what you are driving at, do not ask a series of questions elucidating information on a specific point. There will probably be several points on which you want information. Ask questions upon first one and then another of these. For instance, if you suspect that the trouble may be due to the house in which your patient is living, the last thing you want to do is to rouse his suspicions in this respect lest you should be on a false scent. And even if you should prove to be on the right track, you do not want to disclose the facts to him until you are ready to act, for by increasing his apprehensions you will increase his sufferings. If you suspect that sex plays a part in his trouble, and he guesses the trend of your questionings, he will immediately cover his tracks, and you will find it very difficult to get at the facts at all. Whereas, if his suspicions are not aroused, he will reveal himself to an astute and experienced questioner who approaches him indirectly, without realising that he has done so. By approaching thus indirectly you not only get at the real facts of the case, but spare his feelings.

In taking a case-history you want to look for correlations between your patient's psychic experiences and the circumstances of his life. Dates and places therefore should be sedulously sought for. When did the trouble start, and where? Having obtained as detailed information as possible on these two points, set out to see whether any occult significance is to be found in it. Note the dates carefully, and turn them up in an ephemeris of those years, and observe how the moon stood in relation to them, also the planets. Observe whether they fell on or about the equinoxes or solstices. Note also the days of the week upon which they occurred. If you found that all the crises of the case occurred on Thursdays, or round about the Vernal Equinox, or at the full moon, you would have a piece of information which was of considerable significance. You would be sure of one thing, at any rate, that you were dealing with a case in which the invisible psychic tides played a part.

Information should also be sought concerning the place or places in which the different crises of the trouble took place, and especially the circumstances attending its first onset. It is exceedingly useful if possible to visit the place and sense its atmosphere.

A very great deal can also be learnt from visiting the place where the patient is living.

Having obtained such geographical information as you can, study it carefully in connection with a large-scale Ordnance map. Access to this, and to an relevant information desired can readily be obtained at any public library. Note whether there are any prehistoric remains in the neighbourhood, and if so, how the house bears in relation to them. Observe not only whether it is near any of them, but whether it is in a direct line between any two of them. Look up the history of the district, and see whether it affords any further information. Roman remains are often at the bottom of the trouble, for the legions brought some very queer cults with them in the days of Rome's decadence. Druid remains, too, should be suspect of they are near neighbours.

Enquire also concerning any unusual objects in the house, such as images of the deities of primitive cults or savage weapons. It is quite possible that powerful elementals are attached to these.

Enquire whether the trouble seems to lift when the patient goes away to another place. If the reply is in the affirmative, it may safely be presumed that local conditions are at the bottom of the trouble. But if the reply is in the negative, it does not necessarily follow that the opposite is the case. It may also be that the trouble does not depend upon the place, but upon some person residing at the place. Never forget that in the great majority of cases that person's harmful influence is due to an unfortunate psychic make-up rather than deliberate abuse of occult knowledge. Be very slow to accept the latter hypothesis, for its occurrence is comparatively rare. And even if the person suspected is known to have occult knowledge and can be proved to be antagonistic to the patient, it does not necessarily follow that the attack is conscious and deliberate. It may be unconscious and reflex. It is quite true that an occultist ought to have sufficient control over his vehicles to prevent them from acting independently of his will and consciousness; but this is not always the case. People are at many different stages of development. There is always a difficult period between the awakening of the higher powers and their full control.

Enquiries should also be made concerning the nature of the dreams, and whether the patient is subject to nightmares apart from any question of occult attack. Also whether he has ever had any other psychic experiences, and if so, of what nature.

Finally, a careful enquiry should be made concerning the patient's associates, as to whether any of them are psychic, or students of the occult. Be very careful, however, not to cast suspicion upon any person unless you have conclusive evidence and it is essential to do so in order to save the patient. Remember it always possible that you may be mistaken. A case was reported in the papers not so long ago of a man who committed suicide because a doctor told him that he had organic heart disease and ought not to marry the girl he was engaged to. At the post mortem it was found that there was nothing whatever the matter with his heart. Imagine the feelings of the doctor who had given this rash diagnosis. A person already upset by a psychic attack will be in a state to jump at shadows. He must be handled very discreetly. Be very chary of announcing your suspicions until they are conclusively verified. When all is said and done, the main object is a cure, not an explanation. It is of little value to your patient to fix the blame unless the matter can be cleared up. He is considerably worse off if his suspicions are turned towards some person in his environment from whom he cannot escape, than if he be left to attribute his trouble to unidentified psychic influences. Where ignorance is bliss 'tis folly to be wise is truer in psychic matters than anywhere else. Never open the eyes of your patient to a danger for which you cannot give him an effectual defence. The surgeon who is about to operate covers his instruments with a cloth so that the patient shall not see them. The wise occultist does the same. Do not forget that the Unseen is always suspect to the uninitiated.

Having conducted an enquiry along the lines laid down in the previous pages, you should have acquired a considerable amount of material for investigation. Examine it carefully for correlations of cause and effect. Note if any exacerbation of the trouble is regularly associated with any incident, place, or person. Consider also the various type-cases that I have given as examples in the previous chapters, and see if you can find any that resemble the case you are investigating. Note the explanations given, and see if they throw any light upon the problem, or suggest lines along which enquiry might be pursued.

Working in this way, you ought to be able to arrive at a tentative diagnosis. If this is confirmed by the findings of the psychics to whom you have sent specimens for psychometry, then you may feel confident you are upon the right track and go forward boldly.

Remember, however, that although the psychics ought to agree as to the main points of their investigation, you cannot expect any complete agreement as to details. They are inspecting a composite photograph of the patient's entire life, and there is so much to see that no one person is likely to see everything. The things in which they confirm each other may be held to be established, but the things which the one sees and the other does not are not necessarily illusionary.

17 METHODS OF DEFENCE: PART I

IN WRITING FOR the general reader an account of the methods
to be used in combating a psychic attack, I am reminded of
those excellent manuals upon medicine and surgery which an
enlightened Board of Trade insists shall be provided for the
captains of ships, together with a cupboard full of remedies,
harmless and otherwise. When an emergency arises, the
worthy skipper reads through the chapter he believes to bear
upon the case in hand and goes to work as best be may. On
these occasions the personal factor is a large one.

So it is in dealing with psychic trouble. Wide experience is
needed for diagnosis, and specially trained faculties and
specially developed powers are needed to cope with the
conditions that may be found. This book is more in the
nature of a manual of first aid than a treatise on treatment.

We must also bear in mind that just as the potent drug is
effectual in the hands of the expert but dangerous in the
hands of the amateur, so do the more potent occult formulae
need special equipment for their use. Moreover, a formula
that is used indiscriminately by the uninitiated is apt to lose
its potency and become useless. The popular expletive which
G.B.S. introduced into polite society in his play, *Pygmalion*,
is the worn-out remnant of the once-powerful adjuration,

"By Our Lady." Moreover, no two cases are alike, and the clear-cut, typical case is a rarity and treasure. Common sense, natural aptitude and experience are the exorcist's best equipment.

Having made his diagnosis and being ready to proceed to the handling of the case, the exorcist has to achieve three things: he must repair his patient's aura, clear the atmosphere of his environment, and break his contact with the forces that are causing the trouble. These three things are interdependent, and not one of them is first or last. It is next to impossible to get a damaged aura to heal if you do not clear the atmosphere; nor will the atmosphere remain clear for long if you cannot break the contacts.

Theoretically, the ideal thing to do is to break the contacts as a start. But unfortunately, in actual practice, these often take a good deal of finding, and a good deal of handling after they have been found. Meanwhile, something has to be done to keep the patient going. The exorcist has got to clear himself a place in which to work. Or if the victim of the attack is defending himself single-handed, he has got to throw up some temporary defences while he digs himself in.

The first thing to do when dealing with an occult attack is to make a temporary clearance of the atmosphere and so gain breathing-space in which to re-form the shattered ranks. This is more readily achieved by an organised ritual than by unaided will-power. *Any act performed with intention becomes a rite.* We can take a bath with no more in mind than physical cleanliness; in which case the bath will cleanse our bodies and no more. Or we can take a bath with a view to ritual cleanliness, in which case its efficacy will extend beyond the physical plane. We therefore perform certain physical actions not only as a means of clearing etheric conditions, but also as a means of definitely effecting astral ones through the imagination, a very potent weapon in all magical operations.

Physical objects become impregnated with etheric emanations and retain them for considerable periods as a knife will retain a smell of onions and taint everything that is cut with it. These emanations, magnetism as they are called in the terminology of occult science, profoundly affect any sensitive person who is in contact with them. There is something in the old superstition that it is unlucky to place boots on a table. It is equally inadvisable to place outdoor garments on a bed. You do not know whom you have rubbed shoulders with in bus or train, so why give their magnetism a chance to contaminate your sleeping-place?

Fortunately for all of us, magnetism is a very fugitive force, and although it may be potent when fresh, it soon fades unless it has been deliberately created by means of ritual. The terrible atmosphere that surrounds the victim of an occult attack and permeates all his belongings is not difficult to get rid of, though it will rapidly re-form unless the conditions which gave rise to it are cleared up.

The most effectual way of getting rid of magnetism is to move to a fresh place, taking nothing of one's old belongings with one.

This, however, is a counsel of perfection for most people. Fortunately there are other devices which enable us to attain our ends nearly as effectually. If it be in any way possible, let the victim of an occult attack move temporarily to another environment, taking with him as few of his belongings as possible, and let him make the move in new clothes, or in clothes that are just back from the cleaner. Let him, moreover, keep his whereabouts a secret as far as it is convenient for him to do so.

There is an old superstition that a witch can be thrown off the trail by crossing running water. It is my opinion that many of these old folk-beliefs have a basis in fact, however overlaid by superstition they may have become. I once had a curious experience which gives support to this opinion. I was about to take part in an important piece of occult work to which I knew there would be opposition. A friend who was concerned in the matter asked me to dine with her on the night before the day fixed for the proceeding. We were both conscious of tension in the atmosphere, and she suggested that I should remain the night at her flat instead of returning to my own, informing no one of my whereabouts in order to throw the attack off the trail. The manoeuvre was not wholly successful, and we had a rather trying night, and I was conscious of a good deal of psychic tension next day. I decided therefore to walk to the appointed place across Hyde Park in order to refresh myself. When part of the way across, I suddenly felt that the tension relaxed, and I was able to go through the work in hand without interference. I told my friend of this experience, and she questioned me as to where I was when it took place. We looked up the spot on a map and found that I had just crossed the underground conduit which takes the overflow from the Serpentine. I did not know of the old superstition concerning running water, neither did I know of the existence of the conduit. Nevertheless, the sense of relief was sufficiently marked to cause me to mention it when I saw my friend again, and to be able to indicate the spot where it had occurred.

We have very little exact knowledge concerning these subtle forces which are the basis of both occult attack and spiritual healing, but we have good reason to believe that in their nature they are closely analogous to electricity. They are not inanimate forces, however, but have in their nature something that is akin to life, though of a low type. It has been my experience that if we work on a blended analogy of electricity and bacteriology, we get pretty near the facts; as near, at any rate, as our present state of knowledge permits. In other words, if we act as if thought possessed the combined qualities of electricity and bacteria we shall have a sufficiently accurate method of steering by dead reckoning in the absence of certain knowledge and actual sight. If we consider the various methods used in folk-magic of all ages and races, we shall observe that they are in agreement with these hypotheses.

Running water, we know, has peculiar electrical qualities, as is witnessed by its effect on the divining-rod in the hands of a sensitive person. Whatever it may be that affects the diviner is probably the same thing that affects the occult attack. When we recall, moreover, that running water will throw hounds off the scent just as effectually as it will the alleged witch, we may feel that we cannot be accused of gross superstition if we give the old folk tradition a trial and note the results.

Water, again, is the vehicle of purification. It is used in the rite of baptism by the Church and in the Preparation of the Place by the occultist about to perform a ceremony. Strictly speaking, there should be a trace of salt in the water thus employed, and both salt and water are blessed with powerful invocations when the priest is preparing holy water, whether for a baptism, or for placing in the holy-water stoup for the use of the congregation.

As far as the occultist is concerned, salt to him is the emblem of the element of earth. It is also a crystalline substance, and crystalline substances, in their different forms, receive and hold etheric magnetism better than anything else. Water, on the other hand, is the emblem of the psychic sphere. These two realms, between them, contain by far the greatest part of occult evil. It is rare indeed that spiritual wickedness in high places will reach up as far as the airy realms of mind or the fiery realms of spirit. If we want to get into touch with, or operate upon a particular sphere, we use as base a substance appropriate thereto. Consequently, a solution of salt and water makes a better base than either salt or water could do separately because it enables us to cover the whole of the sphere of probable operations in a single act. It may be interesting to note concerning the magical properties of crystalline substances, that crystals are used in wireless apparatus to pick up the subtle vibrations of the ether. Once again we are close upon the trail of our electro-bacteriological analogy.

It is an excellent plan, when trying to break an undesirable psychic contact, to immerse oneself in a bath of water that has been especially consecrated for the purpose; re-dressing in new or at least clean clothing afterwards, and if it be by any means possible, moving into a different room. If this cannot be done, move the bed into a different position, taking care to turn it at a different angle; that is to say, if you have been in the habit of sleeping lying north and south, place your bed so that you will now be lying east and west.

The following prayers may be used for the blessing of the salt and water:

" (Pointing the first and second fingers at the salt.) I exorcise thee, creature of earth, by the living God (+), by the holy God (+), by the omnipotent God (+), that thou mayest be purified of all evil influences in the Name of Adonai, Who is Lord of Angels and of men.

(Extending hand over salt.) Creature of earth, adore thy Creator. In the Name of God the Father Almighty, maker of heaven and earth, and of Jesus Christ His Son, our Saviour, I consecrate thee (+) to the service of God, in the Name of the Father and of the Son and of the Holy Ghost. Amen.

(Pointing first and second fingers at the water.) I exorcise thee, creature of water, by the living God (+), by the holy God (+), by the omnipotent God (+), that thou mayest be purified from all evil influences in the Name of Elohim Sabaoth, Who is Lord of Angels and of men.

(Extending hand over water.) Creature of water, adore thy Creator. In the Name of God the Father Almighty, Who decreed a firmament in the midst of the waters, and of Jesus Christ His Son our Saviour, I consecrate thee (+) to the service of God, in the Name of the Father and of the Son and of the Holy Ghost. Amen.

(Casting the salt into the water.) We pray Thee, 0 God, Lord of Heaven and Earth, and of all that in them is, both visible and invisible, that Thou mayest stretch forth the right hand of Thy power upon these creatures of the elements and hallow them in Thy holy Name. Grant that this salt may make for health of body and this water for health of soul, and that there may be banished from the place where they are used every power of adversity and every illusion and artifice of evil, for the sake of Jesus Christ our Saviour. Amen."

The water thus consecrated may be used as a bath, or for making the Sign of the Cross upon the forehead, or for sprinkling about a place. When thus using it, the following prayer may be employed:

"In the Name which is above every other name, and in the power of the Father and of the Son and of the Holy Ghost, I exorcise all influences and seeds of evil; I lay upon them the spell of Christ's Holy Church, that they may be bound fast as with chains and cast into outer darkness, that they trouble not the servants of God."

In pointing or making the Sign of the Cross (+), the first and second fingers are extended and the third and fourth are bent towards the palm of the hand and the thumb laid upon their nails. When the hand is extended in blessing over the salt and water, it is held flat, fingers together and parallel, the thumb stretched at right angles to the forefinger.

If there is sufficient occult force at work to produce physical phenomena, it is very advisable to take precautions to prevent materialisations taking place. The physical phenomena are of several types. They may take the form of noises, usually creakings, thuds, or more rarely bell-like notes or wailing sounds. If actual words are heard, auditory hallucinations should be suspected, for in the absence of a medium, spirit messages are given to the inner ear, not to the auditory nerve. Lights may also be seen, usually taking the form of dim balls of luminous mist drifting like soap-bubbles. They may be any size from mere points of light to considerable dimensions, some six feet or more in diameter. In these spheres of dim luminosity psychics can generally see forms, sometimes human, sometimes from the animal kingdom. Whitish grey clouds can also sometimes be seen, rising pillar-wise from the floor like smoke. These are usually fixed to one place and do not move about the room as do the spheres of light, such movement as occurs being within themselves, like the eddyings of smoke caught under a tumbler. More rarely a distinctive odour may be noticed, and still more rarely there may be precipitations of powdery substances or slime. Light objects also may be overturned or thrown about the room.

There are certain substances which experience has proved to be effectual in preventing the condensation of etheric energy from taking place. Consecrated salt dissolved in vinegar and placed in saucers about the room will cope effectually with low degrees of force, but for higher potencies nitric acid is the best thing to use, a small quantity being poured into a saucer and exposed to the air. It is best to use it well diluted to prevent accidents, for it is not the strength of the acid in the saucer that is efficacious, but its evaporation into the air, and it will evaporate just as well when diluted as when neat. In what manner it works I have not the slightest idea, but its value is well known among psychic experimenters.

The methods of occult attack employed in modern Europe are exclusively mental, so far as my experience of them has gone at any rate. That is to say, they work by the mind on the mind, and only affect physical conditions incidentally. In the East and among primitive people, however, other aspects have to be considered, as a much more etheric type of magic is in use under primitive conditions of life and upon virgin soils. For these etheric operations, material substances are required in order that the magnetism attached to them may be made use of. Hair combings, nail-parings, cast-off clothes, objects in familiar use, all contain magnetism. Consequently care should be taken to see that such things are effectually disposed of when discarded. Combings and nail-parings should be promptly burnt. Cast-off clothing should never be allowed to go out of the possession of the owner till it has had at least three days' exposure to sun and air in the open. The magnetism will be more effectually dispelled if the garments be laid on the earth, especially freshly turned earth, than if hung on a line. The same applies to furniture. The chair that has been the accustomed seat and, above all things, the bedding, should be thoroughly aired and sunned before they are parted with. The same precautions are useful if any second-hand article has been purchased.

The disposal of night-soil should also be carefully arranged for and entrusted to reliable servants, abundant disinfectants and deodorants being constantly in use. Precautions should be observed to prevent any native obtaining access to fresh excrete. After the animal heat has gone out of it, its magical value has greatly decreased. A dirty handkerchief, too, is an effectual magnetic link, and so are dressings from a wound. Anything, in fact, that bears traces of any of the by-products of the body.

But apart from any question of psychic attack, there are two substances which are especially prized for purposes of magic, and these are seminal fluid and menstrual blood. The former is used in fertility rites and the latter in certain forms of evocation. These substances are exceedingly hard to come by in primitive lands, because the natives, knowing their significance, guard them most scrupulously; but the memsahib has no suspicions, and allows stained garments and bed linen to go into the hands of the washerman to be disposed of at his discretion, satisfied so long as the garments themselves return safely at the end of the week, and never thinking to enquire what becomes of the water in which they were washed. There are many parts of the world in which the sale of these magical substances is a profitable sideline of the laundering business.

In Europe, menstrual blood and faeces are part of the magical substances of the Black Mass, being made up into patens with wheat flour.

A time-honoured method of clearing a bad psychic atmosphere out of a house, and one which I have known in my own experience to be effectual, is to strew garlic about the place, leave it overnight and then take it up and burn it. Among country people, an onion is sometimes placed in a vase on the mantelpiece as if it were a hyacinth bulb when unpleasant visitors are expected, and solemnly burnt in the kitchen fire as soon as they have departed, it being believed that the onion tribe have the property of absorbing noxious emanations. It is curious to note in this respect that in one coal mine to my knowledge the miners are forbidden to take onions down into the workings as part of their dinners because the onions absorb the underground gases and become poisonous. My informant told me that he and others had smuggled onions down and learnt from bitter experience the wisdom of this rule.

18 METHODS OF DEFENCE: PART II

The meditative method ♦ The invocative method ♦ Value of a combination
of the two ♦ Attack by thought-forms ♦ Attack by thought-force ♦ Magnetic
fields ♦ Formula for making a magic circle ♦ The Qabalistic Cross ♦ The Sword
of Power ♦ The Circle of Flame - Use of incense ♦ The Banishing Pentagram ♦
Incident of the split panel ♦ Formula for sealing the aura ♦ Method of making
astral shields ♦ How to prevent hypnosis ♦ Value of the sacraments.

HERE ARE TWO types of practical psychic work which may
be used separately or in combination, the latter method,
in my opinion, giving by far the best results, though the
exponents of each are apt to decry the other. The method
which we will distinguish as the meditative method consists
of meditation upon abstract qualities, such as peace, harmony,
protection and the love of God. It is the method of the New
Thought school, and its value lies in the harmonising effect it
has upon the emotional state and its counteracting of harmful
auto-suggestions. The other method, which we will call the
invocative, consists in the invocation of external potencies
and the employment of formal methods for the focussing of
their force. This method has many gradations of complexity
and an infinite variety of technique. It ranges from the
simplest prayer which calls upon Christ with the Sign of the
Cross, to the most elaborate rituals of exorcism performed
with bell, book and candle. The essence of the system lies in
the attempt to dissect out from the general force of good the
particular aspect of energy that is needed, and the use of some
symbol to act as the magical vehicle of that force upon the
plane of form. This symbol may be a mental picture of the
blue robe of Our Lady; it may be the action of making the
Sign of the Cross; it may be the consecrated water sprinkled
for token of cleansing; or it may be some object specially

magnetised to act as a talisman. In the invocative method the aim is to concentrate the force, and therefore some symbol of form has to be employed. In the meditative method the aim is to escape beyond the bounds of form into the atmosphere of pure spirit, too exalted for evil to enter, and therefore the use of any form or formula is eschewed as calculated to prevent the soul from rising into this pure air.

In my opinion, and with all due respect to the practitioners of this latter method, much better results would be obtained if the invocative method, with its utilisation of the efficacy of formula, were used to enable the mind to climb into the pure air of spiritual consciousness where no evil is. It is only those who are highly trained in meditation who can rise on the planes unaided. It is exceedingly difficult to "take off" from sense-consciousness without the use of some kind of psychological device to act as a spring-board. There seems to be little object in refusing for purely academic reasons to avail ourselves of a method of proven efficacy. If we realise that the use of forms and symbols is merely a psychological device to enable the mind to get a grip on the intangible, we shall not fall into the error of superstitious observances. A superstition has been defined as the blind use of a form whose significance has been forgotten.

On the other hand, we shall be unwise to rely exclusively upon formal or ceremonial methods unless at the same time we use meditative methods in order to purify and harmonise our own consciousness. If we neglect this aspect of our work, we shall re-infect by our own vibrations the magic circle as fast as we have cleared it. It is not much use sealing a circle with the protective Names if we allow a panic-stricken imagination to run riot, picturing every conceivable kind of evil and leaving blank spaces for the possibility of inconceivable kinds. Equally, however, we shall find it very much easier to perform the harmonising meditation if we are working within the protection of a magic circle. To attempt to perform the work of exorcism solely by means of meditation is like raising a weight by the unaided effort of our two hands. The employment of the magical method resembles the use of a lever, or a pulley and block. Our muscles are still the sole source of energy, but by the utilisation of mechanical principles we have redoubled their Let us, then, in meditation, use symbols to concentrate our attention; we shall find this much easier than meditation in terms of abstract thought. Indeed, in times of stress and crisis, abstract thought may be impossible for us unless we are very experienced in its use; but we shall seldom reach a state when we cannot picture the Cross and call upon the Name of Christ.

Occult attacks may be divided into two types, those which take place by means of thought-forms, and those which operate by means of a current of force. But even in the latter case the current of force soon gathers to itself or germinates thought-forms congenial to its nature. Therefore in every psychic disturbance the thought-form is a factor which has to be considered and dealt with, and which, in fact, forms the readiest means of diagnosis; for it is by the perception of the associated thought-forms that the experienced psychic is able to detect the nature of the attack.

Thought-force is a thing which has no relation to geographical position, but is a matter of pure consciousness and of tuning in to its key-note. We can pick up the forces of dead faiths a thousand years after the death of their last votary, and upon the opposite side of the globe to that in which they flourished. But thought-forms are a different matter. They have position in space, and although they can be moved about with the speed of thought, and can be withdrawn to the subtlest level of the astral and there anchored to an idea and thus prevented from impinging upon the planes of form for all practical purposes, nevertheless, although they do not occupy space, they can be referred to definite positions in space. They can, for instance, be associated with a particular object, and will follow that object about, remaining within its magnetic field. The immediate magnetic field is anything from twelve to thirty feet; the remote magnetic field from a hundred to three hundred yards. Powerful holy centres, like

Glastonbury or Lourdes, have a bigger magnetic field than this, extending possibly to a couple of miles; they are also inter-connected among themselves by lines of force. These things have to be taken into account in practical occult work.

When we are confronted by a disturbing influence emanating from a focus of power, such as the site of an old temple, we have got to deal with the remote magnetic field by means of ceremonial. As this is a method that can only be used by a high-grade initiate, we will not consider it here. For all practical purposes in a psychic attack it is the immediate magnetic field that has to be considered.

The best method to deal with this is to make a magic circle. A mere banishing by itself is not so effective as a banishing performed within a circle, because the circle will effectually prevent the banished forces from flowing back again. There are various methods of performing this operation, but the principle of all valid ones is the same. The more potent conjurations cannot be given in these pages, because their effective use depends upon the grade of initiation possessed by the person who proposes to use them, and to possess a formula without the grade to which it belongs is as unsatisfactory as possessing a gun without any knowledge of shooting. The formula I will give will be found effectual for all ordinary conditions. Extraordinary conditions can only be dealt with by a person who has had experience.

In making the magic circle the operator stands upright facing east. He faces east because the magnetic current on which he proposes to operate runs from east to west. His first procedure must be to steady his own vibrations and purify his aura. In order to do this, he makes the Qabalistic Cross on breast and brow. Touching his forehead he says, "To Thee, 0 God (touching his solar plexus) be the Kingdom (touching his right shoulder) and the Power (touching his left shoulder) and the Glory (clasping his hands) unto the ages of the ages. Amen."

By this formula the operator affirms the power of God as sole creator and supreme law of the universe to which all things must bow, and he establishes this formula magnetically in his aura by the action of making the Sign of the Cross upon himself. This Sign is not an exclusively Christian symbol, and can be used as readily by the Jew as the Churchman, for it is the Equi-limbed Cross of Nature that is being used, not the Calvary Cross, of which the shaft is double the length of the cross-bar, and which is the symbol of sacrifice. The Equi-limbed Cross refers to the four quarters of the globe and the four elements, and the formula associated with it proclaims the dominion of God over these, and thereby occultly formulates His kingdom within the sphere of the operator.

The operator next imagines himself to be clasping in his right hand a large, cross-handled sword, such as is depicted in pictures of Crusaders. He holds it point upright and says, " In the Name of God I take in hand the Sword of Power for defence against evil and aggression," and imagines himself to be towering up to twice his natural height, a tremendous armed and mailed figure, vibrating with the force of the Power of God with which he has been charged by his formulation of the Sword of Power.

He now proceeds to draw the Magic Circle upon the floor with the point of the Sword of Power, and he should see in his imagination a line of flame following the point of the Sword, consisting of small flames, such as spring up when methylated spirit is spilt and ignited, but of a pale golden colour. A little practice should enable this circle of light to be formulated effectually. Keep on going round the circle until it is formulated. The circle should always be, drawn deosil, that is to say, from east to south, to west, to north, in the same way that the hands of a clock would move were the clock laid face upwards on the floor. The contrary way is widdershins, the way in which the witches danced at the Sabbats. The deosil movement affirms the rule of God's law in Nature because it is the Way of the Sun; the widdershins movement repudiates God's rule over Nature by moving against the sun. In resisting an occult attack the whole formula should be tuned to the key-note of asserting God's dominion over all existence, the aim of the operator being to align himself with Cosmic Law and cause the Power of God to deal with the interference.

The circle being formulated, the operator ceasing to visualize the sword but still visualising the circle, clasps his hands in prayer, and raising them above his head towards the east, prays, "May mighty Archangel Raphael protect me from all evil approaching from the east." Turning to the south he repeats the same formula in prayer to Michael. Turning to the west, he invokes Gabriel. Turning to the north he invokes Uriel. Facing to the east again, and thus completing the circle, he repeats the formula of the Qabalistic Cross.

This formulation of the magic circle is especially valuable for protecting the sleeping-place, the circle being drawn around the bed. It is not necessary to move about the room, or shift the furniture in order to draw the circle, it will be formulated wherever it is visualised to be.

It is necessary to reaffirm this circle each time the tides change that is to say, a circle made after sundown will hold good till sunrise, and a circle made after sunrise will maintain its potency till sunset. After the circle has been affirmed a number of times in the same place its influence will persist for a considerable period, but it is advisable to re-formulate it morning and evening during the active phase of an attack. Incense burnt within the circle is very helpful, but care has to be exercised in the choice of an incense. Joss-sticks of unknown composition should never be used, as they are usually compounded with a view to assisting manifestation. Good quality church incense, such as can be bought at most church furnishers, is safe and satisfactory because it is compounded according to traditional recipes; cheaper qualities may not fulfil these conditions.

In dealing with elementals or non-human entities the Pentagram, or Pentalpha, is the best weapon. This is a five-pointed star drawn in a particular way. Pointing the first and second fingers of the right hand, and folding the others into the palm and touching their tips with the thumb, proceed to draw the Pentagram in the air, keeping the elbow stiff and swinging the arm at full length. Start with the right arm across the body, the hand about the level of the left hip, the extended fingers pointing downwards and outwards. Swing it upwards, as if drawing a straight line in the air, until the fingers point straight upwards above the head at arm's length. Now sweep it down again, keeping the elbow stiff, until the hand occupies the corresponding position upon the right side to that from which it started on the left. You have now drawn a gigantic V upside down. Next swing the hand across the body, on a rising incline, until it is stretched on a level with the left shoulder, pointing to the left. Bring it across the body horizontally until it is in the same position on the right, fingers pointing away from the body. Now swing it downwards across the body till the hand has come back to the point by the left hip whence it started. This is an exceedingly potent sign. The value of the Five-pointed Star, the symbol of Humanity, is widely known among occultists, but its potency depends upon the manner in which it is drawn. The method I have given is the correct one for banishing.

The potency of the sign may be illustrated by an experience of my own in using it, which the sceptical are at liberty to doubt if they wish; I merely mention it for the sake of those who may be interested.

I was taking part in some work with an Indian occultist when I became suspicious that all was not as it should be, protested, and was asked to withdraw. I did so, determined to watch proceedings from a distance, and if my suspicions were confirmed, to have an *exposé*. A few days later I was sitting in my room one afternoon chatting with a friend; it was just getting dusk, and we were talking by the light of a gas-fire. Suddenly we were both aware simultaneously of a presence in the room and turned spontaneously in the same direction. My friend sensed an antagonistic presence, and I, being more psychic, saw who it was, and had no difficulty in perceiving the form of my Indian associate in an egg-shaped sphere of misty yellow light. I told my friend to quit the room and wait in the hall, and as soon as the door closed behind her, I made use of the Pentagram I have described, together with certain Names of Power that are unsuitable for disclosure in these pages. Immediately the appearance in the corner by the door shattered and vanished, at the same time there was a resounding crack, which my friend heard in the hall. I called to her to return, and as she entered she exclaimed, "Look what has happened to the door!" and we found that one of the panels had split clean in two. It was this that had evidently caused the loud crack we had both heard. I offer no explanation of this incident for the good and sufficient reason that I do not know what the explanation may be. I merely state what happened. My readers can explain it as they please.

When it is not possible to seal the room, it is a very useful thing to be able to seal the aura. Stand upright and cross yourself, by touching forehead, breast, right shoulder and left shoulder, saying, "By the power of the Christ of God within me, whom I serve with all my heart and with all my soul and with all my strength (extend your hands forward as far as you can reach at the level of the solar plexus, finger-tips touching, then sweep them round to the back and touch the finger-tips together again behind you, saying), I encompass myself about with the Divine Circle of His protection, across which no mortal error dares to set its foot." This is an old monkish formula. It is very effectual, but its potency only lasts about four hours.

There are various other devices which are useful, not only in dealing with psychic attacks, but in any case of undue influence or domination.

If you have to interview persons whose influence you find overwhelming, imagine that they are separated from you by a sheet of plate-glass. You can see them, and hear them, but their magnetism cannot reach you. Visualise this sheet of glass until it appears to you to be absolutely tangible. If you have to associate with persons who distress you, but are not actually interviewing them, imagine that they are separated from you by a brick wall, and say to yourself, "You just aren't there. I can't see you, or hear you, and you simply don't exist."

When dealing with a person who saps your vitality, interlace your fingers, and lay your folded hands upon your solar plexus, keeping your elbows pressed against your sides. Keep your feet touching each other. You have thus contacted all your own terminals and made of your body a closed circuit. No magnetism will go out from you while you maintain this attitude. Your friend will probably complain of your lack of sympathy, however kindly you may speak.

If anyone tries to dominate you by gazing intently into the eyes, do not attempt to return gaze for gaze, for this only leads to an exhausting struggle in which you may get the worst of it, but look steadily at the spot just above the base of their nose, between the inner ends of the eyebrows. If you are merely dealing with an ordinary bully, you will immediately have the upper hand. If, however, your antagonist has knowledge of mind-power, you may not be able to dominate him, but he certainly will not be able to dominate you, and the result will be a stalemate. Do not attempt to dominate him, merely keep your eyes on the spot and wait for him to weary of his attempt to dominate you. You will not have long to wait.

By the use of the methods described in the preceding pages any person of normal courage and mentality, provided he avoids drugs, alcohol and long periods without food, can, if he does not lose his nerve, wear down any ordinary psychic attack; or in the case of attacks of abnormal potency, can at least ensure himself time to make good his escape and seek help. The sacraments are also a most potent source of spiritual power, and a church where the Blessed Sacrament is reserved, or which is sufficiently old to have been consecrated before the Reformation, is an effectual sanctuary.

19 METHODS OF DEFENCE: PART III

Nature of rapports ◆ Effect of rapports ◆ Group rapports ◆ The astral link ◆
The Watcher ◆ Method of ◆ Destroying thought-forms ◆ Method of
absorbing artificial elementals ◆ Method of breaking astral link ◆
Technique of substitution ◆ Illustrative case.

PSYCHIC TROUBLE not infrequently arises owing to the formation of an undesirable rapport. In order to understand the nature of this problem we must consider the whole subject of rapport. We have already considered in some detail the question of telepathic suggestion. Rapport might be considered as the passive aspect of that of which telepathic suggestion is the active aspect. It forms, in fact, the basic condition necessary for telepathic suggestion to take place. Two people who are in rapport might be described as astral Siamese twins. Although the physical bodies are independent units, the astral bodies are linked in such a manner that there is free circulation of astral force between them, just as the circulatory system of the mother is connected through the umbilical cord with the unborn child, and the same blood circulating freely through both.

This fact explains many important occult phenomena. It is the real key to marriage, and explains many facts in the relationship of parent and child. It also accounts for some important aspects of the relation of pupil and teacher.

But not only is it possible for a rapport to be established between two individuals, but between an individual and a group. This fact plays an important part in all fraternity work. It is also possible to establish rapport between a human being and other kingdoms of nature; with discarnate entities, superhuman beings, and, in fact, with any form of life with which an individual can form a sympathetic understanding. There must be some ground of sympathy as the basis for the formation of a rapport, but once formed, it can be developed almost indefinitely. It is a curious fact that if a rapport is long continued, the persons thus united gradually come to resemble each other. We all know the "horsey" type of man also the son of the soil of whom it was expressively remarked, Father's in the pig-stye. You'll know him by his hat.

When two human beings are in rapport, the less positive of the two tends to lose his own individuality and becomes the pale reflection of the other. It is for this reason that the Western occultist, who values individuality highly, does not take personal pupils in the same way as does the Eastern guru, but prefers to work through ritual with a group because this method is more impersonal. But even so, the individual members of a group will undergo certain changes whereby they are tuned in to the group-tone, so that there will be a certain common denominator which they all possess. Who cannot recognise the sign-manual of the Christian Scientist, the Theosophist, the Quaker? Any system which has group meditation rapidly puts its mark on its members.

In this fact, of course, lies much of the value of association with a worthy group. In it, equally, lies the detriment of association with an unworthy group. Let us consider what happens when a person of ordinary good character becomes associated with a group of degenerate moral tone. He will either find himself in such sharp antagonism to the group-mind that he will have no option but to withdraw, or he will rapidly but unconsciously be tuned to the keynote of his new associates. Without his being aware of the fact, his moral sense will have become blunted and he will accept as a matter of course what he would originally have turned from in disgust.

Rapport once established, other things beside the general feeling-tone can be shared. Actual ideas can be transferred from one mind to another as in telepathy; and in the same way, vital force can be transmitted. It is this fact which is the explanation of certain types of spiritual healing. When etheric vitality is being transmitted, it is necessary that the persons concerned should be within the immediate magnetic field of each other; but when astral force is in question, this is not necessary. Transmission is independent of space.

We are not now considering the legitimate use of this force for healing, or for teaching and developing neophytes, so we will not, therefore, consider its modus operandi in detail. Enough has been said to show in what way it works. Let us now proceed to the consideration of the practical methods of breaking such a rapport if for any reason it is desired to discontinue its use.

To astral vision the telepathic link appears as a ray of light, a shining cord, or some similar thought-form, because it is in this form that it is usually formulated by the person who is making the magnetic link. It sometimes happens, however, if the operator has a high grade of initiation, that instead of connecting the ray direct to the person with whom he desires to be in touch, he will formulate an astral animal at the end of it to which he transfers a modicum of his own consciousness. This animal-form is called a Watcher; it does not act on its own initiative unless attacked, when it defends itself according to the nature of the species in whose likeness it is made. The use of a Watcher is to obtain a record of what is transpiring without the necessity of focussing consciousness thereon. When the psychic substance of the Watcher is reabsorbed by the adept, he becomes aware of the content of the Watcher's consciousness. The disadvantage of this method lies in the vulnerableness of the Watcher to psychic attack, and the fact that its projector is affected if it is injured or disintegrated.

In dealing with a thought-form, always bear in mind that it is the product of the imagination, and is in no sense self-existent. What the imagination has made the imagination can unmake. If the maker of a thought-form has thought it into existence by picturing it imaginatively, you can equally well think it out of existence by picturing it clearly and imagining it bursting into a thousand fragments, or going up in flames, or dissolving into water and being absorbed by the soil. That which is thought into existence by the imagination can be thought out of existence by the imagination.

If what was taken for a thought-form resists destruction by this method, it is probably an artificial elemental. Now there are two such elementals, one kind being ensouled by the invocation of elemental essence into a thought-form, and the other by the projection of something of the magician's own nature into it. If it is ensouled by elemental essence, the use of the Pentagram will serve to banish it; but if it is of the kind that is ensouled by the magician's own force, another method must be used, known as absorption.

Now absorption is a very high-grade method, and its successful use depends upon the state of consciousness of the user. Each individual has to decide for himself whether in any given case at a given moment he is in a fit state to attempt it. Unless he can completely steady his own vibrations and arrive at a state of perfect serenity and freedom from all sense of effort, he should not make the attempt.

We will, however, describe the method for the benefit of those who care to try it.

Harmonising himself by meditation upon the Christ, the adept, as soon as he is satisfied that his own vibrations are steady, proceeds to call up before his astral vision the image of the form he intends to destroy. He sees it clearly in all its details and sinks to divine its nature, whether it is a vehicle for malice or lust, or vampiric action: these are the three most common, and it can almost certainly be assigned to one or other of these classes. Having discerned the type of the force with which he has to deal, he then proceeds to meditate upon its opposite, concentrating upon purity and selflessness if the force be lust; compassion and love, if it be malice; and upon God as the creator and sustainer of all life if it be vampiric.

He continues this meditation until he feels himself suffused with the quality upon which he is meditating; until he feels so imbued with purity and selflessness that lust causes him to feel nothing but pity, malice causes him to feel nothing but compassion, and in regard to vampirism, he is so assured that his life is hid with Christ in God that he would willingly let the vampire finish its meal in peace if he could thereby help it. In fact, the adept who proposes to perform a magical absorption has to reach the point where he has clearly realised the nothingness of the evil he proposes to absorb, and no longer has any feeling towards it but pity for an ignorance that thinks it can gain any good thing for itself in this way. He desires to uplift and educate and free the misguided soul from its bondage. Until he has arrived at the point when he has no other feeling than this towards his persecutor, it is not safe for him to attempt an absorption.

Having satisfied himself that he is ready for the attempt, he proceeds to draw the thought-form towards him by pulling in the silver cord that connects it with his solar plexus if it be a vampiric thought-form, or by opening his aura to it and enfolding it if it be one of the other two types. He literally sucks it in. This process should be done slowly and gradually, taking some minutes in the doing. If it be done suddenly, the adept may not find it possible to keep his own vibrations steady, and then he will indeed be in an unpleasant situation.

As the thought-form is absorbed, the adept will feel a reaction in his own nature corresponding to the type of the thought-form. If it is a lust-force, he will feel desire rise, within him; if it is a malicious force, he will feel anger; and if it is a vampire, he will feel blood-lust. He must immediately overcome this feeling and revert to his meditation upon the opposite quality, maintaining it until his vibrations are once more fully harmonised. He will then know that the evil force has been neutralised and there is much less evil in the world. He will immediately feel a great access of vigour and a sense of spiritual power, as if he could say to a mountain, "Be ye cast into the sea," and it would be done. It is this sense of spiritual exaltation and power which tells him that the work has been successfully accomplished. It is, however, advisable to repeat the meditation at intervals for two or three days in case another thought-form is formulated and sent after the first.

As for the sender of the thought-form, when the absorption takes place he will feel that "virtue has gone out of him," and may even be reduced temporarily to a state of semi-collapse. He will soon revive, however, but with his power for evil of this particular type considerably reduced for some time to come; and if he have the possibility of reform in his nature, it may even be that he himself will be permanently freed from this type of evil.

The great advantage of this method is that it actually destroys the evil, root and branch; whereas the mere destruction of a thought-form is like cutting off the top of a weed. On the other hand, it can only be done by an advanced occultist keyed up to the highest pitch. If one is disturbed or harassed or has in any degree lost his nerve, one dare not attempt it.

If the rapport is perceived as a line of light, a cord, or any similar form, attached to the solar plexus, the forehead, or any other part of the body, the best way of severing the rapport is to forge a magical weapon and cut it. In fact, if a rapport is felt, the first thing to do is to visualise the cord and try to see where it attaches; the solar plexus is the commonest place.

Next formulate the cross-handled sword as already described, and invoke God's blessing upon it. Then visualise a flaming torch, and invoke the power of the Holy Ghost, whose symbol it is. Now with the sword hack through the cord or ray until every shred is severed. Then sear the stump with the consecrated fire of the torch until it shrivels up and falls off from its point of attachment to your body.

After such a severing one must, of course, take the ordinary human precautions to prevent the link being re-formed. Refuse to meet the person responsible for its formulation, or to either read or answer letters from him. In fact, cut off physical communications as thoroughly and resolutely as one has cut off astral ones for a period of some months at least.

There are occasions, however, when a person is so completely overshadowed and dominated that he cannot perform this operation for himself. The magical operation of Substitution can then be performed, if he can find a friend ready to undertake the task.

In order to perform this operation, the two friends agree that it shall be done, but the one who is to become the substitute does not tell the original victim when he proposes to undertake the operation lest the latter should be so completely in the hands of the dominator that he should give the game away involuntarily.

Choosing a time at which he is sure his friend is asleep, the substitute concentrates upon him and imagines himself to be standing beside him, and visualises the cord or ray of the rapport stretching from his friend out into space. If he can visualise its other point of attachment in the dominator, so much the better.

He then formulates the sword and the torch as above described, and with these in his hands he imagines himself stepping right through the line of rapport, so as to break it with his body. He must not use either sword or torch for this process, but break it with his own flesh, as it were. Having thus severed it from his friend, he should then go for it with sword and torch with all his strength as it tries to enwrap him, as it assuredly will do, for it resembles nothing so much as the tentacle of an octopus. He should go for it hammer and tongs, making up in zeal what he lacks in knowledge, until it has had enough, and begins to curl up and withdraw. The combat, of course, takes place in the imagination, but if a clear and vivid image is produced it will be effectual.

In illustration of this method I may mention a case I once handled by its means. I was asked if I could help a woman who had been a lifelong invalid, but whose case the many doctors she had consulted were neither able to diagnose satisfactorily, nor to help. They all agreed that there was nothing organic the matter with her, and after trying in vain to get her better, they generally united in saying that it was pure hysteria. She suffered from a chronic condition of exhaustion, indigestion, attacks of vomiting, blinding headache and palpitation of the heart. She was, however, not in the least of a neurotic disposition, but a quiet, sensible, intellectual woman, bearing her sufferings with fortitude.

I made a psychic diagnosis and came to the following conclusion. That for many past lives she had been upon the Path, and that in her last life, a male incarnation, in order to speed up her progress she had travelled in the East, and eventually took initiation into one of the Tibetan Orders, which unfortunately turned out to be upon the Left-hand Path. Here she learnt the Hatha Yoga which gives control over the functions of the body.

In her present life, she retained the powers her training had given her, but not the memory of its technique. Consequently her emotional states affected those automatic systems of nervous control whose functions are normally not under the direction of the mind. Whenever, therefore, she was emotionally disturbed, her subconscious mentation overflowed into the automatic mind and threw certain of the functional systems of the body out of gear. It is my belief that this explanation affords a key to a good many cases of functional disorder. Many people in the course of occult meditative practices obtain control of the automatic mind which controls the functioning of the bodily organs. It may be recalled that the famous scientist, Sir Francis Galton, the founder of the science of eugenics, experimented with mental control of respiration, and having obtained it, found that the automatic function had fallen into abeyance, and he had to spend three anxious days breathing by will power and voluntary attention until the automatic function was re-established.

In this particular case, however, there was more than disturbance of function; there was this peculiar and very marked chronic exhaustion. I formed the opinion that a rapport still existed between her and the Tibetan Order of which she had been an initiate in her previous life. As is well known to occultists, one returns life after life to the Order of which one is an initiate, the rapport being a very strong one. This is one of the reasons why the great Mystery Schools have no need to make themselves known by advertising; they know their own, and pick them up on the astral plane.

But while it is an invaluable thing to be under the aegis of a reputable Order, it is an exceedingly unpleasant thing to stand in a similar relationship to a disreputable Order. In this particular case it was my opinion that the Order to which this lady had belonged in her previous life had sunk to a very low ebb indeed, and its leaders were deliberately drawing upon the vitality of its members.

Acting upon this hypothesis, I projected myself astrally in the way I have already described, and visited this lady at night. I perceived that from her solar plexus as she lay asleep there stretched a black, elastic, stringy-looking substance that resembled nothing so much as a stick of Spanish liquorice that has been well chewed by a small boy. This went off into space. Upon trying to see its further end I had a brief and far-off vision of a monastery with a Chinese type of roof perched on a crag among vast mountains.

I tackled the situation by the simple expedient of passing in my astral body athwart the line of black substance, thus breaking it. It immediately transferred itself to my solar plexus, and for a moment I felt a surge of tempting thoughts urging me to get this woman under my thumb and exploit her to her full financial capacity. I cast these out, and "went for" the rope of astral liquorice in the manner I have described, casting it off and searing the stump, and had the satisfaction of seeing it curl up and disappear into the darkness. I then fell into what I considered a well-earned sleep.

I had told this lady nothing of my ideas because I wanted to see whether I could clear up the case by working solely on the occult hypothesis without any admixture of suggestion. Next morning I visited her to see how she was getting on, and found her sitting up in bed eating a hearty breakfast and looking an entirely different woman to the grey-faced, exhausted creature I had seen the day before.

Without waiting for any enquiry from me, she said, "I don't know what has been done, but I feel as if something has been broken and I am free."

After breakfast she got up, went for a stroll, and met the doctor who was attending her in the street. So great was the change in her appearance that he failed to recognise her until she spoke to him.

I told her that in my opinion she ought to have nothing whatever to do with occult studies lest she re-form the magnetic link with her old Order, and also taught her how to prevent her subconscious mind from giving disruptive suggestions to her bodily systems of functional control. For some years she remained in good health, but later, unfortunately, took up the study of occultism again and relapsed into a condition approximating to her previous one, having presumably re-forged the contacts with the Tibetan Brotherhood which had proved so disastrous to her.

Guardian angels ◆ National Heroes ◆ The Good and Evil Angels of the
Qabalah ◆ The Higher self ◆ The Christ-force ◆ The Occult Police ◆
Experiences·in connection with the Occult Police ◆ The Indian Adept and his
meditation group ◆ How access was gained to the group-mind of the British
race ◆ How the Occult Police were found ◆ Their methods ◆ The sign they
gave ◆ The fulfilling of the sign ◆ Proof that they knew the adept's
movements ◆ The Hunting Lodges ◆ Curious manner in which information
is obtained ◆ How the Occult Police can be contacted ◆ The occult lodges
have no central organisation ◆ The movement is not controlled by Jews ◆
Groundless-ness of the charges brought against the movement in this
respect ◆ Chief abuses of the occult movement ◆ Principal occultists
unknown outside their own lodges.

THERE ARE SO many stories of the appearance of guardian
angels at moments of crisis that even the most sceptical
must admit that there is a case to be answered.

There is a tradition in Devon that if Drake's Drum, which is
preserved at Buckland Abbey near Tavistock, is beaten in a
time of crisis, Drake himself will return to lead the fleets of
England. Newbolt has immortalised this legend in his
famous poem:

> "Take my drum to Devon, hang it by the shore.
> Beat it when your powder's runnin' low.
> If the Dons sight Devon, I'll quit the port of Heaven,
> And drum them up the Channel as we drummed them
> long ago."

The idea of the hero who returns to lead his people, the guardian angel that appears in times of crisis, is sealed deep in the hearts of all nations, and nothing will eradicate it. Innumerable instances were reported by the men returning from trenches during the War.

Let us again refer to the ancient wisdom of the Qabalah, that storehouse of occult knowledge. We learn here of the Good Angel and the Evil Angel of the soul of man who stand behind his right and left shoulder, the one tempting him, and the other inspiring him. Translate the Dark Angel into terms of modern thought and we have the Freudian subconsciousness.

But the Freudians fail to realise that there is also a Bright Angel who stands behind the right shoulder of every man. This is the mystic superconsciousness or, in other words, the Higher Self, the Holy Guardian Angel whom Abramelin sought with such ardour and effort.

We all know that, when caught off our guard, there comes a dark temptation from the depths of our lower selves, something atavistic stirs, and we think thoughts, or even do deeds of which we would never have believed ourselves capable. We have heard the voice of the Dark Angel speaking.

Equally in times of dire stress, when we have our backs to the wall and we are fighting for more than our physical lives, another voice makes itself heard, the voice of the Bright Angel. I have never known this to occur when a man was fighting simply for his physical life. To those who see beyond the veil, death is no great evil; but in times of spiritual crisis, when the very self is being swept away, then it is that the cry of the soul is heard, and Something manifests out of the mists of the Unseen, manifests in a form that is comprehensible to the one who calls. Whether intense stress induces a temporary expansion of consciousness, a fugitive psychism, or whether a Being of its own volition passes through the veil and manifests, I do not know; there are never any details available of these incidents. They take place only in times of dire stress and go as swiftly as they came, leaving no trace except upon the soul.

I maintain that even as the Lower Self can rise up in moments of temptation, so can the Higher Self descend in moments of spiritual crisis. It is the aim of the mystic to live exclusively in the Higher Self. It is the aim of the occultist to bring this Higher Self through into manifestation in brain consciousness; "In my flesh shall I see God." Just as surely as the Lower Self can rise up and betray us to some horrible deed, so can the Higher Self come to the rescue, "terrible as an army with banners."

I have already told of the mysterious voice which instructed me how to extricate myself from grave psychic danger. Upon other occasions of stress and strain I have experienced a sudden expansion or shifting of the level of consciousness. The Higher Self has descended and taken control. From being in the midst of turmoil one is suddenly raised high above it and sees all the circumstances of one's life spread out like a bird's-eye view, as one might see the land from a high place, and one knows intuitively the outcome of the matter. All emotional turmoil ceases, and one is like a ship hove-to, securely riding out the storm. When this occurs to me, the memory of my past incarnations is always vividly present also. It is this simultaneous wakening of the past which makes me feel that the voice is that of my own Higher Self, and not of another entity.

It is my belief that in times of spiritual crisis the man that has faith in the law of God can rise up and invoke its protection and a seeming miracle will be performed for his benefit. Yet there can be no breach of natural law; therefore such a miracle must simply be an example of the working of a law with which we are as yet unfamiliar, just as an eclipse appears to the savage as a miracle, but to the astronomer as a natural phenomenon which he can forecast with accuracy.

What is it that induces this change of control in our lives? We are familiar with the fact that the engine of a car has three speeds and a reverse. May it not be that our minds are also geared, and that it is a changing of gears which induces psychism? Are there not times when we get into reverse and the ape and tiger within us take charge?

Behind the physical plane lies the astral plane, and behind the astral plane lies the mental plane, and behind the mental plane lies the spiritual plane, each plane acting as plane of causation to the one beneath it, and each in turn being controlled from the subtler plane above it. When we "change gear," consciousness is shifted from a denser to a subtler plane and we begin to move among remoter and remoter causes of which the happenings upon the physical plane are the end-results; we manipulate these causes and the results are immediately effected.

When we change gear from the physical to the astral, we find ourselves upon the plane of psychic consciousness and the lesser magic. Supposing a psychic combat is taking place between two occultists, if one of them is of such a grade that he can change gear again, so that consciousness is lifted from the astral to the mental plane, he will be in the sphere of the greater magic and be in full control of the situation. The other can make no stand against him. But what happens in the case of the rare and mystic soul who can shift consciousness once again and engage the gears of a purely spiritual power? He has outclassed the adept. There are many souls who have this mystical spiritual consciousness although they have no occult knowledge. Between the higher and the lower modes of thought there is a great gulf fixed across which they leap precariously. If in a time of crisis they are able to rise up in faith and enter into this mystical consciousness and be still, they will have the upper air of any occultist who relies upon nothing save the technique of occultism.

The question of mystical consciousness is, however, outside the scope of our present enquiry, which is concern with psychic methods and the traditional technique of the occultist. Different temperaments will employ different methods, and the mystical method does not appeal to everybody.

The occultist does not ignore the Christ-force, however; he recognises it as among the hierarchy of supreme forces of the universe, although he may not be prepared to assign to it the exclusive position which it occupies in the heart of the Christian mystic. In the Western Tradition it is symbolised by Tiphareth, the central Sephira of the Ten Holy Sephiroth of the Qabalistic Tree of Life.

The Christ-force is the equilibrating, compensating, healing, redeeming, purifying factor of the universe. It should be invoked in every operation of psychic self-defence where any human element, incarnate or discarnate, is concerned. Where non-human elements, such as elementals, thought-forms, or the Qliphoth, have to be dealt with, it is the power of God the Father, as Creator of the universe, that is invoked, His supremacy over all the kingdoms of nature, visible and invisible, being affirmed. God the Holy Ghost is the force that is employed in initiations, and it should not be invoked during times of psychic difficulty, as its influence will tend to intensify the condition and render the Veil yet thinner.

There is a very curious aspect of the occult field concerning which something must be said in the present pages, though not a great deal can be revealed, and, to be frank, I do not know a great deal about it myself, but only such aspects as I have actually come across. I have always heard it called the Occult Police; others may know it by different names but I believe it to be a very real and concrete thing, though its organisation is not upon the physical plane, nor, so far as I know, are its mundane activities gathered up into any single pair of hands. I have crossed its trail upon a number of occasions, and played my part in its activities, and I have talked with others who have also been concerned in it, and they have always said as I do, that it is the inner voice and circumstances that direct our activities when we cooperate with this mysterious organisation.

I think myself that it is organised in national units, for people seem to go in and out of jurisdictions, or to be passed on from one to another. In my experience it has no particular political bias, but concerns itself solely with occult methods applied to criminal ends and offences against society.

One or two illustrative cases may help to make the matter clear. Some complications arose at one time over an Indian occultist who was visiting this country in order to found a school. He was deeply involved in the politics of his own country, and there could be no doubt about it that he disliked the English and all their ways very much indeed. I think that I was the only pure-blooded Anglo-Saxon who was in touch with him. As far as I know, he did not concern himself with mundane plane political activities, his idea being to organise a meditation group which should pour the regenerative spiritual force of the East into the group-soul of the British Empire, which he declared was in a very bad way indeed. I maintained, however, that the group-soul was not dying, as he held, but very tired, for it was immediately after the Great War. Moreover, I could not see how anybody who disliked it so very much was going to be able to regenerate it. Nor was I sure that the regeneration was going to be to our taste if we were to get it. This man, whom I will call X., was of an intense spiritual pride, and his root-idea was that England must acknowledge the spiritual supremacy of India and take her spiritual inspiration from the East. I was young and inexperienced at the time, but I began to ask myself what manner of spiritual force was going to be poured in through the channel we were constructing. Supposing during the Great War a group of English occultists had tried to perform a similar service for Germany, what line would they have taken? Would they not have tried to influence the German group-mind to give up its militarist ideals and concentrate on the League of Nations? Was it not more than likely that our Indian friend was trying to disabuse us of our Imperialistic tendencies? Would it not appear to him, smarting as he was under the race prejudice of the white man, that the world would be a much better place for humanity if the English cultivated their own garden and let other people alone? I got more and more uneasy, and X., being a good psychic, detected my uneasiness, and I was asked to withdraw from the group he was organising.

I felt quite convinced that something sinister was being attempted against the group-mind of my race, but I had no means of gauging its extent or potency. This was not the kind of tale one could take to Scotland Yard; moreover, several of my personal friends believed in the bona fides of X. and were taking part in the group he was organising, and I was very anxious not to involve them in any unpleasantness. In my perplexity I resolved to do nothing upon the physical plane and to invoke the Masters upon the Inner Planes.

At this time I was not of a grade which is supposed to have direct access to the Masters, but I determined to try and get them telepathically, though I did not know whether those to whom I was trying to telepath were human or non-human, incarnate in physical bodies or discarnate entities, for at that time I was not very advanced in my occult studies.

All I had to hold on to was an abstract idea and the knowledge that in previous difficulties I had been able to get in touch with Something on the Inner Planes which had proved a powerful friend.

In telepathing, the usual method of getting in touch is to visualise the person you want to communicate with and call him by name. I had nothing I could visualise and I knew no names. However, I determined to make the attempt as best I might and, metaphorically speaking, I put my head out of the window of this fleshly tabernacle and called for the police. And I got an answer. The Inner Voice replied to me very clearly and distinctly:

"You are to go to Colonel Y."

I was taken aback at this, for Colonel Y. was a rather eminent person to whom I had once been introduced, and the last person in the world one would invite to go mare's-nesting. I had no desire to make myself ridiculous by bearding this formidable warrior in his den. My psychological studies had made me familiar with the workings of the subconscious mind and what it can do when dissociated, and I felt that the situation required handling with considerable caution because the results of a mis-step might be unpleasant.

I therefore replied to the Inner Voice, "I cannot trust you unless you will give me a sign."

The reply came through, "Colonel Y. will be at your next lecture. Tell him then."

To this I replied, "I know that Colonel Y. cannot be at my lecture because his regiment is ordered abroad, and he will have left before it takes place."

The answer came back, "Colonel Y. will be at your next lecture."

"Very well," I said, "that shall be my sign. If Colonel Y. is there, I will tell him, and if not, I shall leave the affair to take its course."

The day duly arrived when I was to give a public lecture at a certain town. I arrived at the hall in due course, and the firstthing I saw was Colonel Y. going up the stairs! So I determined to take the bull by the horns, and immediately after the lecture I went straight to him and said, "I have got a message for you."

"I know you have," he replied, "for I have been told to expect it."

It appears that he was sitting in his quarters one evening with his two dogs. They suddenly became disturbed and began to investigate something that wasn't there. He heard a voice saying distinctly to his inner ear that I should come and ask his help and that he was to give it. He was so impressed by this occurrence that he went to a mutual friend and asked her whether I was in trouble of any sort. At his request she wrote to me to enquire how I was faring, but mentioned no names, and I, not realising the significance of the incident, returned a non-committal answer.

He heard my story and told me to leave the matter in his hands, which I did. This is a queer enough story of coincidence, but the sequel is even queerer. After leaving Colonel Y., I enquired once more of the Unseen whether I should take any further steps. The reply came through that for the present I was to do nothing, but that I would be told when further action was to be taken. I learnt afterwards that X. had left the country a few days after my interview with Colonel Y.

Nothing happened for about five months, and then one evening when I was sitting over my fire in the dusk I distinctly heard the Inner Voice telling me that now was the time to make a move in the matter of X., and that I was to go to Mr. Z, and tell my story. Now Mr. Z. was a very eminent person indeed, whom I knew of as being an advanced occultist, but whom I had never met. I replied to the interior voice that for me to approach Mr. Z. was impossible, I should merely be shown the door, and that unless they could open up that way from their end, I did not see how it was to be done. The answer came through very clearly that the way would be made plain. And it was.

A couple of days later a visitor was announced, an old friend whom I only saw occasionally, and after the usual greetings and exchange of news, he said, " I should very much like you to meet a friend of mine who I think would be interested in your work. May I take you to see him? His name is Mr. Z." Needless to say I agreed.

When I came to the appointed meeting, I said to Mr. Z., after I had been introduced, "I have got a message for you," thinking I might as well be hung for a sheep as a lamb. He listened attentively, and when I mentioned the name of the Indian, my friend who was present, exclaimed, "It is a curious thing that you should be moving in this matter at the present moment. X. landed in England a couple of days ago."

It will be noted that as soon as X. left England, I was instructed to hold my hand, and as soon as he returned after an absence of five months, I was instructed to commence action again. Unless we are prepared to pull the long arm of coincidence clean out of its socket, we must conclude that some directing intelligence was at work. This is but one among many instances in my experience. Limitations of space forbid me to mention any more.

In addition to the Occult Police, who function solely on the Inner Planes, there also exist certain groups of occultists who have banded themselves together for the purpose of combating Black Occultism. I suppose they give themselves different names, but I do not know what these are; I have always heard them referred to generically as the Hunting Lodges. Upon various occasions I have skirmished on their flanks and looked on at some lively forays. I imagine them to be organised in conjunction with the Occult Police, and they certainly possess means of obtaining information which point to cooperation from the Inner Planes. They appear to possess alliances in unexpected quarters and to be able to pull a remarkable number of strings. What psychic weapons they use I do not know, but upon the physical plane they appear to rely largely upon newspaper exposés, and upon keeping undesirables on the move, never allowing them to settle down and organise. Knowing what I do of their methods, I have from time to time recognised their sign-manual in various transactions for which decent citizens have every reason to be grateful.

I came across them in a manner which serves to illustrate the way in which occultists can "call" for information they may be in need of, and the fortuitous train of circumstances that will supply it.

As a young girl, at the commencement of my interest in occultism, I came in touch with an adept whom I soon realised to be on the Left-hand Path, and with whom I soon severed my connection. Shortly after I broke with him, I was watching a gymkhana in company with some friends, among them a student of occultism, and we began to discuss matters of mutual interest. Impelled by I know not what impulse to confide in him what I had never told a soul, I told him of my experiences with the adept I have referred to. To my surprise he knew all about him. It seems that my new acquaintance was connected with a group of occultists who had taken for their work the hunting out of Black Lodges; they had already crossed the trail of my black adept and had compelled him to close down, and he had sworn not to reorganise his Order. They had had reason to believe recently that this oath was not being kept and that he had again organised a Lodge and was working his rituals, but they did not know where to lay their hands on him. Then here came I, a bit of human flotsam tossed up on a sports field to give them the information they needed at the very moment when they needed it. These things happen too regularly in occultism for one to be able to look upon them as chance.

It is my belief that it is possible for anyone who has need of them to get into touch telepathically with this occult police force. The symbol I was taught to use was a black Calvary Cross with circle on a scarlet ground. This is pictured in the imagination, and while gazing at it mentally the call is sent out into the Unseen, projecting it from the centre of the forehead.

Various attempts have been made to prove that the occult fraternities are all directed from a single headquarters, said variously to be situated in Germany, Tibet, Mongolia and South America. Personally I do not believe it. I suppose that I have a pretty varied acquaintance with the inner workings of the occult movement, and I have never seen anything whatever that indicated any centralised control, whether for good or for evil. Everything, in fact, points the other way, and indicates that there is no connecting link save that of a common literature, a common idealism, and a set of symbols which, if not common to all sections, are readily translatable by means of well-understood equivalents. The position in the occult field is analogous to that of Protestant Christianity, not Roman Christianity. Occultism has no Pope.

Nor do I think that Bolshevism ever gained any foothold in the Lodges, though I believe it tried; as witness the application to my own fraternity. The average occultist is not interested in politics, his concern is with things invisible. Moreover, the occult fraternities are too uncoordinated and scattered to be formidable political weapons even if they were imbued with Bolshevism.

It has also been said that the occult fraternities are controlled by the Jews in the interests of Zionism. This is quite untrue. There are very few Jews in the occult movement. It is true, however, that the Qabalah, the traditional mysticism of the Jewish race, is one of the principal sources of Western occultism, and that any occultist working on that tradition must know at least enough Hebrew to be able to transliterate Hebrew script. The study of the modern mystical Qabalah is almost exclusively in the hands of Gentiles, and orthodox Jewish scholars know little or nothing of its literature and nothing whatever of its mystical significance.

No one has said harder things of the occult movement than I have, and if I thought that there were any organised system of evil influence, I should not hesitate to say so, for I have the integrity of the movement very much at heart; but I honestly do not believe that there is any generalised organisation of the occult movement, whether for good or evil, whatever may be one's conception of good and evil.

One can, of course, only speak of that which one has seen, but I think it would have been impossible for me to have been as intimately associated with that movement as I have been and never to have crossed its trail at any point. I have crossed so many trails, and seen, I will not deny it, so much that was evil, but this particular evil I have not seen, and I do not believe it exists outside the imagination of people with bees in their bonnets. The true nexus of the occult movement is devotion to a common ideal, but this ideal is approached by an infinite diversity of paths, as many as the breaths of the sons of men.

I am sorry for the hypothetical person who has the task of organising the occult movement, for occultists of different schools cannot be induced to cooperate. Any technique which differs from that which they are used to is suspect; any unfamiliar contact is black. The great majority of the heads of schools that I have known have sat each in his own circle of light and damned everybody else. Like the old lady who watched her son march past with the Territorials, they exclaim,"They're all out of step except our Jock." I had once dreamed of a federation of occult societies with an annual convention, but I soon realised that it was unworkable. If occultists cannot be got to organise to serve their own interests, it is very unlikely that they would ever be got to organise to serve anybody else's.

The most prevalent abuses of Western occultism are immorality, drug-taking and the bamboozling of silly women. Its worst faults are credulity, a slipshod scholarship that verges on illiteracy, and a widespread sappiness of intellect. Fortune-telling in all its forms and some very spurious spiritual healing constitute another slur upon what should be holy ground. It is difficult to do justice to ideals which one does not share, but it has always seemed to me that the highly-coloured humanitarianism with which certain sections of the movement are soaked is not an ornament. "By their fruits ye shall know them." Such fruits of this as I have seen have appeared to me to be somewhat over-ripe.

The finest minds in occultism are totally unknown outside their own Orders. A very common clause in initiation oaths binds the candidate not to reveal the names of his fellow-members. If this oath were broken, the general public would get some surprises. Occultism not being in good repute with the general public, men in public positions cannot afford to have their names associated with it; their interest is therefore carefully concealed, and they only speak of it to those upon whose sympathy and discretion they can count.

Those who know what to look for, however, can pick them out readily. Anyone who is accustomed to the analysis of literary style can detect the regular reader of the Bible. Anyone who knows the occult rituals will detect their flavour in the literary or oratorical style of a man who is habituated to their use. Perhaps at this length of time I may be forgiven if I break the Oath of the Mysteries that binds to secrecy concerning the names of initiates and suggest that the key to the Bacon-Shakespeare controversy may lie in the fact that Bacon and Shakespeare were members of the same Order?

CONCLUSION

IN THE PRECEDING pages I have endeavoured to discharge a difficult task, one that is almost impossible to discharge satisfactorily. Limitations of space prevent me from explaining my concepts step by step and offering proofs thereof. To have done so would have required a library, not a book. I have had to presume in my readers not only an acquaintance with the literature of occultism but, what is much rarer, some experience of its practice. At the same time I have endeavoured to offer sufficient explanation as I went along to make my pages comprehensible to those whose, acquaintance with the subject is but cursory.

This book is not, and cannot be, a satisfactory handbook for the treatment of psychic disorders. All it can do is to point in directions where enquiries might be pursued with advantage. If it serves to direct attention to certain subjects that badly need investigation it will have fulfilled its purpose.

I may be charged with having revived the superstitions of the Middle Ages. To this charge I must plead guilty. But I must put forward as a counter-claim the plea that there could not be so much smoke without some fire, and that the superstitions of the Middle Ages may repay examination in the light of the recent discoveries concerning the psychology of subconsciousness.

Whoever is familiar with the literature of psychic research, abnormal psychology, and the baser aspects of that movement which took its rise from the inspiration of Christian Science and spread into a hundred uncontrolled cults, cannot fail to be struck by the fact that the old witch-finders were getting exactly the same phenomena as we meet with in all these different movements and fields of thought.

It has been said that since we find the stigmata of hysteria liberally distributed among those unhappy beings charged with witchcraft that the witch-cult is explained and disposed of. But we may find that a study of the real motives underlying the witch-cult would throw light on hysteria and the allied mental states.

It has also been said that history moves in cycles. At the present moment we are seeing a great revival of interest in psychic and occult subjects. We shall not have to look very much further to find that there are also the very promising beginnings of a witch-cult in our midst.

Let it be remembered that the cases I have quoted in these pages are from the experience of a single person, and I am by no means exceptional in the range of my experience, though I may be less cautious than most in committing myself to paper. If one dip of the bucket reveals so much, what might not be brought up by systematic dredging?

Since my treatment of my subject must necessarily be cursory, I should like to direct the attention of my readers to certain books which throw a great deal of light upon the question from various angles.

Not only occultists, but psychologists, alienists and students of psychic matters owe an immense debt of gratitude to the scholarship of the Rev. Montague Summers and the enterprise of Messrs. Rodker for making available exact and complete translations of the principal books upon witchcraft that were written by the men who were actually concerned in stamping out the witch-cult and had first-hand knowledge of its nature.

BIBLIOGRAPHY

IN ADDITION TO these I would direct my readers' attention to *The Projection of the Astral Body* (Weiser, 1968), by Muldoon and Carrington, which throws a very interesting light upon the manner in which genuine witches attended the Sabbats. I do not mean by these words to imply that Mr. Muldoon is addicted to wizardry, but he certainly possesses the traditional powers, and if he can do these things at the present day, why could not the witches have done them in days past ? At any rate, I do not think there is much doubt that the Holy Inquisition would have paid him the compliment of burning him if he had lived during its hey-day.

Thirty Years Among the Dead (Health Research, 1996), by Dr. Wickland, is another book which gives chapter and verse for personal experience instead of citing authorities and theorising about them. It is the record of an asylum doctor whose wife is a trance medium, and who made a most remarkable series of investigations concerning the nature of obsessing entities.

In Dr. Moll's book, *Hypnotism* (Da Capo, 1982), some remarkable phenomena are recorded such as do not find their way into modern books, whether because the investigators are less expert at eliciting them, or more cautious in communicating them, having profited by the experience of the earlier investigators. Some of the earlier books on hypnosis and mesmerism yield some very interesting reading to the psychic investigator.

Dr. T. W. Mitchell's *Medical Psychology and Psychical Research* (Methuen, 1922) is another book of value to the student, who should be familiar not only with the signs of psychic attack, but also with the signs of pseudo-attack in order that he may distinguish between them and not be misled into some very uncomfortable errors. To find one has been successfully hoaxed by a lunatic is a humiliating experience.

Myers' *Human Personality* (Ayer, 1975) is of course a classic with which every student of psychic phenomena ought to be familiar. There is an excellent abridged edition available for those who do not feel equal to coping with the two massive volumes of its original form.

Nicoll's *Dream Psychology* (Weiser, 1979) and Hart's *Psychology of Insanity* (Cambridge University Press, 1923) are two exceedingly illuminating little books, both written for the layman and readily comprehensible by him. They throw a great deal of light upon the mechanisms of the mind, and no one should attempt to deal with a psychic attack unless he understands those mechanisms. My own little book, *Machinery of the Mind* (Weiser, 1980), written under my maiden name of Violet M. Firth, will, I think, be found a useful general introduction to modern psychology.

Let us approach the subject of modern witchcraft neither in a spirit of incredulity nor of superstition, but from the standpoint of the psychologist, seeking to understand the workings of the mind and prepared to discover much that had hitherto passed unsuspected.

AFTERWORD

Christian Gilson

Christian Gilson holds a degree in theology and a masters in cultural philosophy. He has been a teacher of religious studies and a student of the occult for over thirty years. Christian began studying the published works of Dion Fortune twenty-five years ago, and has recently been granted access to the Society of the Inner Light's archives. For the last seven years he has followed in Dion Fortune's footsteps as the Editor of *The Inner Light*, the journal published by the Society.

To best understand the importance of Dion Fortune's *Psychic Self-Defense,* it is essential to remember its place in the body of her work. Fortune had written four short books on psychological issues before it. It was the second of these, *The Esoteric Philosophy of Love and Marriage* (1924) that famously precipitated her departure from the occult group known as The Hermetic Order of the Golden Dawn. She was openly accused of having broken her oath as an initiate by revealing one of the central concepts of magical practice. It was later shown that Dion had not in fact knowingly done so, but that she had independently stumbled onto this teaching. However, the damage was done. Her next three books are tamer than their titles suggest. The first, *The Esoteric Orders and Their Work* (1928) was to all intents and purposes an advertisement for her newly formed fraternity, and the second, *Sane Occultism* (1929) explored the value and problems with more commonly known forms of occultism, such as astrology, numerology, and past lives. She mixed in several chapters on the danger of the left-hand path and the need for secrecy. It is in *Sane Occultism* and her novel *Demon Lover* (1927) that lay the seeds for *Psychic Self-Defense.*

What Dion Fortune appears to have been doing was to interest people in occultism and at the same time direct them towards occult schools, such as her own. To do this, it was necessary in part to use fear to lead them away from works that had already been published on ritual magic, such as Aleister Crowley's *Magic in Theory and Practice* (the first part of which was published in 1929). In *Psychic Self-Defense* she offered strange events in order to engage the reader but also to sow the fear of accidentally stirring up trouble. Yet she was careful not to fully divulge any of the ritual methods of ceremonial magic.

The second reason for publishing *Psychic Self-Defense* was Dion Fortune's fundamental concern with the validation of her present and future esoteric development. The use of psychic ability to gain insight into the spiritual dimension is the foundation of her approach to ritual practice, as can be seen from her novels. In *The Sea Priestess* (1938), Miss Le Fay Morgan puts William Maxwell through a fairly strict program of psychic development prior to the ritual that is the climax of the novel. The importance of psychism is very much present in the papers of the Golden Dawn, however, in *Sea Priestess* it is referred to in veiled terms, as scrying in the spirit vision, and going forth in the body of light.

As a member of the Theosophical Society, Fortune would have been aware of the teaching of the Masters through psychic means. Indeed, it was claimed that a series of instructional letters, now known as "the Mahatma Letters," were psychically delivered to A. P. Sinnett. Colonel Ollcott, co-founder and first president of the society, claimed that one of the Masters physically manifested himself to him through psychic means. And Fortune must certainly have been aware of the story told by Helena Blavatsky about a senior lama who was said to be able to project his soul out of his body and into that of a child. This may have motivated her to write the following letter that was published in the *Quarterly Transactions of the British College of Psychic Science.*

Pioneer Club
March 12, 1924

Dear Mrs McKenzie,

I shall be very pleased to give you any particulars of my apparent death in babyhood as I have heard my mother tell the story, for naturally I cannot recall it.

I believe I was about four months old when I had to be weaned suddenly. This caused serious intestinal disturbances and I became very ill. For three days I lay at death's door, and my nurse, who was very devoted to me, went out each day to burn candles in Brompton Oratory and to pray for my recovery, for she was a devout Catholic.

On the evening of the third day the doctor pronounced me dead, and both he and my mother tried to persuade the nurse to accept the fact of my death, and to lay me aside, for she had sat for many hours with me on her knee. This she refused to do and declared she would not let me go out, and rather than make a disturbance with her they let her have her way and she sat with the apparently dead child in her lap all through the night.

During the three days of my illness there had been a dense fog, and they had not seen the house opposite for the whole of that time, but with the dawn of the fourth day the fog lifted and the sun came through, and with the coming of light I revived.

I did not, however, make a complete recovery, as in the case recorded in your magazine, and the effects of the illness remained with me all through my childhood.

It was only recently that I knew of this incident, but when I heard it, it threw a curious light on feelings I had had ever since I can remember. I have never felt any ties of kinship with my relatives, I like or dislike them according to their qualities as I do my other friends. I have never identified myself with my name, if you can realize what I mean by that, and I have never had an intimate friend who made use of it, they also have felt it was not 'me.' My face in the glass has never from childhood seemed familiar to me, I have always looked at my reflection quite impersonally, it also does not seem to be 'me.'

With regard to my supposed death, my own belief is that the soul of the baby V.M.F. really went out; that my nurse's vitality, impelled by the determination that I should not die, supplied some faint and elementary life to the unsouled form in her lap, and that a mature soul, which had recently passed out, took advantage of the opportunity to reincarnate because it had some work it wished to do. All through my childhood I knew that I had some work to do, and I trained my mind and will for that purpose, though I did not know what purpose it was. Later on, I knew that I should start this work, whatever it would be, when I was thirty-three, and this has proved to be the case. This leads me to the speculation that the soul which entered the child's body was possibly thirty-three years of age at the time it disincarnated.

I do not know whether these speculations are of any use to you; to me, personally, they are interesting, but I hold no brief for them, because I know that they can never be anything but speculation.

> Yours sincerely
> (signed) Violet M. Firth

Just like Dion Fortune, we must take care not to read too much into this fascinating tale, for it is as she clearly argues merely 'speculation.' However, her letter also suggests that it is possible for souls to move from one body to another and if unchallenged, take possession of them. This highlights the importance in protecting the whole self when engaging in magical work which is the basis of *Psychic Self Defense*.

If we are to take anything from this letter, it is the importance of being well grounded and secure in yourself before engaging in psychic work. Also, that there is a duty to protect the innocent and respect the personhood of all those we encounter, whilst guarding against becoming too detached from the physical body and the incarnatory personality. This comes into perspective when we read the second of two articles that Fortune wrote for the *Journal of the Fraternity of the Inner Light*, on the Masters and how to communicate with them. The article discusses the use of trance mediumship within a ritual setting and is reproduced in an abridged form below.

The Masters and the Fraternity
II
How communication is made.

Those who have some acquaintance with the inner workings of the Fraternity of the Inner Light know that it possesses a quantity of teachings that have been received psychically and that are referred to generically as "The Words of the Masters."

Those communications were received by means of trance mediumship, myself acting as medium and various Masters who are behind the Order which is behind this Fraternity acting as controls.

Mediumship consists in the power to disconnect the rational mind from the subconscious mind, leaving the latter swinging freely, like a compass needle. The subconscious mind, which is normally capable of perceiving thoughts and influences psychically with varying degrees of clarity—being, in fact, the seat of the psychic faculties—can be influenced by means of telepathic suggestion.

Some explanation of the psychology of mediumship will be useful in enabling us to understand the nature of these communications and assess them at their true worth, being neither superstitious nor unduly sceptical. I will therefore give the explanation that was given us, together with such psychological comment and explanation as shall make it more easily understandable.

The person who is to act as medium picks up the contact of the Masters psychically, either by "calling up" a particular Master, as it were, or being "called up" by a Master wishing to communicate. At the appointed time a curious sense of power begins to gather, as if one were waiting for the race to start, and those present who are familiar with the procedure can generally recognise who the communicator is going to be.

Whoever is going to be medium must then open a channel of communication by disconnecting the conscious mind from the subconscious mind and going into trance.

The first stages in this operation consists in completely relaxing every muscle of the body; a dim light is necessary, and relative quiet. Light, in my experience, affects the aura and not merely the eyes, for bandaged eyes and a thick rug are no protection against it. Absence of noise is necessary in order to enter into trance, but once

depth of trance is obtained, a reasonable amount of noise is imma-
terial, with the sole exception of sharp percussive sounds, such as a
car back-firing or a chair being knocked over. Light has a far more
drastic effect than sound; a shade slipping slightly on a lamp will
break a trance that street noises do not affect.

The next stage in the proceedings consists in building up in the
imagination a picture of the Master who is going to communicate
and concentrating on it. This imaginary picture, as I watch it with the
mind's eye, takes on life and absorbs my attention to the exclusion
of all else; it is no longer a case of concentrating, though that is the
necessary preliminary—it is a case of being held fascinated with the
same kind of fascination that one watches a street accident taking
place—unable to look away even if one wanted to. All consciousness of my surroundings blots out; there is a curious squinting sensation behind the eyes, which is probably caused by the eye-balls
rolling up as they do in deep sleep; then comes another, and none
too pleasant sensation of going down in a fast lift. I seem to lose
consciousness for a moment, and then recover to find myself floating about two feet above my own body, wrapped like a mummy; or
sometimes, when the trance has been particularly deep and there
is a great deal of power, of standing upright behind my own head,
facing the communicator, who stands upright at my feet.

The next move we are told, is for the communicator to build
up a mental image of himself and superimpose it upon the passive
subconscious personality that remains as a kind of psychological
residue in the physical body, the higher, directive faculties being
in abeyance or withdrawn. The whole process can be described in
psychological terms as a form of hypnosis, with a discarnate entity
as the hypnotist, or it can be described in traditional psychic and
occult terminology; the two are not contradictory or mutually exclusive, but on the contrary throw much light on each other.

The personality thus built up in the subconscious mind that
has been deprived of the guidance of its rational self, appears to be
the vehicle of communication of the controlling entity. It is, in fact,
a 'dramatisation' such as the work of the Salpétierre has made us
familiar with in the literature of psycho-pathology, the only difference between my dissociation of personality and that of the unhappy
patients at the Salpétierre being that in my case it remains under my

control; I can take my personality apart at will, though I need cooperation from the Inner planes if there is to be communication; but, on the other hand, I have never known my personality to come to pieces involuntarily, which, of course, is what happened to the Salpétierre patients. Equally, I can do what those poor souls could not do, and get the component levels of consciousness accurately co-ordinated again after the operation. This power, to take my personality apart and join it up again, has been perfected by years of practice, after I had been taught the method by my first guru. It always requires considerable effort, but of recent years I have acquired the skill to do It quickly and neatly and without fuss. It can be described as auto-hypnosis or as astral projection according to whether the terminology employed be that of psychology or psychic research.

Re-coordination appears to take place in two ways. If there is no "spirit-control," and I have shifted the level of consciousness in order to work on the inner planes, I connect up the two levels of consciousness by retracing link by link the association-chain of picture images that I used in coming out. Thus, if I used a mental picture of an Egyptian pylon to pass through and go out, I would use the same mental picture to pass through the reverse way when returning this serves to re-associate consciousness and keep memory intact, and, after all, personality is entirely a matter of memory. When, however, there is a control in charge, I go into deep meditation once I have "handed over," and it is his responsibility to see me safely back into my body again. I do not know exactly how this is accomplished; I simply find myself waking up out of deep sleep, feeling very cramped, and with a vague and rapidly fading memory of incoherent dreams. My memory is a very uncertain quantity on these occasions; sometimes I remember a little; sometimes I remember nothing, nevertheless, a residuum seems to remain in the background of the subconsciousness and sometimes reappears in my writings, or even in conversation, though I am quite unaware of its connection with the trance until I am told of it.

Trance mediumship fell out of fashion during the second half of the twentieth century, and much was made of the fears about the medium becoming possessed, or of spirit becoming attached to them in such a way that the medium would be unable to restore their natural sense of self.

The skill of trance mediumship is developed slowly over a number of years, the medium often working with the same inner plane contact or group of contacts. This is what she meant when Dion Fortune described her Fraternity as contacted, and her particular group of inner plane contacts are well known. These contacts give teaching and guidance through the medium to the group, and this was the way in which the Cosmic Doctrine was first communicated to Dion and her group. This method continued to be used by the Fraternity after her death.

However, such a practice does raise some important questions in relation to the reliability of the process and the veracity of the material received in this manner. There can be no doubt that unscrupulous individuals exist who through a great force of charisma and confidence lead people astray, claiming to be communicating spiritual wisdom. It is perhaps for this reason that Dion wrote *Psychic Self-Defense*, to arm the reader with the awareness and tools to defend themselves against such people. This reaction clearly arose from her own experiences, and yet there is also the realization that these very processes can, if used with care, training, and great discrimination, bear tremendous spiritual fruit.

Fortune's care about this may well have been stimulated by the work of Blavatsky and Olcott in revealing the fraudulent practices of many spiritualists of the late nineteenth century, such as Jenny and Nelson Homes. It would have been important to be sure that what was happening was genuine and not merely some psychological by-product. The question being whether the communication gained in this manner is just the product of a fertile imagination or a genuine communication. In the 1920s Dion published a substantial article on the relationship between psychology and occultism in the *Quarterly Transactions of the British College of Psychic Science*, an abridged version is reproduced below.

Psychology and Occultism
By Violet Firth

PSYCHOLOGY is the youngest of the sciences to assume a scientific form; its development was slow and tentative until the publication of Freud's book upon the interpretation of dreams and his system of psycho-analysis gave us an instrument of precision for the investigation of the human mind. In its early days it was considered the science which investigated the soul. In Professor McDougal's definition, however, which has had much currency of recent years, this bold undertaking has been modified, and psychology is declared to be the study of behaviour.

To my mind this definition is too narrow, unless one includes all forms of mental activity from intuition to phantasy-making under the heading of behaviour, and I propose, for the purposes of this essay to use the term psychology from the standpoint of inductive science.

By the word OCCULTISM I indicate that body of doctrine, method and data which has come down to us by the tradition of the initiates, and I also include under this heading the phenomena which this tradition has always regarded as its especial territory, but which is now being investigated by Spiritualists and psychic research workers.

No one who has attempted the practical exploration of these two subjects can fail to note the extent to which they overlap. Psychology approaches the human mind by the empirical method, and occultism makes use of it according to certain theories handed down by tradition.

It is my belief that each of these fellow-workers in the same field can be of enormous assistance to the other if they will lay aside their mutual pride and suspicion and consent to co-operate. Psychology regards the occult manifestations as the fraud of charlatans and delusion of hysterics, and occultism resents this attitude towards its phenomena by those who, in the great majority of cases, have never troubled to investigate that which they condemn, and despise psychology for its limitation of outlook.

It is my contention that psychology can be of great service to occult investigation by counterchecking its results, and that the occult theories can give psychology much light upon the organization of the mind.

For the purposes of a rough classification I have divided the occult phenomena into the following five divisions:

I. The poltergeist type. Table turning, spirit rapping, levitation, the moving of objects, and materialization mediumship.

II. Phenomena of the transmission or translation type such as automatic writing and trance speaking.

III. Direct perception, without the intervention of any of the physical senses, such as telepathy, psychometry, and the reading of the 'Akashic' records.

IV. The action of individuals that do not possess a physical vehicle and of individuals that have the power of withdrawing from their physical vehicle.

V. The theory of reincarnation or metempsychosis and the doctrine of Karma or causation.

These are the phenomena of which occultism claims the existence and offers its own explanation in accordance with its traditional doctrines, whereas orthodox science sweeps the whole lot away as fraud and delusions and refuses to investigate them.

With regard to my own position in the matter, I may say that I have personally seen enough of such phenomena to convince me that they do occur, and that I largely accept the occult theories with regard to them. I also believe that these occult theories, robbed of their verbiage, can be translated into terms of psychology without any contradiction between the two schools of thought.

But it has been my experience that much of the phenomena presented to us as occult phenomena though not of a fraudulent nature, is purely subjective and can be best interpreted in terms of psychology.

CLASS I is of extraordinary interest, because, to my mind, it represents the point of contact between mind and matter. All these phenomena point to the existence of a substance which, while not material in the usual understanding of the term, is yet capable of acting upon dense matter, exerting pressure and sustaining weight. [. . .] It is my belief that this substance, either visible or invisible, which exudes from the medium and also very frequently from the sitters, belongs to what occultists call the etheric subdivision of the physical plane and it is believed by them that this form of matter is capable of being moulded by mind, and is used by them as the basis of certain of their phenomena.

The spirits of the dead, which are minds without bodies, would be able to use this medium as a means of influencing dense matter and so making themselves apparent to the physical senses, but the minds of incarnated spirits, the living would likewise affect it, and just as the discarnate mind can mould a representation of itself in this form of matter, so the living mind can form an image of its memory of the dead upon which it may be concentrating. And although we may get the actual spirit entity functioning through this form, we may also get nothing but a product of the subconscious mind of a sitter in the séance, a concept much more acceptable to many of us who believe that the great majority of the dead are in a subjective or sleeping condition after death, and that only the more developed type of individual is capable of active functioning upon other planes; that is to say, the man who is incapable of functioning actively after death, and will not, therefore, make himself known through the séance medium; on the other hand, if he be capable of functioning on these planes of activity during life, then he would go over in full possession of his consciousness, and would be quite capable of manifesting through a suitable medium, or even directly upon the subconscious minds of those still in the flesh, though whether they were aware of it or not depends upon their capacity to get in touch with their own subconscious minds.

II—Automatic writing and trance speaking. These two phenomena are regarded as being methods of communication with planes other than the material and with the beings that function upon those planes. It is the occult theory that the medium who submits to this method of manipulation either lifts right out of his body and permits other minds to act upon his material vehicle, throwing the vocal chords into vibration, or he becomes so passive that his mind is acted upon by other entities and translates their messages. To these I will add a third hypothesis, that a second personality of the medium may come into function under certain conditions, and that this secondary personality may be of superior calibre to the normal personality because it has the subconscious memory storehouse to draw upon.

It will be seen that all trance work is not of equal value, it depends upon the level upon which the medium is working, and mediums usually have their special level; for instance, one will specialize upon the etheric plane and produce materializing phenomena, while another will use the lower mental plane and have access to an intellectual type of communication. I do not propose to enter upon the study of these hypnoidal states, and I have merely enumerated them in order to enable myself to point out their relationship to psychology, and show where the criticism of the psychological method can be of great value in determining the objectivity of phenomena; I do not say "the genuineness of phenomena" because phenomena can be perfectly genuine examples of subconscious conditions, and yet have no connection with other planes of existence, and therefore be valueless to those who are seeking to investigate those planes, therefore it is that the occultist pays great attention to the subjective aspect of this phenomena, because he knows how liable it is to falsify his results, and the initiate of an occult school is taught that he must know his own subconscious before he can function upon another plane, because he has always to go out through his subconscious on to that plane, and return by the same road, and unless he can correlate his conscious and subconscious minds, he will not be able to carry through his memory.

III—Direct perception. Upon the hypothesis of telepathy the bulk of occult phenomena is built up. If we admit the possibility of a mind sending forth a thought which can affect another mind, then the whole structure of occult phenomena follows. We have enough evidence of telepathy for even the material scientists to accept nowadays, and a great many of them do. To what then does this theory lead? Upon this assumption we admit, in the first place, that a thought is a thing, formed by the mind and projected outside itself, that it is a manifestation of force, in its turn manifests force, and is capable of producing reactions under certain conditions. We conceive of thought as a form of force capable of objective activity.

I fully admit, however, that the factor of conscious suggestion, whether deliberate or otherwise, plays a great part in these transactions, also the subconscious reaction to a suppressed wish along sex lines; these factors have all to be considered, hence the importance of psychology and occultism working hand in hand and counter-checking each other.

The question of the psychic reading of the "Akashic" records is of absorbing interest. Herein it is claimed that the psychic can decipher the memory of nature and so reconstruct past scenes in the world's history, and several books exist that purport to contain the records derived from this source. Scott-Elliott's "Atlantis" is an excellent example of this type of work, and so is Steiner's "Atlantis and Lemuria."

IV—With regard to the action of discarnate and disincarnating spirits, an hypothesis long familiar to occultism, I cannot enter here upon the evidence, but must merely say that if you accept the theory of the survival of bodily death (and it is a doctrine to which all Christians nominally subscribe, whatever their attitude may be towards its logical implications), then you must admit that there may be souls in existence which have not got bodies, and if you also admit the hypothesis of telepathy or thought-transference, then you must admit that if a mind can function apart from its physical vehicle during life, then it can continue to function apart from it after the connection is severed, providing it retains its organization, as an entity, and it is one of the doctrines of the Christian faith that it does.

We now come to the problem of Thought-forms, as the occultist calls them, or thought transference or telepathy, as the psychologist calls them if he condescends to think about the problem at all. Here we must depend upon experimental evidence, and there is much available, though we could do with more taken under test conditions, but be it remembered that practically the whole theory of widespread phenomena of Christian Science and other forms of mental healing, whose existence no one can deny, is based upon the assumption of thought-transference, and therefore of the Thought-Form.

It should also be observed in this connection, that suggestion and "rapport" could be set up between discarnate entities and the living, and may play their part in psychopathology.

V—With regard to the doctrine of reincarnation, and its con-comitant, Karma, here we come to an extraordinarily interesting and important psychological point; in fact, it may be said to form one of the foundations of psychology. Are we to construct our doctrine upon the hypothesis of a single life? Is the mind to be regarded as deriving its pabulum from the short span between birth and death? Or shall we take for our unit the reincarnating soul, and think, not in terms of an incarnation, but of an evolution? There is a profound difference between the two attitudes. I need hardly say that I subscribe to the latter, and work from that point of view. For me it has thrown a profound light upon the problem of psychology. How, under the ordinary hypotheses, can we account for the innate disposition of a child, which begins to show itself within a few hours of birth, and perhaps might reveal itself from the moment of birth to an acute observer? Science explains it by the theory of heredity, but it cannot explain one thing which must have struck other observers, namely, that the circumstances of a man's life seem to be appropriate to his character; that is to say, if he has some weakness, his environment will conspire to play upon it, not once, but repeatedly, and he will have opportunities of yielding to his fault which are not forthcoming for the average individual. I have been repeatedly struck by this fact in examining the life histories of the cases that pass through my hands, whether as actual patients undergoing medical treatment, or as those who wish to be analysed for the sake of self-culture and not for any remedial purpose.

I believe that psychology is steadily being forced towards the occult standpoint and that the present generation will see the theories of thought-transference and reincarnation incorporated among the body of orthodox scientific doctrines. How anyone who works upon the human mind can escape their significance is a mystery. I only know that to me they came as a flash of light upon the darkness. I had felt as if I stood in the centre of a small circle of illumination cast by scientific knowledge and that the darkness of the unknown pressed in upon every side. A number of threads were placed in my hands, and I was bidden unravel them, but the ends thereof disappeared into the darkness, and those threads were human lives. I had come to the point when I felt I could no longer carry on my work as a medical analyst owing to the poor percentage of success that attended our efforts, when the doctrines of occultism were brought to my notice. Immediately on this realization, the circle of light was widened, and I could trace the run of threads; I could see whence they came and whither they were tending, and from the segment could calculate the circle.

I commend the occult doctrines to psychologists, not as natural laws, but as working hypotheses, asking them to take them in that spirit and see whither the facts will lead them. We should think nothing human as alien to us, and if the phenomena presented by the human mind resist the accepted classification of science, shall we amend our science or reject the evidence of our senses? No one who investigates the matter can doubt the existence of these phenomena, it is only those who have never seen them who repudiate them—the witness cannot do so. What an irony it is that when an eminent scientific man examines the evidence and pronounces in its favour, far from his dictum being accepted, as it would be upon any other subject, it is his reputation that suffers.

No fact can be subversive of the truth, and if this mass of data known as psychic phenomena should take its place in natural science, knowledge would be the richer.

Little has changed since Dion wrote this article and psychology has continued to look to occultism with derision. The only difference today is that her work has encouraged occultists to make use of the tools offered by psychology. This article is a clever attempt to defend the exploration of occult phenomena through the scientific discipline of psychology. In it, she suggests that she is very concerned about the validation of these phenomena and is seeking to use documentary reports as validating evidence, assuming that the reader will accept such validation without hard evidence.

The carefully constructed argument used to justify the phenomena in Class I gives great insight into some of Dion Fortune's personal concerns. She is at great pains, in these lines, to try to convince the reader that such phenomena not only can and do occur, but that they can be brought about by the active mental power of a living person. In this way she is attempting to secure a solid basis for the work of the magician, using a trained mind to focus on the etheric and produce changes within the physical world. This section clearly relates to many of the occurrences that she goes on to write about in *Psychic Self Defense*. By establishing that it is possible for the mind of both manifest and non-manifest entities to manipulate matter at some level, then it is possible that they can be working for ill rather than good, and anyone may be affected by their actions, especially the more sensitive initiate. Therefore, the sensitive person needs the protection and skills that are suggested in the book, and which are attainable by training within a genuine and effective occult school.

The use of trance was central to much of Dion's magical work, as the teachings received from the Fraternity's contacts at this time were obtained in this way. It became important then, to argue that this was a genuine phenomenon and that with the right precautions, potential issues such as falsification of contact, could be avoided. Yet in *Psychic Self-Defense* we have the warnings that use of this method without appropriate training could and probably would result in at best a false result, at worst a very misguided communication. This section on Class II dominates the article and is important not only to Dion's continued work in the Fraternity but also to the communications she had received and was to later publish.

The perception of psychic attack whether actual or imagined is the same. The individual needs to have the discrimination necessary to understand what is happening, and not jump to conclusions. The subject needs to see when the experience is an attack and when it is a challenge set from the inner planes in order to encourage the development of either the incarnatory personality or evolutionary personality.

The opening of the section on the third class of experience is interesting and makes some sweeping claims about the acceptance of telepathic phenomena which has certainly not gained such widespread credence in the scientific world. Dion Fortune is correct in seeing it as the basis of many of the occult phenomena. On the simplest level the occultist or magician creates a thought form and empowers it, sending it out into the world. This idea is central to many of the experiences that she describes in *Psychic Self-Defense*.

The perpetrator of the attack has often knowingly or unknowingly felt so strongly about another that they have created an idea and given emotional force to it, sending it out to act upon the recipient. This will function regardless of the recipient's awareness, but its intensity will vary according to the amount of force that the recipient lends to it. If the person is oblivious to the idea of thought form or embodied anger then the thought form will have little impact upon them. If, however, the subject realizes that this is occurring and expresses fear or concern, then they will project emotional force towards the source, so empowering the thought form and reinforcing the channel along which the thought form travels between themselves and the source.

Dion talks about the problem of thought-transference and the resultant pathologies, explaining the connection between her work as an occultist and a psychoanalyst. But more importantly she is explaining the nature and purpose of *Psychic Self-Defense*. The techniques she talks about teaching to her clients are the very techniques laid down for sealing the magical working space, for securing the aura, and for dismissing thought forms that have been attracted or directed towards the individual. The article does not go into these techniques, whilst the book goes a little way in doing so.

It will come as no surprise that the first degree of the Fraternity is much linked to these ideas expressed here, the use of both occultism and psychology to examine the personality and to address those defects that hold the individual back from spiritual development. The training offered at this degree is to Dion the essential foundation, without which the initiate can easily become unbalanced and inflict psychological damage upon themselves.

Many of the conditions described in *Psychic Self-Defense* have come about because the individual has been exposed to spiritual power without necessarily understanding how to control or manage such power. It is this idea that she put forth when talking about thought-transference, or in other terms, psychic attack.

It is with class V that we find ourselves back to Dion's letter regarding her own experience with near death as an infant. Rather than seeing this as the vacating of the body by one soul and another taking occupancy, we could argue that the incarnating soul had reached a point of development such that its continued development could only be accessed at a particular point in life. This offers an important interpretation of those events in life which can often be interpreted as psychic attacks. The individual needs to exert a specific kind of discrimination to recognize whether this is the action of a maleficent being or simply just the effect of their own development, and the opportunity given to confront those weaknesses that need to be overcome if the individual is to develop spiritually.

Later in her life Dion Fortune wrote a three-part essay entitled "The Secret Tradition" that was published in *Light: A Journal of Spiritualism: Psychical, Occult and Mystical Research*, appearing in the April to May editions of 1942. By this time she had moved away from her concern about revealing those things she had been taught, demonstrating how far she had come since publishing *Psychic Self-Defense*. The full text is not needed here but there are some relevant passages:

The Secret Tradition
By Dion Fortune

The principal source of trouble is the secrecy, which prevents the useful sharing of knowledge and the wholesome criticism of methods. The solution of the problem cannot, owing to the nature of occult work, be solved by the wholesale application of publicity. The initiate, engaged in practical experimental work which is called magic in occult circles and psychic phenomena in spiritualistic ones, knows by experience that he must work with carefully selected people if he is to get good results. His working is apt to be more easily disturbed than the working of a psychic developed by spiritualistic methods because his techniques are more intricate and elaborate, being enshrined in traditional rituals. Personally, I think that occultists could profit by an acquaintance with the method of developing Mediums used in well-conducted "home circles," which would enable them to cut away a great deal of the traditional ritualistic paraphernalia.

The occult dove-cots, however, were badly fluttered a few years ago when the secret papers of one of the most famous of the occult fraternities, the "Golden Dawn," were published in four volumes in America; but anyone who reads these books in the hope of learning the occult secrets will be sadly disappointed, for they are quite incomprehensible to the outsider, though an invaluable encyclopaedia of reference for the initiated. I had all this material in my possession many years ago, laboriously copied by hand.

The more advanced occultists and spiritualists are nowadays well aware of the value of modern psychology in counter-checking psychic experiences; perhaps the day is not distant when psychologists will realise what the psychic-sciences could give them in the way of data and technique.

Occult organisations vary enormously in both the quality and quantity of their teachings; and though they are in general agreement as to first principles, differ widely in their practical methods. There is no secrecy nowadays about the occult philosophy—it is published in innumerable books; but the practical technique is carefully guarded by each organisation, partly on grounds of traditional secrecy and partly as a trade secret of value in competition with rivals. These methods consist firstly in the knowledge of the ancient symbols and their use, though it is not infrequent to meet with teachers who know the symbols but don't know their use.

There are psychics who are simply primitive sensitives with no critical faculties, and there are sensitives whose natural psychism works through the vehicle of an intellect developed by the discipline of philosophy.

This article, published twelve years after the publication of *Psychic Self-Defense,* shows Dion Fortune supporting a very different view of secrecy. She would be pleased to see the continued publication of materials, including books which present practical techniques, and others that share the symbols. Yet many of these books suffer from the same problem that she expresses above; they do not go much beyond the first principles and often fail to discuss the next steps.

Whilst many argue that as a society we have grown beyond the power of sympathetic magic, this is not entirely true. The argument is that as human beings develop intellectually, they fall away from simplistic beliefs in the power of omens and charms. However, for most individuals within a range of societies this cannot be held to be fully true. The continued sale of varied amulets and talismans, from the simple cross to the more intricate forms, attest to this. For if we had become less concerned with such effects, then these objects would have become unnecessary and meaningless.

The individual today has wide access to occult wisdom and can learn a whole magical system from a book, even self-initiate. This seems to be the point at which Dion would have become concerned. Putting the question of genuineness aside, the concern is for the psychological well-being of the individual who has been exposed to this material without the benefit of reliable guidance. The simplest consequence is that nothing will happen and the individual will be left disappointed, and discouraged. However, those whom she says are naturally sensitive may find themselves experiencing a range of problems, and it is not important whether these problems arise in the mind of the person or beyond them. What is important is that they do arise and for the individual experiencing them, they can be and often are very real. The person believes themselves to be under attack, and that is all they need in order to suffer a whole range of unpleasant consequences. Here lies the central importance of the teachings given, albeit in a veiled way, in *Psychic Self-Defense*.

The protection of the individual engaging in magical or spiritual activity is essential. Firstly, it is about focusing the mind of the participant, as when random thoughts are allowed to enter and doubts arise, the practitioner begins to encounter unbalanced force. On occasion this imbalance arises from within the individual, at other times it will be the result of turbulent situations that they find themselves in in their daily lives impinging upon their minds. Equally it can be imbalanced energy projected by another person who has some form of relationship with the practitioner. It is for this reason that all magical schools teach a basic system of protection, from the casting of a circle to the use of the Lesser Banishing Ritual of the Pentagram. Whilst a member of the Golden Dawn, Dion Fortune was taught this ritual as a way in which to ensure the integrity of any magical ritual. She later adapted it for use within the Fraternity of the Inner

Light, and the following teachings are taken from her training documents on this ritual.

The Use of the Pentagram

The Pentagram is a powerful symbol representing the operation of the Eternal Spirit and the four Elements. From each angle issues a Ray, representing a radiation from the Divine, and therefore it is called the Flaming Pentagram or Star of Great Light.

Traced as a symbol of good, the point must be upward, but traced with the point downward, it is a symbol of evil, and its use as such must be very guarded.

Whenever it is necessary to prepare for any magical work or operation, it is desirable to clear the place and consecrate it by performing the Lesser Banishing Ritual of the Pentagram.

Its use is permitted to Neophytes that they may have protection against opposing forces, also that they may be assisted to attract and come into communication with Spiritual and invisible things.

The Lesser Banishing of the Pentagram is reproduced in a number of books, but what is important is not simply the words but the way they are said and the accompanying meditation or visualization. Dion did go on to create her own variation of the ritual in which she puts aside some of the Hebrew words, however, such developments should be determined by the practitioner and will not be reproduced here.

This ritual though may be seen by some to be cumbersome, as often when experiencing stray or unwanted energy, we do not have the time or wherewithal to perform a ritual of this nature. Indeed, it could in the wrong circumstances leave the practitioner looking rather strange or even foolish. However, in 1922 Dion received a very clear communication on simpler methods of psychic self-defense from her Inner Plane contact, David Carstairs.

from David Carstairs (1922)

From Dion Fortune's personal record:

Learn to stiffen the edge of your aura. Visualise a glass sphere. What you visualise in the imagination is built in astral matter, and if you want to get rid of a person, build a brick wall between you and him. Build brick by brick, and see the courses go up.

If you want to break a rapport, see yourself with a flaming sword chopping away the thread; then sear the ends with a flaming torch. Make the mental pictures clear and you can manage it.

If you want to keep a person from interfering, get a guardian angel on the door. Ask Our Lady to [send] one from Our Lord. Make one with astral matter—a thought form—with flaming sword turning all ways, this will be ensouled.

You must use fire, not love, to clear some things. Keep evil influences off by making a line of fire. The boy in the office is a petty thing, but the widow is different. Fire is a wonderful purifier. It is not generally recommended, but is the right thing in this case. You can cut back a numberof times, but if the ends are not burnt, it can grow again.

You have learnt the lesson of love. This will go far, but there are circumstances when this will not work. Never let love upset justice. Nothing but fire may be able to destroy the evil manifestation. You may hate and destroy the evil, but still see the soul, the essential part, as always divine.

If a loved soul manifests evil, it must be dealt with as evil, thereby helping the soul and the world. Don't be too easy going, it is bad for you and the other people. You must not be unjustly kind, any more than unjustly harsh. You don't help the person by letting him off easily. Others who don't love will administer what is due, and probably more harshly.

Now I'll get along.

This communication from Dion's inner-plane contact David Carstairs contains the foundation of modern techniques of psychic self-defense that are tremendously effective and yet exceedingly simple. The most important key to their performance is missing as it would already have been well known to Dion and the Fraternity; any magical action that is undertaken must be done with the right intention, focus, and emotion.

The first technique that is described above is very similar to the idea of casting a circle, a familiar technique used by most practitioners. It is well to remember that it is not just about drawing a line with salt or chalk or whatever comes to hand. Rather it is about creating a sphere of intention, a space that extends in all dimensions around the practitioner and those with whom they are working. The simplest form of this sphere of protection, or magical circle, is the boundary of the aura itself.

The edge of the aura often becomes ragged and permeable through our continual interaction with the world. We allow experiences to enter and their energies to be exchanged so changing us. The initiate must learn to discriminate between these energies, recognizing their source and intention. To this end the edge of the aura needs to be more focused, and less permeable. Carstairs gives us a technique for this, through strong emotional visualization we can reinforce the edge of our aura and create a filter or reflective system. Once aware of the nature of an incoming energy we are able to repel it or absorb its influence at will. The aura edge then is the first true magical circle.

The still and focused mind is described as the magical mirror, the place where the energetic and spiritual actions that impinge upon the initiate can be seen and understood. It is the most important tool that helps us to exercise the virtues of discretion and discrimination. It is in this mirror that we see the impact of energies and discern whether they are there to challenge and develop us or simply seek to undermine our sense of self. It is the latter that we can describe as being forms of psychic attack.

There is much to be said for sympathetic magic, and external actions can help to reinforce these intentions. The simplest of these is the use of a physical mirror. Such a mirror is bought for magical use only and after consecration it is placed in a window of your dwelling facing outwards, preferably on the same side as the entrance to your home. The intention is that this mirror will reflect unwanted negative energies so keeping you safe. For this tool to be fully effective it is important not to use it for mundane purposes or its association with magical protection will become diminished in your own mind and so the force of sympathetic magic will as a result also diminish.

In the same communication David Carstairs talks about the use of the flaming sword. This is another tool of the mind which acts to break connections. The human energy body builds connections with others of varying kinds. These connections can be perceived by the psychic as cords or cables running between the auras of those connected. There are times when these relationships become damaged or turn toxic, and we find the need to move on and leave those relationships behind. But whilst we move on the other may not, or at some level we may continue to try to hold onto the other. In such cases the connecting energetic cords have remained in place, and energy has continued to flow between you. It is in such cases that we need to use the flaming sword, cutting the cords and searing the ends so that they cannot reattach, and cannot be restored.

Should the incoming energy have been given shape as a thought form, then the flaming sword becomes even more important. By seeing the thought form in the magic mirror of the mind we can take the flaming sword and strike it, and if it is but a thought form, the shock of the impact will shatter the form so releasing the energy that has ensouled it. If the image does not shatter, then the practitioner must examine it again and consider what they are being presented with.

Dion Fortune realized that there are times when these simple yet powerful techniques are not enough, and the individual needs a more ritualistic way of rejecting negative forces. To this end she created her own ritual formulation of exorcism. Such a ritual, performed with a focused mind and emotional intent, will repel other sources of negative energy.

Unlike the Lesser Banishing Ritual of the Pentagram, this ritual will clear the place in which it is operated of any and all forces both positive and negative. It will, if worked effectively, create a clean slate in which new energies will need to be invited in and a new working atmosphere created. In a living space, it will cleanse the space and may rarely be used by the occupants unless new energy is intentionally brought in. The use of such a ritual should be a last resort.

Psychic Self-Defense marks a bridging point in much of Dion Fortune's work. It serves to highlight the dilemmas that she was facing in her own spiritual development. Firstly, there is the tension between the scientific discipline of psychology and the spiritual nature of occultism. Secondly, the tension between the initiate's promise of secrecy and the healer's desire to share wisdom that can help those who are struggling with mental illness. Finally, there is the tension between revealing enough to be of help but not so much that the information could be used in a way that harms its user as well as others.

The first tension is apparent in the way that, writing as Violet Firth, she seeks to find a harmony between psychology and occultism. In doing so there is the obvious desire to justify her own experiences with communication from the inner planes and show it to be reasonable and reliable, even if it cannot be proven as scientifically or academically acceptable data. *Psychic Self-Defense* does this by presenting the arguments through a series of examples or case studies. Each one seems packaged up for the scientist and framed in therapeutic style, as if to say to the world "I have such experiences, they can be interpreted through occultism, they are for me genuine, and so I invite you to examine them and apply them so that you may come to see the value of psychism as a tool for not only psychology but for life."

The second tension is also evident in the production and use of case studies, and the reluctance to give direct magical ritual instruction. Earlier publications were less forthcoming, but later ones became more and more open. This shift seems to have been brought about by a desire to use her knowledge in the service of others whom she saw as suffering from neuroses that could be addressed through occult understanding and the use of magical techniques.

The final tension explored in *Psychic Self-Defense* is clearly a turning point. The publications of Aleister Crowley and Israel Regardie had thrown open the doors to magical practice, yet unlike these writers, Dion was not prepared to conceal by dissembling nor was she ready to tell all. The result is a book that remains highly relevant and is a cornerstone for the more practical texts that explain what to do. *Psychic Self-Defense* looks at why and when to do it; it is a foundation that is rooted in the virtues of discretion and discrimination.

—Christian Gilson

INDEX

THE SOCIETY OF THE INNER LIGHT

The Society of the Inner Light is a society for the study of Occultism, Mysticism, and Esoteric Psychology and the development of their practice.

Its aims are Christian and its methods are Western.

Students who, after due inquiry, desire to pursue their studies further, may take the correspondence course. Their training will be in the theory of Esoteric Science, and they will be given the discipline, which prepares for its practice.

For further details apply for a copy of the WORK & AIMS of the Society from:

The Secretariat
The Society of the Inner Light
38 Steele's Road
London NW3 4RG
England

The Inner Light Journal, a quarterly magazine, founded by Dion Fortune, is devoted to the study of Mysticism, Esoteric Christianity, Occult Science, and the Psychology of Superconsciousness. Inquire with the Society at the address above for subscription rates.

Also in Weiser Classics

The Book of Lies, by Aliester Crowley,
with an introduction by Richard Kaczynski

*The Druidry Handbook: Spiritual Practice Rooted in the
Living Earth*, by John Michael Greer, with forewords
by Philip Carr-Gomm and Dana O'Driscoll

A Handbook of Yoruba Religious Concepts,
by Baba Ifa Karade

*The Herbal Alchemist's Kitchen: A Complete Guide
to Magickal Herbs and How to Use Them*,
by Karen Harrison, with a foreword by
Arin Murphy-Hiscock

*Psychic Self-Defense: The Definitive Manual for Protecting
Yourself Against Paranormal Attack*,
by Dion Fortune, with a foreword by Mary K. Greer

*Taking Up the Runes: A Complete Guide to Using Runes
in Spells, Rituals, Divination, and Magic*, by Diana L.
Paxson

Yoga Sutras of Patanjali,
by Mukunda Stiles, with a foreword by Mark Whitwell